Zen *and* *the* Lady

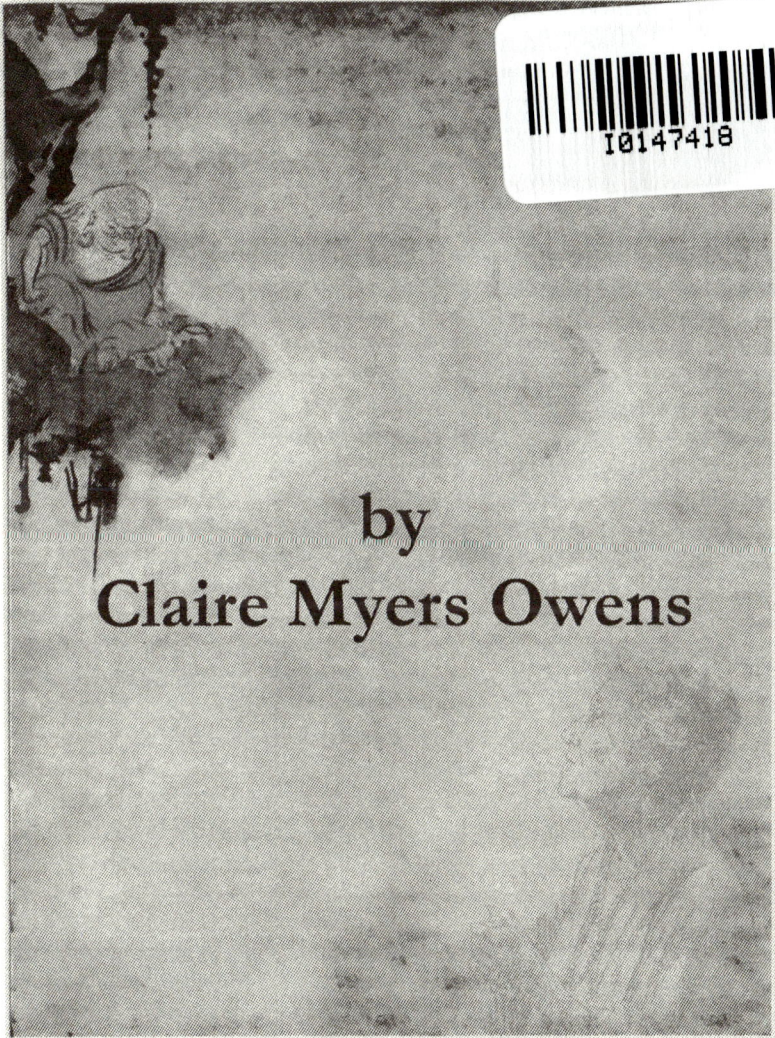

by
Claire Myers Owens

The Book Tree
San Diego, CA

Originally published 1979
Baraka Books Ltd.
New York

© 1979
Claire Myers Owens
Reprinted by special arrangement
with John White

ISBN 1-58509-203-7

Cover layout and design
Lee Berube

Printed on Acid-Free Paper
in the United States and United Kingdom
by LightningSource, Inc.

Published by
The Book Tree
P O Box 16476
San Diego, CA 92176

We provide fascinating and educational products to help awaken the public to new ideas and information that would not be available otherwise.
Call 1 (800) 700-8733 for our *FREE BOOK TREE CATALOG*.

DEDICATION
to
JOHN WHITE
with
gratitude and affection
for
his unshakable faith
in
my writings

Grateful acknowledgement is made to the following publishers and authors for permission to quote from their publications:

Harper and Row
Heaven and Hell, by Aldous Huxley, 1955.

Macmillan Co.
Meeting of East and West, by F.S.C. Northrop, 1946.

Aldus Books Limited, London
Man and His Symbols, ed. by C.G. Jung et al., 1964. Chapter, "Conclusion: Science and the Unconscious" by Marie Louise von Franz (Doubleday edition)

Princeton University Press, Bollingen Foundation
Plato, *Collected Dialogues*, ed. by Huntington Cairns & Edith Hamilton (Pantheon), 1961.

Rider & Co., London
The Way of the White Clouds, by Lama Anagarika Govinda, 1971. Reprinted by special arrangement with Shambala Publications, Inc., 1123 Spruce St., Boulder, Colo. 80302

Beacon Press
Forms and Techniques of Altruistic and Spiritual Growth, ed. by P. Sorokin, 1954. Chapter, "How Altruism is Cultivated in Zen" by Kita and Nagaya

Table of Contents

"The new era we are entering will require a shift from the exclusively personal to one that includes the transpersonal, a shift from an egocentric position to a universal orientation."
—June Singer, *Androgyny*

"Science does not need mysticism and mysticism does not need science but man needs them both."
—Fritjof Capra, *The Tao of Physics*

"It is not the Zen or Buddhist or Hindu religions that are so wonderful —not Plato's philosophy, nor Jung's psychology. It is the human mind itself. They are man-made systems that have formulated universal principles of the human psyche common to all men and have offered methods for actualizing man's noblest potentials."
—Claire Myers Owens

FOREWORD

This is a simple American story of Zen Buddhism as I experienced it, told in simple American language. It is based, however, on the fundamental principles of Zen, as I understand them. I entered Zen too late in life, or am too obstinate, to become adept in the intricacies of Japanese Zen terminology.

But why write such an *intimate* story, some may ask? For several reasons. The general reason is that many people today are confused and afraid in a world they themselves have made. Yet there is a way to solve life's apparently insoluble problems. One longs to share with others the profundity and joy of experiencing another way of life.

Specifically, there are three purposes in presenting this true story of my seven years in Zen training. The secondary purpose is to demonstrate the difficulties encountered by a mature, more or less intellectual person of the West, like me, in submitting to the rigors and rules of training in a Zen Buddhist Center.

The third purpose of this book is to demonstrate the even greater difficulties encountered by a conventional woman brought up in the old South to be a "lady", as I was, in adjusting to the infomality of the young people of the counterculture.

The primary reason for these memoirs, however, is to demonstrate with living examples:

—how meditation (zazen in Zen) can quiet the discursiveintellect and awaken the True-self;

—how this process can —intermittently and briefly —induce joy unlike any other, the certitude we have been seeking, the creativity for which we long, a detachment from material possessions that astounds us, a desire to serve others and a score of other virtues inherent in all people but often dormant in our rational scientific culture of the West:

—How meditation can arouse profound love between a man and a woman despite disparity in ages —which may be an unconscious desire to return to one's source;

—How love for one beautiful young man may precipitate universal love for all mankind, exemplifying the Socratic principles of "the ladder to perfection" enunciated in Plato's Phaedrus;

—How oneness between a Zen spiritual teacher and his student can awaken oneness with art and with ultimatereality;

—How "your work can be your practice", that is, how work can produce the same effects as meditation —joy, strength and purification;

—How work can become effortless play —one of the goals of Zen Buddhism.

These memoirs —personal and transpersonal —reveal:

—The way anger, hate and jealousy gradually disappear until one is able to cope with human relations with compas sion and wisdom;

—The way cosmic energy can pierce one's chest like an arrow, diffusing exultation;

—The way intense zazen (in sesshin) penetrates the different levels of the unconscious;
—The way nature can play a role in one's inner development and a single simple palm tree can induce a numinous experience.

This autobiography reveals the way zazen can bring freedom from the tyranny of society's conventions, from the compulsive need of a spiritual teacher and even of the Buddha, freedom from compulsive dependence on love, people and the world. It shows how one may walk the earth in a state of quiet bliss, enter a state of nothingess that is everythingness, a state of contentedness that Buddhists believe is a beautiful preparation for a beautiful death.

An attempt is made to describe enlightenment, the promised land of which meditation provides many a provocative glimpse along the path. One may seem to witness the death of one's own ego in the ocean of the deep unconscious, behold a great light, then the individual consciousness identifies with universal consciousness, ecstasy is ineffable, purification seems complete, one is reborn. One is capable of intuitive insights into the nature of the universe and finds it good. One experiences the unity of all things, realizes the interrelatedness of all things and that everything is a manifestation of reality. A surge of love for all people arises regardless of age, sex, or race, social or marital status.

Afterward, spontaneous integration of spiritual principles occurs in daily life without one's volition. One displays a selflessness of which one did not imagine oneself capable, transcends fear of old age, sickness and death. Reason isactivated —in some cases —and functions harmoniously with intuition —in some cases. The actualization of one's finest potentials brings harmony with the laws of life and the law of the universe, the Dharma, with which most of us are in conflict hence our suffering.

Realizing the self does not add anything new to one's character. It awakens the True-self so that one becomes what one already is. The highest state of consciousness brings the eternal into the now. It reveals the secret of happiness, the meaning of life. Self-realization is the supreme experience of which human beings are capable, surpassing the joy conferred by youth or beauty, love or passion, fame, wealth or power.

It all sounds too miraculous, does it not? It is not. It is as real as this morning's breakfast once one actually experiences inner transformation. Zen Buddhism is not theory, not philosophy, not psychology. It is immediate, living, personal experience.

Skeptics today can validate —and have —the spiritual experience. Scientists inform us that the two hemispheres of the brain perform different functions. The left hemisphere is concerned with reason, language, mathematics and analysis —cultivated almost exclusively by the Western scientific world. The right half of the brain is concerned with intuition, imagery, creativity, spiritual experiences and synthesis, cultivated almost exclusively by Eastern religions. Neuroses also lurk there.

"Science does not need mysticism and mysticism does not need science but *man* needs both," according to the atomic physicist, Fritjof Capra. The cultures of the rational West and the illumined East are interchanging values today. Mysticism and science are becoming reconciled. The reconciliation and transcendence of opposites occurs in Nirvana —eternal bliss.

All the characters in this book are real. Some of the names have been changed to protect the innocent. The sequence of events has been altered occasionally. Nature does not always arrange events in the order man considers consonant with the rules of literary art.

I trust my friends will forgive me for including them in this book. What other way could I tell the story of my inner development? My personal life is unimportant but my inner development may possess some universal elements, consequently they may be of help to others, in today's frightening and confusing world.

Claire Myers Owens
Snowbound, New York
1977

Chapter 1
END AND BEGINNING

"The only people in this place who look happy are the widows." This observation was offered by my ever-skeptical husband. We were spending the summer at a seaside hotel north of Boston.

Every evening I watched incredulously as the widows paraded through the lobby on their way to the cocktail lounge. They were decked out in brightly colored evening gowns and were always laughing gaily. How, I asked myself in dismay, can a woman ever learn to laugh again after she had lost her husband?

Now it had happened to me.

I was sitting in our living room in New Haven, Connecticut at the memorial service for Thurston, my husband. I felt as if at any moment I might be shattered into a thousand pieces. I was holding myself together by sheer will power attempting to listen to the eulogies delivered by his friends.

But I was thinking how utterly helpless one feels against the cold finality of death. A few years ago I might have confronted the ordeal more bravely. A beautiful experience of spontaneous self-realization had been visited upon me. I had expected it to continue unabated forever. To my dismay it had gradually faded away. So long as it lasted I felt no fear of old age, illness, or death—my husband's or my own. I longed to recapture that glorious mystical state—but how?

Seymour Tate, the president of the company, was talking. "And Thursty was also a shrewd business man. In the Great Depression the business he brought us was one third of our total volume. We have never forgotten that. He was with our company for nearly sixty years —first with my father and then with me.

"Thursty was an extremely reserved man. He attempted to conceal his virtues. He possessed a dry sense of humor that was sometimes delightfully bawdy. If he had any religion, I think it may have been the arts —the seven arts. He seemed to possess an unerring sense for excellence, especially in the theater, music and painting. But not in poetry, Claire tells me. He had a passion for beauty. I think probably that's one reason he married his beautiful young wife. Yes, we in the Michigan plants shall miss Thursty Owens but his good deeds will live after him."

This eulogy was delivered by Seymour Tate who had flown to New Haven to be present at the memorial service I had arranged for my husband. However meritorious it was to donate one's cadaver to a medical school, to those left behind it seemed impersonal, almost inhuman. It made it doubly necessary to mark a loved person's passing with some kind of ceremony, however secular.

Thirty of our mutual friends were sitting in small uncomfortable folding chairs in our living room. Flowers were everywhere. One friend had telephoned and said, "I assume you do not wish any flowers sent to the house. What is your favorite charity?"

"I am," I replied promptly. "The more flowers the better. I can't imagine anything on earth that might banish the smell of death in a house like flowers."

The next speaker, a member of Thursty's club who often played bridge with him, ended his remarks by saying, "Thursty was an uncanny bridge player. He always won but by his own rules."

Last, our intimate friend, Ina, stood to deliver her eulogy. She spoke of the way Thursty cherished and protected Claire. It was so beautiful it loosed the flood of tears I had been struggling to restrain. I sobbed uncontrollably for a few embarrassing minutes. I sat there with conflicting emotions surging through me as if to tear me apart. Despite its many difficulties I had found marriage a deep, nourishing relationship. Thursty was my father and mother, my brother and friend, lover and husband. Some people said he was hard. But to me he seemed as strong as the Rock of Gibraltar. I depended on him excessively in practical matters. He was a shield that protected me from the harshness of life and people, in a way no man ever understands or desires for himself. Behind this shield I could safely write the kinds of books I wished to write that did not sell very well and together we could enjoy the beauties of nature and the arts. Already I had experienced many altered states of consciousness, which I called "small ecstasies," the significance of which I did not understand.

Thursty refused to read my book about them, *Awakening to the Good*, and laughed at the warm responsive letters they elicited from all over the world. He often reminded me of Browning's *My Last Duchess*, which I had memorized in high school.

As Ina continued talking, I clasped my hands fiercely together in my lap. How, oh, how could a woman continue to live without a husband? Without love? Without someone to live for? And how much longer could I sit here so politely without collapsing? Not only the shock of his death but the sheer fatigue of long years of nursing him left me drained and empty.

The service was mercifully brief. Jerry, our part-time gardener who had been with us for thirty years, quickly and quietly whisked the folding chairs out into the hall. Margaret, our cook of ten years, who was a great comfort to me, served the diminutive sandwiches. Molly, our part-time upstairs maid, passed the sherry. Everyone tried to speak a few consoling words, pressed my hand and left soon.

Before the ceremony had begun, Seymour had offered to act as my financial advisor. This was a great relief. I understood nothing about money — except that it was necessary —and even less about investments. He had suggested that after the service we hold a meeting of the president of the bank, my trust officer, lawyer, Seymour and myself.

He also had said, "You won't need two cars. So I'll send a man to drive the car Thursty's been using back to the plant. But you are welcome to use the red Buick so long as you like. He must have told you that the company has already paid for it and the insurance. You pay for maintenance and repairs. All right?"

"Oh, more than all right. Seymour, you really are generous. I do appreciate it to no end."

The company had always furnished us both with cars. But why me, why now? I was indeed fortunate.

I struggled to brace myself for the financial meeting. As the four men sat in a circle, I understood nothing of what they were discussing. The lawyer warned us. "There may be a gift tax on the house because Mr. Owens did not give it to Mrs. Owens until the last minute —though I shall work on that problem."

Actually, the bank president had spent one Sunday afternoon persuading Thursty to deed the house to me. Seymour had called from Michigan and told my husband he must deed the house to his wife who had kept him young all these years. He was nearly ninety when he died.

They were unaware that Thursty's previous wife had been ill when they were divorced. Expecting her to be ill forever he had given her their house and most of his money. She had promptly recovered her health, sold the house and married again. It left Thursty very bitter and distrustful of all women.

Nevertheless for the first twenty-six years of our marriage we had been blessedly free of the usual marital bickering concerning money. Thursty had allotted me an over-generous allowance. He seemed to enjoy giving me diamonds, mink coats, original model dresses, and frequent trips to Europe. Frankly, I usually enjoyed these material luxuries yet somehow I felt like "a bird in a gilded cage," an old song Thursty often sang to me with a wicked gleam in his eye. I was not free.

During the last few years, however, everything was different. He stopped my allowance altogether and changed his will repeatedly.

Sometimes hardening of the arteries transforms a kind loving person into something of a sadist, his cruel words and actions being beyond his control apparently. As his illness increased, Thursty frequently remarked, "After I'm gone you can live in some little hole in the wall." After thirty two years of marriage had my husband left me destitute? Could a woman of my age go out and get a job? Or had he left me a wealthy widow?

Forcibly I brought my attention back to the discussion of my finances and my future fate. Vaguely I heard the men discussing death duties, estate taxes, probate court costs, lawyer's fees, assets and investments. Seymour listened silently and then cut to the very bone of each problem in what appeared to me brilliant decisive strokes. Suddenly it became clear why Thursty had always regarded Seymour as a financial genius. His grasp of complicated problems, ability to isolate essentials, and offer simple concrete solutions amazed me. In addition to running several manufacturing plants, he was working for his Ph.D. in economics, taking piano lessons, was a collector of first editions and modern paintings.

My trust officer, who was very young, now launched forth confidently into suggestions for a portfolio of certain growth stocks for me. Again Seymour listened quietly then said, "Mrs. Owens at her age does not want growth stocks but income. I suggest she buy bonds. Any bank is likely to invest her money conservatively at four and one half percent. Here is a list of bonds that yield 7, 8 and 9%. And I think they are safe. This should increase Mrs. Owen's income considerably."

I sat in a silent daze. Everything was still unsettled. The lawyer said it required three years usually to settle an estate. In the meantime there would be insurance money for immediate expenses. Three of the men left soon.

I lay down on the sofa in utter weariness and listened to Seymour pour out his own troubles. I was pleased that he thought of me as a confidante. But, I reflected, all his millions, all his ability, attractive face and figure, good mind and good education can not preclude troubles. I expressed sympathy for his predicaments and intense gratitude for the willingness of such a busy man to assume responsibility for my investments. Why did he wish to do it? He derived no benefit from it. Unless he actually enjoyed helping other people.

Now the long ordeal of Thursty's illness was over. I was alone in the world. Day after day, hour after hour, I lay motionless and silent in the reclining chair in our sun porch. My eyes were fixed hypnotically on the green leaves of the bushes, pressing against the glass on three sides, as if they might produce a magic cure.

It was June 1969. The doors were open. The gentle breeze that touched my cheeks seemed to possess a healing power. Perhaps nature could heal me; nothing else could, I feared. If my physical endurance or sanity were strained one inch further they might both be shattered irreparably. I was exhausted beyond the danger point. I feared I might be plunged into a black abyss of despair —or worse. I was frightened as never before in my life at losing my grip on life. I had instructed the maids to answer the telephone and the doorbell, to inform friends that I was resting, too exhausted to see anyone.

I could not bear to sit in the dining room opposite *his* empty chair. Margaret brought a tray and set it beside my chair without a word. It always contained some of my favorite dishes. My appetite had disappeared. She understood my problems as well as I did. Her silent devoted presence emanated a soothing atmosphere. She was a simple, uneducated woman of innate nobility. I not only respected but loved her as if she were the sister for whom I had always longed. She had never once lost patience with Thursty during his angry spells.

Days, weeks, months passed. I was unaware of time. There existed only each painful moment of the present to live through somehow while waiting, wondering if the surge of life would ever return. After lying there for weeks in that reclining chair, sodden with grief and weariness, gradually I began to recover from the death of my husband three months earlier. My mind, if not my body, commenced to come alive.

Everyday I asked myself in desperation, what do I do now? How can any woman live without someone to love, someone to love her? All my life love had been more necessary to me than the food I ate, the air I breathed. Without it I was certain I would die, wither away like an autumn leaf. How can a woman alone make any sort of life for herself when she has no husband, no children, no relatives nearby? I can't live with my dear cousin, Laura, in California —bless her. I visited Imperial Valley once. Desert country is not for me.

At times I rung my hands despairingly. Oh, God, is my life absolutely finished forever? It can't be! I *feel* like a person of forty. I refuse to just sit in this big empty house and vegetate for the next ten or twenty years. Is it possible for a person to die of sheer loneliness? What do other widows do with themselves? Lunch at the club. Bridge or matinees. Cocktail parties. Charities and civic work. Travel. Indulgence of their grandchildren. No, no, that's not for me.

Well, Claire, I asked myself, what do you *enjoy* best in the world? Certainly the most wonderful thing that ever happened to me in my entire life was my spontaneous spiritual awakening at fifty-four. The joy of it surpassed everything life has to offer —love, passion, marriage, wealth, creativity, youth, beauty —everything. And if it could last for twelve years as it did, could one perhaps learn to live *permanently* on that high plane? But how?

Vaguely I recalled references in my reading to systems purporting to induce the highest state of consciousness. I had dismissed such ideas as too fantastic to merit credibility. I had once subscribed to a small magazine, *Vedanta and the West,* published in California. I became interested because Aldous Huxley was one of its editors briefly. He was the only modern intellectual I knew of in the early 1950's who possessed sufficient courage to be interested in the mystical experience. It was both praised and satirized in his novels and essays. When he wrote me concerning my book, *Awakening to the Good,* he said, "Maybe I can learn from you." Was that an indication that he had failed to find all he needed in Hinduism?

Nevertheless I dragged myself to New York to consult Nikhalananda, director of the Ramakrishna Order. He also had written an encouraging letter concerning *Awakening,* although warning me that the spontaneous spiritual experience did not last. But he was now in India. So I took a train to Boston to consult another teacher of Hinduism. My friend who accompanied me, an old lover, was politely certain I had gone off my rocker. The swami in Boston was not the answer to my problem. Then I, who loathed driving alone through the country on unfamiliar roads, drove to Franklin, New Hampshire to call on Baba Ram Dass, recently returned from India. He was away that day.

Frustrated, I wondered if I should become a Catholic nun? But I should never be able to accept some of the doctrines or the severe training. Should I go on an Episcopal retreat? But was their discipline severe enough to effect inner transformation? Or should I ingest psychedelic drugs? But they were injurious. Or enter Jungian analysis? But I did not need analysis, did I? Had not the penetration of the religious level of the unconscious during my awakening cured my neurosis connected with my mother? Where, oh where, on earth could one turn for training that would induce the spiritual experience?

It was not only an acceptable system I sought but also I longed to devote the major portion of my time to spiritual training —but how? To live in a community of like-minded aspirants —but where? Most of my friends — except Judy —were atheists who did not even believe in inner development. In truth, they considered that I had gone off the deep end when I revealed my self-realization experience in my books. So now I had not only lost my husband but also became estranged from many of my friends.

At night my husband's absence was a palpable thing. To be alone in a large empty house was truly terrifying. I felt like a child afraid of ghosts. Margaret's husband was too ill for her to sleep in as all our other cooks always had done over the years. During the day, however, she was infinitely comforting and solicitous.

Social unrest presented another danger in being alone. 1969 was a period of great racial turmoil in Connecticut, especially in New Haven. As a Southerner I felt guilty about the exploitation of blacks by whites. I believed they should be given education, jobs, and opportunity, but I abhorred violence. The Black Panther trial had recently been held at the courthouse on the Green. The Panther organization had threatened to bring 15,000 people into New Haven and raze the city to the ground if the court did not release the two black prisoners. Rocks were thrown through the windows of white people's houses. Harassment on the telephone occurred frequently. At this time it was not safe for a white woman to go downtown alone.

By 1969 a few Growth Centers had sprung up across America. I received various announcements. One arrived from Bucks County, Pennsylvania. A couple had purchased a farm house where various workshops and seminars were conducted by spiritual leaders in the human potential movement. Ram Dass was scheduled for the next session. I telephoned the farm house. Every series was over-subscribed far in advance. They were able to sleep only twenty-five people. They said they anticipated one possible cancellation for the three-day seminar to be held by Ernest Kolberg, founder of the Zen Buddhist Center of Snowbound, N.Y. I had never heard of it.

"I'll take it," I said promptly. I had no knowledge of Zen and even less interest. But why not investigate all systems of self-realization?

On Labor Day weekend, I embarked for Pennsylvania. It was the most strenuous trip I had ever been subjected to. Every possible difficulty arose. I hoped it was not indicative of coming events. First I took a train to some town in New Jersey. The August heat was unbearable, the humidity enervating, no porter to carry my bag up the steep flight of stairs at the junction where I changed trains. Halfway up the steps a black man volunteered to carry it. He was in the Pentecostal religion, refused a tip but accepted a donation to his church. Then an incredibly rough and crowded commuters' train ride through Pennsylvania, ending in a long circuitous taxi drive through the woods to the farm house —so circuitous it left me slightly nauseated. Ordinarily I might have been defeated and returned home.

Instead I rehearsed my little speech to Kolberg, describing my spontaneous awakening. It would prove to him my serious interest in self-realization. I would say to him, "In 1950 I was confronted with two problems that were insoluble by my rational conscious mind: the fearful state of the world that distressed me deeply after the atom bomb was exploded, and a personal tragedy that put me to bed for three months. One day I crawled out of bed, climbed up to my writing room on the third floor, 'died' and was born again —psychologically and spiritually. At the time I thought I was dying. After reading Jung I realized it was my ego that had drowned in the ocean of my collective unconscious. The surrender of my conscious mind evidently released my unconscious so that it flowed forth freely.

"Then a great golden light filled the whole world. The good immanent in me seemed to dissolve, to mix and mingle with the transcendent good until they were united indistinguishably. The ectasy was ineffable. The sense of purification incredible as if all my faults were being washed away. I felt reborn. Then came intuitive insights into the nature of the universe, into my own nature and that of others. And I found them all good. I experienced a oneness of all things and all peoples. I loved the whole human race irrespective of sex, age, race, or social status. In fact, I longed to sacrifice my life to save others. Afterward I lived in a state of exaltation for twelve glorious years. It changed my entire life style."

Then I planned to repeat to Kolberg, as nearly as possible, the passage I had written in *Awakening to the Good* describing the incredibly beautiful life style that followed: "Self-realization awakened the certitude I was forever seeking, the courage I wished I possessed, the creativity for which I longed. It evoked a selflessness of which I did not know myself capable, a love of the human race that astounded me, a sense of union with the life force my rational mind had assured me was not possible. It brought greater rapport with nature, deeper response to the beauty of the arts and a joy exceeding all others. But it faded away recently." Surely this would demonstrate to Kolberg that I understood something about enlightenment.

At the farm I discovered most of those attending the seminar were teachers. Never in my life had I slept in a room with strangers. There were five of us in one room. Seven strangers used the same bathroom. (I laughed to think that at home my husband and I had separate bathrooms and separate bedrooms.) All meals were eaten in silence. The atmosphere was unbelievably harmonious. Something mysterious had already happened to all of us.

A large barn had been converted into a meditation hall (zendo). We sat there on hard cushions on the floor, silent, motionless for nearly half an hour practicing the Zen form of meditation, zazen. We suffered agonies of pain in our knees and back. Kolberg gave a talk on Zen Buddhism. His manner suggested that it was a matter of supreme indifference whether we joined his group or not. I studied this man sitting in full lotus posture —small, about sixty years old, with shaven head, and wearing a Japanese robe —highly intelligent face and bright, alert eyes. Rumor had it that he had renounced everything, trained in a Japanese monastery for several years, come to enlightenment and been ordained as a Zen monk.

Later Nat, Kolberg's disciple, led us in yoga exercises on the lawn. It was four o'clock on a hot suffocating summer afternoon, the humidity thick enough to hold in your hand. No one even mentioned the weather. Kolberg did a prolonged headstand, waving his legs about over his head as nonchalantly as if he were sitting right-side-up in a chair.

After the exercises I noticed Kolberg was standing alone. I walked up to him. "Mr. Kolberg, may I tell you why I came here today? Years ago I was visited by a spontaneous enlightenment experience which —"

His face looked blank and uninterested. But surely it was only logical for any teacher who was leading others on the spiritual path to be deeply interested in *all* forms of realizing the self. I struggled on. He turned his face away. My voice trailed off and stopped. I felt hurt that he refused to listen to the beautiful story of my spontaneous awakening. Never had I received a rebuff like this in my whole life. (Only long afterward did I realize that he might have sensed too much ego in my approach. I didn't know since he never explained. But later in the workshop he talked to me personally for a long period of time —though not about my awakening.)

At the time, however, I walked away consoling myself by the thought of all the hundreds of warm responsive letters the book describing my awakening had elicited from scholars all over the world: Albert Schweitzer in Africa, Raynor Johnson in Australia, Aldous Huxley in California, Maslow at Brandeis, the Yale scientists Sinnott and Margenau and philosophers Northrop and Sheldon. How strange that these men were interested and Kolberg was not.

At that time I knew nothing of the Rinzai Zen policy of never complimenting anyone for fear of inflating his or her ego, chief enemy of the self. I knew nothing of the practice of discouraging potential aspirants in order to test the strength of their urge to enter Zen training. Also, I was yet to learn that in Zen, matters are seldom explained theoretically or intellectually. In Buddhism one must learn experientially.

At that moment, however, I was unutterably weary from grief and prolonged loss of sleep. I longed for gentleness and understanding. But I felt desperate. Nevertheless I was surprised to hear my own voice saying to Kolberg later, "Are there any groups in New Haven practicing zazen now?"

"There is a group of students at Yale but they can't find a suitable place to meet."

"Well, I have a large empty house —perhaps —"

I was not drawn to such a severe system as Zen but I was determined to sample various disciplines. Kolberg gave me the name of the Zen leader at Yale whom he himself had trained at the Snowbound Center. The university, however, would not open until later in the Fall.

Chapter II
LOVE AND MEDITATION

After I returned home, I answered the telephone one morning to hear a young man's voice say, "Are you the Claire Myers Owens who wrote *Awakening to the Good* and the 'Mystical Experience —Facts and Values'?"

"Yes, I am."

"Wow! I think they're wonderful. My name is John White. I'm calling to request permission to reprint your *Main Currents* paper in a book I am compiling. It's called *The Highest State of Consciousness*. I have already signed the contract with Doubleday for a paperback."

I granted him permission and we talked animatedly at great length. Finally he said, "I should like to take you to lunch tomorrow."

"Well, I do not usually go out to lunch with a man sight unseen. But you do not sound *too* dangerous."

We met and he proved to be literally "tall, dark and handsome" (the phrase Mae West had made famous) also kind and gentle, highly intelligent and a writer. He showed me the picture of his pretty wife and three young children. We talked of our writing, of the whole self-realization movement that was now burgeoning mightily, of Abraham Maslow, pioneer of the human potential movement in America and Jung who fathered it in Europe. It was not necessary for us to become acquainted. It was as if we were resuming an old friendship, not commencing a new one. After finishing Dartmouth, John had joined the Navy where he was visited by a tremendous inner experience that changed the direction of his entire life.

Often when strangers meet who are both on the spiritual path a bond is forged between them almost as strong as a blood tie. This had happened the first time in my case with those scientists and philosophers at Yale after they read *Awakening to the Good*. When John and I parted he suggested that we go to lunch again next week. He kissed me on the cheek, much to my surprise and delight. We lunched together every week after that and discussed our work and the higher states of consciousness in general. During the day he wrote a house organ for a large business firm and at night edited his prospective anthology.

Once he invited me to meet his mother, a brilliant woman from California. Sometimes on Sundays I spent the day with his wife and children at their place in the country. To those not involved in the inner development process such unorthodox relations as John's and mine were inexplicable. Once one of his friends remarked, "Well, if you think Claire Myers Owens is so wonderful, why don't you marry her?"

Could anything be more absurd? John was thirty. I was seventy-three. Of course he was not aware of my exact age but it was obvious that the lady was well over thirty. The last thing I wished was to cause friction between husband and wife. I endeavored to reassure him that my intentions were honorable. John's understanding, respect and friendship came at a time when I needed them badly. Later after he had published several of his own books he offered to become my literary agent. This was a great relief to me.

One afternoon on his way home from the office he stopped at my house. A caller was present, Lois Triffin, wife of the master of one of the Yale colleges. As he rose to leave he said to her, "Well, Mrs. Triffin, you have come to the wisest woman in New Haven."

"I know that. That's why I'm here. I've just read her *Awakening to the Good*.

What did they mean? I did not feel wise at all. I knew nothing of the mysteries of life except the joy of experiencing an involuntary spiritual awakening. But, alas, I knew no way to assist others in attaining it—a miraculous feat many people appeared to expect of me after reading *Awakening*.

In October, Bob, the leader of the Zen group at Yale, called on me. He was a pleasant, neatly dressed young man with short hair, a senior majoring in English literature. He had written a number of poems, and appeared seriously dedicated to Zen. We agreed that he would bring his Yale group to my house to practice zazen three afternoons a week. There would probably be six to ten at each meeting.

On the appointed day the group descended all together like an army, arms full of pillows and mats, looking as if they expected to stay all night or indulge in some kind of oriental orgy. Their gypsy rag-tag bobtail clothes took me aback. I had never seen anything like it before. Their long hair — unwashed and uncombed —long beards, villainous moustaches, and —in some cases —need of baths left me speechless. What would the neighbors think had happened to this recent widow?

After the students left I called on my neighbors to prevent their being offended —no, the primary reason was so that the neighbors would not look at me askance. I did not explain that the young people were Zen Buddhists —the mere words frightened orthodox people —I explained that they were all Yale students and were coming to sit in spiritual meditation. As most of my neighbors' husbands were connected with the University they were obliged to accept this strange invasion. My friends and neighbors considered godliness next to cleanliness and being well-dressed and well-groomed a sacred law of civilization and good breeding.

After a few weeks, however, the genuine idealism, alert minds, spiritual aspiration, kind hearts and delicious sense of humor of these young men and girls caused me to forget their unsavory appearance —almost. I continually reminded myself that their slovenly way of dressing, their unkempt hair and beards were to them badges of courage. They had rejected the values of the Establishment created by their parent's generation —and mine —which laid excessive emphasis on clothes and other material possessions.

Two of the students moved all the furniture out of my largest and best guest room as easily and quickly as if they had been children's toys. We sat for two hours in meditation on our cushions on the floor, counted our breath, concentrated fiercely, attempted to silence our discursive intellect, and thereby liberate our True-self with its many potential virtues. We did walking zazen (kinhin) after every thirty-five minute round of sitting.

We listened to Bob read from one of the Mahayana Buddhist scriptures (sutras) and terminated our practice by chanting the four vows:

All beings One Body, we vow to liberate;
Endless blind passions, we vow to uproot;
Dharma gates without number, we vow to penetrate;
The Great Way of Buddha, we vow to attain.

I had no idea what these vows meant.

The students very seldom talked except Bob and one other young man. I asked Bob the reason.

"They're overwhelmed."

"Oh no, that can't be. But why, for heaven's sake?"

"Oh, your large elegant house, servants, your age and dignity, the fact that you are a published writer and most of all because you have experienced the state of enlightenment we are striving for. They're all reading your book."

I redoubled my efforts to put them at ease. I asked them about themselves. Many of them had difficult relationships with their parents who, if Christian, felt outraged at their son or daughter for practicing Zen. Yet all the students seemed to long for a home. On Thursdays, the cook's day off, I frequently invited half a dozen of them to dinner. They would do most of the work so quickly, so efficiently, it filled me with admiration.

When I asked, "Would you rather have a ham sandwich or cheese?" "Both," they said. "Milk or coffee?" "Both." Their appetites were enormous, especially the tall thin ones. It did one good to watch them eat. The only problem was they never knew when to go home. I became so exhausted I almost collapsed on the floor from fatigue. But who would have the heart to send such dear young people away? I soon learned that there is nothing so touching, so endearing as youth. The young are so enthusiastic and inexperienced, so eager and vulnerable, so gullible and trusting, one longs to help them and protect them from all hurt and harm.

I wished to invite some of them to a civilized dinner at one of our clubs. Their strange appearance, however, would have offended the members who in turn would have been offended with me. "Hippie" clothes and long-haired men were not yet a commonplace in 1969, at least not in New Haven. The trouble was their soiled clothes were soiling my delicate satin damask chairs. It was necessary to set out a row of hard uncomfortable but unsoilable folding chairs in the hall. Some of the same chairs used at Thursty's memorial service. I shuddered to think of his reaction to these young people. He himself was always immaculate, never appeared in public without his jacket, and was always clean shaven. After one glimpse of these slovenly young students he would have slammed the door in their faces. Zen he doubtless would have pronounced nonsense and refused me the fee for membership.

It was difficult, however, for me to concentrate entirely on Zen and meditation. There was one special young man —Dexter. He was quite tall and

thin, rather awkward but with beautiful blonde hair, large blue eyes with long
lashes that were not blonde but literally golden, an aristocratic aqualine nose
and very red full lips. He was the type William Sheldon would designate an
ectomorph in physique and cerebrotonic in temperament. For years I had
found Sheldon's constitutional psychology of great assistance in understanding the mysteries of human personality.

Dexter resembled the Blue Boy or the portrait of some young English
duke painted by Gainsborough. All the freshness and bloom of youth was
still on him as on a ripening peach. He seemed blissfully unaware of his
extraordinary beauty. But then youth is always wasted on the young, as some
wag once remarked. Dexter had graduated from Yale and was now an instruc-
tor in physics.

The first moment our eyes met across the room a spark was ignited
between us that flamed and later flared until we were both almost consumed.
Soon he began to arrive at my house before the others and remain after they
all had departed.

He and I laughed at everything, at nothing, smiled into each others eyes,
were tender, considerate, wounded at every imagined slight. We scarcely
dared to be alone. We never dared to touch. Incredible as it seemed, passion
boiled underneath the surface of propriety. I feared a volcanic explosion any
moment. Each time he took his departure he kissed me quickly, almost fear-
fully, on the cheek and rushed out the door, going down the steps backward,
endangering his life, his eyes never leaving mine.

We both strove to be very circumspect in the presence of others. But when
alone he would stand looking down into my eyes and it was as if a stream of
golden light flowed from his eyes into mine. It bewildered, disoriented,
intoxicated me. I scarcely knew what to say, what to think, what to do. I had
been in love several times in my life. Never had the charisma of a man so
overwhelmed me. I felt like an inexperienced high school girl.

"Claire, how old are you?" Dexter took it upon himself to call me by my
first name. All the others called me Mrs. Owens, which I preferred. More dig-
nified.

"How old do you think?"

"Oh, about fifty."

"Fifty is a nice age. I always feel a permanent forty." I was seventy-three.
He was twenty-nine.

On the days the group was not scheduled to practice I sat alone in the living room attempting to read the *New York Times*. I was too aware of Dexter
to concentrate on anything else. Day after day a storm of desire swept over
and through me until I was shaken from my mooring, like a small ship in a
tropical hurricane. Waves of passion engulfed me with a force I had not
known existed —I who had always found passion a delight.

I was bewildered but grateful that I was able to experience such intensity
of desire. Each time the waves subsided I felt purified strangely enough.
These storms of passion continued for months.

One night Dexter was driving me through the country to have dinner with
a friend of his. "Well, Claire, what do you plan to do about your sex life now
that your husband is gone?"

"Oh, sublimate it, I reckon."

"That may not be necessary. We both know how we feel. The honest thing to do would be to follow our natural impulses."

Good Lord, I thought, is he blind? Can't he see my graying hair and the lines in my face? Aloud I said, "But the disparity in our ages —it might seem like incest to you and haunt you all the days of your life."

He laughed. "Nonsense."

I reminded him of Oedipus Rex in Sophocles. When the king discovered he had killed his father and married his own mother he burned out both of his eyes with red hot irons.

At night I lay awake struggling with the problem. If we had an affair and afterward he discovered my real age he would feel betrayed. Therefore, it would not be fair to commence an affair unless I did tell him —in which case I might lose him. It was an impasse. But why be afraid? There were plenty of historical precedents. Byron and Lady Oxford —she was twenty years older; George Sand and Chopin —he was seventeen years younger. And Diane de Pettier was loved all her life by a man twenty years her junior. There was another private reason that caused me to hesitate.

Yet each time Dexter went down those front steps backward, I would lean back against the closed door overwhelmed by longing to feel him hold me in his arms. After my husband's death it was not sex I missed so much as the comforting sweetness of a man's strong arms around me. I was utterly lost without it.

Yet if I succumbed would not Dexter appear ridiculous in the eyes of his peers? Would not I? Yet every newspaper carried stories of men of sixty marrying girls of twenty. The men were not ridiculed. They were congratulated. Didn't the women's liberation movement declare men and women should be offered equal opportunities in everything? Men of course from the beginning of time had always supported young mistresses and no one laughed. But then men had always arranged life for men's benefit. Every woman knew that.

I often discussed the matter with a friend who was in her fifties and having an affair with a man in his thirties. She was a brilliant intellectual, a member of the state assembly. Her lover had said to her, "If I don't mind the difference in our ages, why should you?" She and I laughed at the whole stuffy world —privately.

One day Dexter declared his love —not with his eyes or tone of voice but verbally, explicitly. "Claire, I want you to know I love you."

I sat across the room motionless, my whole body throbbing like a gigantic heart.

"Do *you* love *me*?" he asked.

"Oh, Dexter dear, do you need to ask?" I whispered.

After this declaration I walked about the house in a state of ecstasy for months. I had known love before but never in my life anything so intense, so all-consuming, like a wonderful conflagration.

It is abnormal, unnatural, unhealthy, I chided myself.

I don't care, I don't care! Love is love wherever it occurs.

I could not sleep. I could not eat. I did not care. I was floating on a rosy cloud of rapture. I learned to laugh again. My cook said it was the first time she had heard me laugh in the last seven years. A compulsion such as I had never experienced toward any man all but overwhelmed me. I was seized by an almost irresistible urge to give Dexter everything I owned —my car, my house, my money, my body, my life. For some unknown reason my heart did not run away with my head. But I felt a sudden understanding compassion for the middle-aged women one read about in European novels, never American. They fell hopelessly in love with a handsome young man many years their juniors. Vivian Leigh played such a role in a movie, the name of which I forget. Naturally the story ended with her destruction by the experience. But why?

I had no intention of allowing it to destroy me if I could prevent it. At the moment I felt nourished, rejuvenated by it. I was deeply grateful to Dexter for arousing such an intense love in me.

As we all sat in our make-shift zendo, engaged in zazen, my awareness of Dexter's presence enveloped and penetrated my entire body, mind and heart like a powerful fragrance. One day I was walking in front of him in the kinhin line. I stumbled and quick as lightening his hands were thrust out to support me. My whole being melted, suffused with ineffable sweetness. Oh God, I moaned inwardly, how can Zen offer anything so sweet as this?

Then we had a quarrel. He had related to me the story of his work in the civil rights movement for the blacks down South. He was proud that he had been jailed for his activities. This confused me. I was brought up to consider being thrown in prison a disgrace. Later he was to purchase a house in the black section of town to demonstrate his sympathy for the Negroes. This particular quarrel, however, concerned homosexuality. He announced he had planned to rent a room in the house of a wealthy homosexual.

"Are you a homo?" I asked bluntly.

He laughed. "You should know better."

"But my dear Dexter, everyone will assume that you are."

"I don't give a damn what everyone assumes about me. It's a protective measure for a class of men who are ostracized by society. Homos and blacks, Jews and women and other disadvantaged people have just as much right to a place in the sun as other people."

I knew he was right and courageous but his news distressed me. He did not know the world as well as I did. Later he informed me that he had taken a girl friend into the man's house to stay overnight. Then I felt sorry for the older man.

Dexter discussed his various girl friends with me. They all seemed to have serious emotional problems and his chief interest appeared to be in helping them. He displayed a slight messianic complex at times. He did not seem to love any of these girls particularly, consequently I felt safe. I feared that if he married any one of these emotionally disturbed girls, she would wreck his life. I told him so.

He took me out to the Greasy Spoon where I ate chili con carne as he did, fully expecting to become poisoned, but I never was, to *avant garde* movies where sex was made de- generate not beautiful, to guitar concerts (though the guitar was not my favorite instrument), to ride in his small open foreign car where the roar of the engine drowned out all conversation and the wild wind reduced my elegant coiffure to a wreck. Privately, I laughed at myself for being a lovesick idiot.

Finally Dexter evinced signs of inner conflict. His anomalous position of involvement with an older woman —filial but dangerously passionate at the same time —disturbed him and me. We were both caught in a whirlwind of forces beyond our control or comprehension. I strove to clarify this strange situation for him and for myself, equally mystified. I repeated to him Jung's and Stein's explanations of such phenomena. What might appear incestuous, they said, is innate in all men everywhere. 'The longing for the mother' is symbolic of man's desire for union with the deepest level of his unconscious, a desire to return to the cosmic source from which he sprang.

The incestuous feeling may be the vehicle of psychological rebirth, the union sought for is not necessarily with another person but with that other person within oneself. The taboo against incest in nearly all countries in all ages forces an internalization of the feeling. This taboo transforms sex, making it no longer merely a biological urge but a vehicle to induce spiritual development. It sounded beautiful but Dexter looked dubious.

Then a very strange incident occured. One day as we all sat in meditation, the muscles of my eyes suddenly strained painfully in an attempt to converge on a spot between my eyebrows. Images began to parade before my astonished eyes though I realized they were projected from within. There appeared a score of small beautiful images, all outlined as if by a pencil of golden light —flowers, urns and ships, dolphins and Grecian columns. It was delightful but what on earth did it mean?

The following day in the synchronistic way nature is so fond of displaying, as Jung points out, a strange coincidence occurred. One of the young men in the group (who had been gazing startled and wide eyed at Dexter and me for months) presented me with a little book for my birthday. It was by Edgar Cayce. It issued a warning to beginning meditators. Often in meditation erotic passion is aroused to an extreme degree of intensity. In India it is believed that often the cosmic energy enters the individual body through the reproductive organs. At the base of the spine is stored a tremendous reserve of energy coiled there like a serpent ready —through a proper form of meditation —to uncoil. It then may ascend through the seven chakras of the body, psychic or energy centers, finally rising to the 'third eye' between the eyebrows. Then, if one is fortunate, it reaches the crown of the head and brings enlightenment. In India this is known as *Kundalini*. It is considered extremely dangerous unless one has proper guidance by an enlightened teacher. It can be like playing with fire. Was this what had been happening to Dexter and me—a spontaneous rising of the Kundalini? It had not, alas, induced enlightenment. I felt relieved and cheated and delighted.

Chapter III
THE OLD SOUTH

Often half a dozen of our Zen group would sit around the dining table after dinner on Thursdays drinking endless coffee and milk.

"Did your generation rebel against anything?" they asked me.

"Not my generation so much. Rebellion came later —at least in the old South. Although personally I was a rebel at twenty. The minute I finished college I announced to my mother that I was going out to earn my own living. 'Why?' she asked. 'We will give you a new piano and a horse of your own, maybe a car later and a debut.' 'Because,' I said, 'I want to be free to be myself.' How I could have uttered these words of wisdom I can't imagine. I had not the faintest idea what they meant. I was as ignorant as only a Southern girl of that period could be. To tell you the truth, I was taught very little except how to be pleasing to others —especially men. In our town I was only the second girl of 'good family' as we called them, to leave home to get a job. Southern ladies did not do such things. To be a lady was the highest ideal offered to us. So my father disinherited me and my mother never forgave me."

"What kind of job did you get?"

"Well, I wanted to save the world and abolish poverty overnight. So I found a social service job in a mining camp in Alabama —coal mining. Later I worked in the slums of Chicago and New York."

"Where were you born in the South?"

"I hesitate to tell you. Nobody understands it. Some don't even believe it. You see, all my people on both sides originally came from Virginia. My mother and grandmother were descended from Martha Washington and Governor Spotswood who was the Royal Governor of Virginia for twelve years. He built the governor's palace in Williamsburg, now restored. My father's people were from Virginia too. Professional people —lawyers and doctors, teachers and preachers."

"Did you live in Virginia?"

"Only in a commune later on. But my grandmother and all her cronies were exiles from Virginia. She had owned slaves at sixteen and tried to bring me up with all the prejudices and traditions of the antebellum South. Actually I was born in Texas."

"What! With all the cowboys!"

"No, I never saw a cowboy in my life except in the movies. That's western Texas. Our central section of Texas was called the Black Belt —a crescent of rich black land. Our town was surrounded by cotton fields, and filled with countless Negroes, excuse me, black people. All my mother's servants were always black. There were no other kind down there but we loved our servants."

"But you didn't treat them as equals," Dexter protested somewhat belligerantly.

"We didn't treat anyone as equals without education, breeding and compatibility. My father, however, had a long line of blacks coming to our house to ask his help with their divorces, razor slashings on Saturday nights, and boys in jail. He repeatedly deplored the injustice shown black men in court if their cases were against white men. He was way ahead of his time."

"You evidently were too," Bob remarked.

"Only in some ways. My father's ideal was Thomas Jefferson. His watchwords were freedom and democracy. Jefferson, although an aristocrat himself, as you know, destroyed the aristocracy system in America. He deemed it unjust to other classes. My father instilled Jeffersonian principles into me everyday. My mother and grandmother, however, upheld the caste system of the aristocracy. Money, believe it or not, was not respected in our circles. Once I was not allowed to attend a very elaborate ball given by a rich banker. He was the only man in town who could boast of a real ball room. I longed to go. But my mother said, 'Why, I saw his wife as a girl picking cotton in her father's field —barefoot!' All manual work was *infra dig* for a Southern lady as it once was in England. No one went barefoot except poor whites and Negroes who could not afford shoes. But nowadays —."

"Nowadays we go barefooted, because it's natural," a girl said.

"And in the Zen Center, it's required," Bob remarked.

I laughed. "Well, you see we indeed are in a world of transition where values change in one lifetime. My mother loved to cook but if she did, it might ostracize her socially. So she left the kitchen to the negro cook while she organized a gourmet cooking club —sort of Cordon Bleu. And my father often said to me, 'I would enjoy the slow rhythmical exercise of mowing my own front lawn. But no gentleman ever does such menial work. So I walk in the woods instead.' He knew every woods, cave and river for a radius of fifty miles. It distressed my mother, who was a Baptist, because he went to the woods on Sundays instead of going to church. He said the woods were his cathedral."

"Oh, that sounds like Walt Whitman," a girl murmured.

I smiled at her. "Yes, it does. And my mother saw to it that I never lifted a little finger in housework. I never sewed on a button, washed a pair of stockings or boiled a kettle of water as a girl. She believed that a lady should sit on a cushion and *not* sew a fine seam but simply eat strawberries and cream, as it says in the old nursery rhyme. Isn't that an awful way to bring up any girl?"

"But now you run this big house," one of the students protested, looking about him.

"Oh, but my father insisted that I attend a college that emphasized the domestic arts and sciences. Besides the excellent maids I have now know far more about household matters than I do —fortunately."

"I never heard of such a thing!" a girl muttered.

"Why," I exclaimed, "didn't they teach you the social history of America in college? Have you never heard of WASPs? White Anglo-Saxon Protestants, WASPs for short. They were referred to constantly in papers and books a few years ago. We considered we were the group that settled

America, gave it its form, freedom and laws and therefore possessed every right to run it. But in the South, WASPs were narrowminded. They were prejudiced not only against all Northerners and Catholics, Jews and Negroes, but Chinese and Japanese, Italians and French, in fact anyone who was not a WASP and what's more, a Southern WASP, and with aristocratic lineage."

"More milk for you, Claire?" Dexter asked with the carton poised over my glass.

"Yes, thanks." He placed the empty carton on the table. "Do you mind taking it back to the kitchen?"

"Didn't such prejudices interfere with your social life?" John asked.

"It certainly did," I replied. "I had a good friend in high school named Ruth, the smartest girl in the class. She was an Irish Catholic so my mother would not allow me to visit in her home. Also because she was afraid I might meet their next door neighbor, a divorcee. Divorce was worse than leprosy. So I brought Ruth up to our house. My parents liked her so much I was allowed to visit her. And that's where I learned to dance —a pleasure strictly forbidden by my mother when I was sixteen."

"It all sounds like something in a novel."

"It was very real to me, I assure you. And because I loved books I chose to work in a bookshop when I went to New York, but I did not dare tell my parents and grandmother. They believed that being 'in trade' was socially demeaning. You find this is in all the classic English novels. And when my husband and I were in England not too long ago, the most noticeable characteristic of the country seemed to me to be class distinction. This seems so odd in America —now almost a classless society."

"As it should be," Dexter added.

"As it should be," I repeated. "The trouble was my grandmother and her 'exiled' friends considered no one on earth their superiors except the titled people of England whom of course they did not even know."

"Zen Buddhism," Bob remarked quietly, "sees everyone in the world as equal because everyone possesses the Buddha-Mind with all its potential virtues —compassion and wisdom and —"

Several of the people at the table murmured, "Hear! Hear!"

"I saw the movie of *Gone With the Wind*. Do you think that is an authentic picture of the old South?" a girl asked.

"In many ways, yes. Certainly every Southern girl, when I was young, was still raised to be a belle. She was a flat failure socially unless she was besieged by male admirers night and day. Remember, that is the scene with which the picture opens. I have been flirting with every personable male from seventeen to seventy from the time I was ten."

"How did your husband like that?" Dexter asked.

"He didn't, so I endeavored to restrain myself —without too much success. Men are so stimulating. They make life so exciting. But to return —the wonderful thing about the mystical experience is that —"

Bob interrupted. "Zen does not like the word mystical. It prefers enlightenment or self-realization."

"But Bob, the spiritual awakening is a mystical experience. All the intellectuals who are writing about self-realization in the scholarly journals nowadays use that word too. Anyway, the enlightenment experience, whether spontaneous or induced by meditation, is —"

"They don't like the word meditation either. Kolberg says that is the function of the rational mind."

"Oh, dear. Well, I suppose I must become accustomed to the unaccustomed word, zazen. Though most philosophers and psychologists use the term meditation. Anyway, spiritual enlightenment, whatever the method or means, causes prejudice against other classes, races and religions to fall away like empty husks —even in a Southern WASP like me."

"Someday there will be enough enlightened people to change society," a girl suggested. (At the time I knew everyone's name. I've since forgotten.)

"Both have to be changed simultaneously —people and society," Dexter stated firmly. "The more I hear about Claire's aristocratic childhood the gladder I am that I'm just poor white trash." The others laughed.

He rose, motioned to one of the other men. They carried the soiled plates out to the kitchen. We could hear them rinsing the dishes and putting them in the washer. Dexter was always considerate. Also he preferred action to conversation any day. The others made no move to leave the table. I often wondered when and if these students ever studied. The conversation continued.

"The old South sounds like the dark ages to me," a student from New York City remarked.

I laughed. "No, not really. Like all societies the deep South was a mixture of good and bad. It taught dignity and self- confidence, integrity and honor, hospitality and graciousness. Some of its faults are superficial and some sections received an infusion of Puritanism. My mother was a puritanical Baptist, my father a free thinker who instilled Jeffersonian democracy into his daughter and my grandmother attempted to sustain the antebellus traditions of plantation Virginia. A nice conflict of values for me, I assure you."

Dexter came back through the swinging pantry door. "Ready, Bob?"

They all left. But the next Thursday at dinner we continued the conversation. "Speaking of values," Bob said, "don't most people live —often unconsciously —by the values imposed on them by the society in which they live?"

"Yes," I laughed. "For years I made the mistake of assuming that the highest value was social status —based on breeding and ancestry. Don't forget, that was the value which ruled most societies of the world for centuries."

"Marx has proved for all people that the highest value is economic." This was said by Earl, a handsome young man who never spoke except to interject a remark in favor of Communism. He was quite handsome, with exquisite manners, always immaculately groomed, the son of a wealthy prominent Philadelphia family.

A quiet girl spoke up. "I had a course in valuation. According to the philosopher, Wilbur Urban, no value system can be adequate that fails to do justice to all our values —because they are inherent in the structure of reality. The kind of society we have seems to depend on the hierarchy in which they are placed, don't you think so, Earl?"

He stared into his coffee cup. He had shot his bolt and refused to talk any more.

We all gazed at the shy girl admiringly. "You're so right," I said. "It required many years for me to realize that my family, church, school and even my grandmother were actually trying to instill ethics into me. I am keenly interested in values because I seem to have lived under all six systems which the philosophers suggest. Ethical, in the South that I knew. Aesthetic, in New York City. The circle I knew believed that art was all that mattered. In Connecticut today it appears that people's social status is determined primarily by wealth. To liberal intellectuals nothing matters except politics. In my courses at Yale I realized that the cognitive, the intellectual, was primary. Nowhere in America have I found the metaphysical or religious experience regarded as the highest value in life except in Zen."

"Other Eastern religions, too."

"Oh, yes, undoubtedly," I said. "So you see I have lived under all the values men value."

They laughed politely at my feeble little joke.

"What about love?" one pretty girl demanded.

I sighed, "Ah yes, we women have placed romantic love as the chief value of our lives. That is why we have suffered so much. It never endures. Our value system was established by men. They omitted love."

"In all the higher religions, love of mankind is one of their values," Bob said.

I rose from the table all too ready to go to bed. The others rose slowly. "One more thing I must say. You young people of this generation are beginning at the point it has required a lifetime for me to attain. You can't imagine how extraordinarily intelligent and intellectually mature —if not otherwise —you seem to a person of my generation. At your age I was interested in nothing but dances, pretty clothes and men." They were all in stocking feet. These young people with such beautiful minds pulled on such ugly clumsy shoes.

"Goodnight, goodnight. See you Tuesday," they called as they went down the front steps.

Chapter IV
MACHINES TO ALTER STATES
OF CONSCIOUSNESS

One day I informed the group that it would be necessary to change the day of meeting. Dr. Jean Houston had asked me to come to her laboratory of the Foundation for Mind Research in New York which she and her husband, Robert Masters, directed. She wanted to experiment with my mind. Our leader, Bob, frowned disapprovingly. Zen Buddhists are not supposed to stray from the straight path.

When I returned from the city they eagerly asked me to describe what had happened. "It was really extraordinary. I have always been reluctant for her to experiment on me. I feared I might not perform well enough and so disappoint her. She really is a genius. I admire her tremendously. She has read my books and articles and says she likes them. Well, anyway, she placed me behind a transparent screen —curved for some reason. She used an audio-visual device environment machine that threw slides on the screen. She and her husband had painted abstract designs on them in all sorts of colors. On the screen they moved, swirled and swirled endlessly like clouds in the sky but faster. She placed some kind of sound receiver over my right ear with modern music playing every minute.

"At the end of half an hour Dr. Houston came for me. 'My body feels so heavy, I can scarcely walk,' I heard myself say in a slow thick voice.

"'That's because you are nearly in a trance,' she replied.

"She asked me to lie on a couch, close my eyes and relax while she sat beside me. In a low calm voice she began to make suggestions. 'Imagine yourself on a raft floating slowly down a broad calm river.'

"I did and to my astonishment I saw it as plain as day.

"'Now stop and step out on the bank. Do you see a meadow?'

"'Yes, yes,' I heard myself saying in a slow, sleepy voice. 'Full of beautiful spring flowers. Texas flowers I saw as a child. Indian heads, paintbrushes, nigger toes but no blue bonnets. And, oh, there's my father! He always took my brother and me every spring to see the wildflowers.'

"Then Dr. Houston asked me to see and enter a great tree with a door. Inside was a pool. She told me to visualize myself diving into it. I saw myself vividly swirling round and round in a vortex. A small white figure though at the moment I was actually wearing my favorite color, red. She asked me to step out of the vortex onto flat land. I did.

"'What do you see?'

"'Nothing in all directions.'

"'Keep looking.'

"'Oh, yes, there's a man sitting over there. He looks exactly —why, he looks exactly like Michealangelo's painting on the ceiling of the Sistine chapel —the one of God in swirling draperies, pointing a finger at Adam, but Adam is not there.'

"'What does he say?'

"'Nothing.'

"'What of nonverbal communication?'

"'Oh, yes. Now I am laying my hand on his knee and he is saying silently to me, "You must not expect me to bring you to self-realization again as I did before. You yourself must work for it this time.'"

"'All right,' Dr. Houston said. 'Now I am going to count to twenty-five very fast and at twenty-five you will wake up.'

"I awakened feeling rejuvenated, exalted. I remained in New York for three more days, as you all know. I almost wished there would be a riot in the streets that night so that I could go out and lose my life to save others. I loved absolutely everybody. But it didn't last."

At that time I was completely ignorant of such mental phenomena. Later, however, I read with amazement in Charles Tart's book, *Altered States of Consciousness*, a chapter by Wolfgang Kretchmer. He described Carl Happich's method of symbolic visualization where archetypal images are evoked. A meadow with flowers, a mountain, chapel and forest. The meadow, for example, is Mother Nature, the world of the child, a return to the creative basis of life. It seems that a healthy man will have a satisfying experience of a meadow in the flush of spring. The psychically ill find it impossible to visualize a meadow.

Chapter V
TWO GENERATIONS

Often after the others had put their shoes on again and left, Bob and Dexter and I would sit in the hall talking. Dexter would sit patiently, sigh and look hungry. He was waiting to drive Bob back to the University. He was not overly fond of conversation.

"How did your rebellion differ from ours?" Bob asked me.

"Well, basically it was the same with superficial differences. All my life, for example, I was seeking freedom and certitude and truth, unconsciously in the beginning. I was never certain about anything but passionately longed to be. Uncertainty frustrated me horribly. In fact, my first published book, a novel, was an adventure story of a woman's search for the highest mountain in the world, Mt. Certitude."

"Did she —did you —find it?" Dexter asked with a smile.

"No. She thought she did at the time. But that was an intellectual search and now —"

"Now Zen is the search for wisdom through awakening of the True-self," Bob murmured like the conscientious teacher he aspired to be.

I smiled at him. "But what I rebelled against was the domination and the values of family and class, school and church, society and marriage. Especially against male domination of women, double sex standards and all the conventions imposed on women. My generation, however, rebelled within the framework of existing society. We did not withdraw and develop a counterculture as you-all have done today. And we did not dress differently to advertise our differences. Another point is that today many young people rebel against their parents' materialistic values yet are willing to be supported by them. It is considered okay as long as they hate their parents. I do not understand that. We worked for our living in order to be free to rebel."

"It seems to me," Bob said, "that every generation rebels against the older generation. But never in all history has there been such a complete break with the values of society as our generation has made, isn't that true?"

"It deserved to be broken away from," Dexter murmured.

"Yes," I said, "but it is more than that. It appears to me that you young people have literally skipped a few stages in evolution. If it is evolution. And I think it is. Teilhard de Chardin and Sinnott, the Yale biologist, say it is. My theory is that nature herself was so appalled at the dangerous crises produced by the almost exclusive worship of reason, science and materialism in the West that she felt it encumbent on her to do something drastic —and quickly. So she produced you religiously-oriented young people of the counterculture. I honestly believe you're the hope of the race."

They smiled and looked embarrassed.

"But," Bob said, "the religiously-oriented young people are not violent like those political radicals in the counterculture. The ones who throw bombs and burn down houses."

"Thank goodness," I murmured. "But did you-all read that article in the *New York Times* recently by a psychiatrist at Columbia University? He discovered the reason the politi- cally radical students were so violent. He analyzed 200 of them. In every case their unconscious motivation was intense hatred of their parents, primarily because they had not been loved or understood."

"But," Bob continued, "we want to change people by helping them to awaken their Buddha-natures. That might do them more good than Freudian psychoanalysis."

"Yes, Freud did not penetrate below the neurotic level, although Jung did and —"

Our conversation was usually terminated by Margaret appearing in the door of the dining room saying with offended dignity, "Dinner is served, Madam." She did not approve of anyone who did not know when to go home. She was very fond of Dexter, however. He was the only one of all the Yale students who ever paid the slightest attention to her. He always went out to the kitchen to speak to her, offered to drive her home, carried the piles of blankets she was taking home to rebind for me, went in and talked to Margaret's sick husband.

About this time I began to read Kolberg's *Introduction to Zen*. It was unlike any book I had ever read before. Half of it I failed to understand. It was obvious that Zen Buddhist values were the opposite of the prevailing Western philosophy of life based on materialism, rationalism, individualism, science and lip service to Christianity. Buddhism offered the profoundest ideas I had ever encountered. In some instances they were similar to those that had emerged during my spontaneous awakening, yet were more systematized.

At least three of the basic principles of Buddhism proved easy to accept: the existence of a True-self, enlightenment, and the oneness of all things. I translated True-self as similar in meaning to the collective unconscious in the Jungian system. It was a reservoir of virtues inherent in all men but suppressed in the West for centuries by the domination of our rational conscious minds. The True-self had emerged to an incredible degree during the actualization of my potentials when I was fifty-four. This self was now in sore need of activation again.

The second Zen principle of enlightenment was similar to self-realization in Jungian therapy. It was induced, however, by one's own efforts in zazen, not by the aid of an intermediary like a therapist. Self-realization involved the discovery of the self, return to one's source and identification with mankind, to use Jung's terms that I understood better. To me it was terribly exciting and important that both systems were based on the same laws of the human psyche. However much the terms, means or method varied, the results were apparently similar —at least theoretically —in Zen, in Jung, and in the spontaneous variety of spiritual awakening and each strengthened the other in my doubting mind.

The third principle, the oneness of all things, was a truth I had experienced without my own volition after, or was it during? my awakening. The

Western concept of the separateness of Creator and creature, subject and object, man and nature, man and the universe constituted a dualism which I had abandoned, in theory if not in continuous feeling.

Kolberg's editorial comments and his translation of the teachings of Yasutani and others proved that he was a fine Zen student, understood the intricacies and subtleties of Zen more thoroughly than I ever could. He wrote the English language exceedingly well. But the unfamiliar Eastern terminology, the Japanese and Sanskrit words were very frustrating. Nirvana, dharma, karma, reincarnation were beyond me at that point.

With all its negativism, paradoxes and ambiguities and, what seemed to me, its unnecessary peculiarities, Zen did not appear too alluring. If, however, zazen could induce a second self-realization experience in me, I might be willing to devote myself to it —maybe —sometime. But it must conform to those truths that had emerged in my spontaneous spiritual awakening. Otherwise I could not accept it. For was not the spontaneous union of the individual self with reality the most natural and trustworthy guide? I was not fully aware at this time that most of the higher religions were established on the *spontaneous* mystical experiences of their founders —though Buddha's was *induced* by meditation.

I had planned to read the *Introduction to Zen* again after I had further experience with zazen. Then I might be able to comprehend it more fully. I was impressed by one review, however, that compared Kolberg's book to William James' classic, *Varieties of Religious Experience*. That explained the mystical experience psychologically. Years ago that book had offered validity of my own mystical awakening that my rational mind had doubted.

One cold winter night —it was Thursday, the cook's day off —we all sat around a roaring fireplace after dinner. We continued our non-stop conversation between the generations. They sat on the floor. I was the only one who sat in a chair.

"How old are you?" I asked a girl with long straight hair, which she told me she sometimes flattened with a hot iron. A curl was regarded as a disgrace in the counterculture.

"Twenty-two," she replied.

"Well, when I was twenty-two every woman in America had long hair piled on top of her head held up with hairpins. A few bold young women bobbed their hair short. I was one of those. You girls protest by wearing your hair long and straight, even if naturally curly, while your mothers wear theirs short and curled unnaturally. I suppose you would not be caught dead at a hairdressers?"

They laughed.

"Well, I may be a rebel but I don't want to be enslaved by the fashions of the counterculture any more than those of the conventional world. I try to choose the best of both worlds. So I go to a hairdresser. Another thing. You all deny the mores of the times by smoking marijuana. My generation had a similar problem. When I was a girl your age no decent woman smoked cigarettes —only the 'fancy women' as we called prostitutes. I loathed the taste of cigarettes but I smoked in a misguided attempt to be equal to men. I was asked to leave several New York City restaurants because women were not allowed to smoke in them."

"Oh, no!" several voices moaned.

"Oh, yes. And once a nice Canadian man came up to my apartment in New York. We had had a delightful evening —dinner and dancing. He made passes at me which I did not consider justified by my behavior. I asked him why he assumed so much. 'Well,' he said, 'any girl who smokes and cuts her hair and lives in an apartment alone —she's just asking for it.' I gave him a little lecture he never forgot. He assumed everything a woman did had a sex connotation. The only way a girl can protect herself from ravenous wolves is to see to it that they fall in love with her."

"Easier said than done," a girl murmured, glancing meaningfully at the man next to her who stared straight ahead.

"What about marriage and sex and all that?" another asked.

"Well, I for one rebelled against marriage, though my generation did not at that time. I pronounced it a form of imprisonment for a woman. Now, of course, I know it can be the most wonderful human relationship. At twenty-two I joined in a 'companionate marriage' as we called it then or 'free love'. You-all call it a 'relationship' today. The man wanted a ceremony but I refused though we told our parents and the world that we were married. No one was able to rent an apartment in those days without being married. I refused to wear a ring unless he did. I said, 'Why should a woman advertise to the world that she is bought and paid for?' My views were very extreme then. I saw no reason why a woman should lose her identity and name and assume those of the man. So we hyphenated our two last names."

I laughed and continued. "But what our poor children would do for a name I don't know. Hyphenate the hyphen, I reckon. Actually it turned out to be a common law marriage and legal."

"Did you have communes in those days?"

"No, I knew of only one —the one I lived in with my so-called husband. It was in the Blue Ridge Mountains of Virginia. We called it a cooperative colony."

"Was it a success?"

"A dismal failure in all ways. Not enough money and too much sex. I doubt if such a venture can ever succeed unless the members are motivated by serious religious aspirations. Too many egos clashing."

"What about sexual freedom for women in general?"

"There wasn't any. Even the word sex was forbidden to be spoken except in a whisper. In my college only one girl, who the authorities imagined, suspected, assumed, might have gone to bed with a man, was expelled —secretly."

"Today they'd have to expel the whole college," one of the men murmured. All the other men laughed. The girls did not.

"Why," I continued, "in my senior year I was engaged but I did not even know what a man and woman did in bed. A stupid way to bring girls up, isn't it? I hope the sex freedom of girls today will not bring unhappiness to them. Theoretically it all sounds wonderfully fair. But we have yet to see how it works in practice. It has already wrecked the lives of many high school girls. Girls of fourteen with babies or venereal disease. Tragic."

We talked on and on about the different generations, new values, and Zen. The self-realization movement, if sufficiently widespread, might some day prevent the world from destroying itself, we hoped.

One afternoon some of us sat in the hall waiting for the laggards to arrive. Earl went up to reclean the zendo although I told him Margaret had cleaned it thoroughly that morning. In Snowbound the zendo and entire Center was at all times incredibly, shiningly clean.

"Mrs. Owens," Bob remarked, "you were certainly many years ahead of your time. The counterculture has just now caught up with you. In many ways, you are more like us than we are ourselves."

I laughed.

"No, I mean it." He counted on his fingers. "We are more interested in inner growth than in materialism, in intuition than reason, cooperation than competition, compassion rather than criticism of others. We believe in man's innate Buddha-nature and goodness and in zazen as a way to release it. Except for you and Roshi Kolberg I've never met any mature person who has values like ours and yours." He glanced inquiringly around the circle. "Have you?" They shook their heads.

I had not rejected all the values they rejected so much as altered the hierarchy and diminished their emphasis in some instances. All except cleanliness and good grooming. I longed to mention this one grave fault of these wonderful young people but I could not bear to hurt their feelings. When any of the students invited me out to dinner or a movie, however, I would say, "I'll wear my prettiest dress and you will pretty yourself up too, won't you?" And they would.

As the months passed, the changes that meditation effected in these young men and girls was plainly evident. They became less competitive, more cooperative, less selfish. They assisted each other with cars, money and offered various services quite spontaneously. There was no coercion, no friction. It was an exhilarating lesson for me. It not only proved that Zen's postulate was correct that everyone's True-self contained many inherent but dormant virtues, but also that they could be awakened by zazen. The chief effect zazen had on me was the *Kundalini* experience. These months of Zen practice with the Yale students were joyous and stimulating. I knew I liked and admired the young people. I was not sure about Zen yet.

Chapter VI
THE OLD AND THE NEW

Bob and Dexter and some other members attended the intensive training sessions (sesshin) at the Snowbound Center. Some returned in a glow, others deeply disturbed. I was now a member but not yet eligible for sesshin or ready to undergo the hardship of rising at 4:30 every morning, sitting in zazen nine hours a day for seven days, eating little and sleeping less. Members were not allowed to discuss their inner experiences that occurred during sesshin. Consequently its value was still a mystery to me.

When Spring arrived Dexter urged me to visit Snowbound to attend the annual picnic and meet various members. He drove us up in my car. The spring day was perfect, the car purred like a happy cat. Dexter drove with ease and therefore pleasure. We detoured to visit some married friends of his in Pennsylvania. The woman's name was Clare. She had received her Ph.D. at the Sorbonne and was now deep in Zen.

The Dutch towns and streets through which we drove had very amusing names. We laughed, feeling we had not a care in the world. Everything in life was absolutely perfect at this moment. Perfection is such a rare thing in life that my heart sang. We were free. I was with the man I loved, who loved me. I wished we could drive on forever —perhaps into sweet oblivion.

Late that afternoon I was shocked to see Dexter sitting on Clare's porch looking very strange as if overcome by sleepiness. He admitted that he and one of the other men had taken some sort of psychedelic drug. It made me sick at heart, disappointed in him. And I felt he had betrayed me. I considered the ingestion of drugs a sign of weakness, injurious to mind and body and a refutation of the efficacy of zazen. In fact, Zen members usually "took the ten precepts" (similar to the ten commandments), that included proscription of liquor and drugs. Dexter had endangered our drive to Snowbound tomorrow morning. Now I should have to do all the driving.

He was well aware that driving on fast highways with heavy traffic made me extremely nervous. When he drove I relaxed. I could not bear to speak to Dexter. Next morning he appeared to have recovered so we continued our trip to Snowbound in virtual silence.

After arriving in Snowbound he took me through the Center building. Formerly it was a fine private residence now remodelled into a Zen Center with a large impressive zendo. A gold figure of Buddha was on the altar with flowers and fruit offerings placed before it. The interior of the house was as simple, austere and immaculate as Japanese houses were reputed to be. Everyone in Zen referred to vibrations. I did not understand what they meant. But that zendo certainly emanated something —not holy exactly —but indescribable —different.

That afternoon I met Blanch, a tall attractive woman in her forties —well-dressed and well-groomed. She had been a charter member of the Center in 1967. She drove the Roshi and me out to the country estate of Harriet, a Center member, for tea. Both women were warm and cordial. Roshi was pleasant but non-committal. I had expected him to welcome me with open arms. That is not the way of Zen, I was told. One must display an urgent desire to train at the Center. I was not at all sure that I wished to do so.

I described to the Roshi some of the strange *Kundalini* experiences in New Haven. He suggested that I write it up for the *Zen Voice*, the Center quarterly. Later I did so. All I remember, however, is that it was a difficult task to write about such a delicate matter as the relationship of Dexter and myself. I did say, "Being in love is like walking in a garden of eternal Spring."

The next day we all attended the annual picnic on the grounds of a large estate of another member. Many of the young people who had never even seen me before urged me to move to Snowbound. Bernadine, a fine violinist who played for us, said to me, "We need older people here, Claire. We are all so young and inexperienced. We don't know nothin' 'bout nothin'!"

Susie, Roshi's secretary (surnames seemed to be unknown at the Center) had invited me to stay in the Center's guest room. I wished to be free, therefore I stayed at an inn nearby. I certainly entertained no slightest intention of abandoning my beautiful home and garden in New Haven but I was curious about Snowbound as I always was about every new city I visited.

I walked up West Avenue, the wide spacious street that was the main residential street in earlier days. It is lined with a few architecturally fine Georgian houses and many large ugly Victorian mansions. Snowbound has a great deal of wealth derived primarily, I am told, from two large factories, one of which employs about 50,000 people and the other many thousands.

Could anyone live in any city without flowering trees and shrubs, I wondered? On West Avenue I saw tulip trees in bloom, dogwood just beginning, forsythia just gone by, hawthorne, and one wisteria vine in bloom. The street has many magnificent tall trees. Beeches —copper, weeping, and otherwise —amusing ginkgoes, spruces, white pines, hemlocks, small Japanese maples, lindens, locusts —every kind of tree imaginable. The houses are all set unusually far back from the street providing spacious grounds around them. But I was more than happy to return to my colonial home with its eighteenth century furniture and small garden in New Haven.

In June the school year at Yale was nearing its end. Dexter left me speechless one day. He announced he was leaving New Haven and moving to Snowbound. "I need the strict daily discipline of the Zen Center. So far in life, families and schools have all been too permissive [implying that I had been also]. So I'll get a job in Snowbound. Now, Claire, you must sell your house and move to Snowbound."

"What! Leave my beautiful home where I lived for thirty-two happy years with my husband! Give up my friends and my three devoted servants! They are irreplaceable! No, my dear, you go. I shall miss you terribly, but moving is absolutely out of the question."

"But, I *need* you, Claire. The young people at the Center need you. The Center is where you belong. You won't have to do a thing. I'll find an elegant apartment for you near the Center. I'll rent one of those U-Haul trucks and move all your furniture for you. Then I'll come back on the bus and drive you up to Snowbound in your own car."

I laughed. "My dear boy, thank you, but you're out of your mind. But if by any remote chance I should move up there, which I have no intention of doing, what would you want me to do?"

"I don't want you to *do* anything, just *be*. Why don't you consult your financial adviser. What's his name?"

"Mr. Tate."

"Doesn't the man have a first name?"

"No." I could not bear for young people to call mature people whom they did not even know by their first name.

I telephoned Seymour. He held no brief for Zen although his own son was a teacher of Transcendental Meditation and he himself had introduced it for the executives into several of his plants. The deciding factor he said must be my happiness. If I was absolutely certain this was what I wanted then go ahead. But be positive before I placed my house on the market.

Dexter soon left town and all the other Zen meditators scattered far and wide. It was as if the world had suddenly come to an end. I attempted to console myself—unsuccessfully: You are fortunate, Claire. You have been given a wonderful year with young people and laughter, love and ecstasy and meditation. And just when you needed it most after Thursty's death. So be grateful, for heaven's sake.

I walked about my home seeing it with new eyes. Never had the eighteenth century decor looked so elegant. It was inseparable from my marriage to Thurston. There was his empty chair in the living room where he sat in the evenings reading or listening to music. Remaining in this house kept him alive—and kept the pain alive too. Surely any woman who would deliberately abandon such a beautiful home had lost all sense of values, I admonished myself.

The very furniture and shelves of books seemed to look at me in an accusing manner. The crystal chandeliers, the Hepplewhite side-board with its glossy mahogany luster, the sweeping red damask draperies. We have served you faithfully for over thirty years, they seemed to say, we have given you pleasure and comfort and now at a whim you want to discard us.

I know, I know, I moaned silently. I love you, I cannot leave. You're part of my life, part of me. Then a faint voice sounded, but Zen teaches that attachment to transient material things is not wise. And the garden. I went out and walked slowly around it as I did nearly every day. Never had it looked so lovely. I had watched the growth of every tree and shrub for over thirty years.

If you take an apartment in Snowbound, Claire, I chided myself, you will have no garden to walk in, no flowers to bring in the house, no trees to watch as they grow.

I went around and touched the forsythia bushes—always like a burst of sunshine in Spring, the poplar that I loved to watch swaying gracefully in the wind, the white pine, the gigantic oaks, the dogwoods that lighted up the green garden with their white blossoms, and the hemlock hedge that Thursty had planted for me all across the front of the lawn because I could not bear to look at bare trees in the winter.

Then I stood at a front window as I had a hundred times before and watched the rays of the late afternoon sun touch the East Rock palisades to a luminous red. And what of the park and river opposite where we had walked so many happy times? No more, however, too many muggings there nowadays. I lived in a beautiful green bower of trees—how could I ever abandon it?

The next day I drove through the grounds of the elegant Lawn Club where Thursty and I had been to many pleasant social functions. I always enjoyed the sight of its red brick Georgian entrance. Then I went on to the Quinnipiac Club for lunch—the best food in town. The building was something like the Governor's mansion in Williamsburg, Virginia—most pleasant to the eye.

Would there be some fine clubs for me to join if I should ever move to Snowbound? Public restaurants in the provinces everywhere were too often impossible. That was certainly true of New Haven.

After a delicious lunch I left the car at the Club and walked slowly around the Yale campus. Was it perhaps for the last time? I wondered. I revelled in the beauty of the college Gothic and Georgian buildings that had given me continuous joy over the years. I recalled the many stimulating courses I had taken and lectures I had enjoyed here.

I stepped into the entrance of Sterling Library. It was exciting—the Gothic doorway, the great corridor like a cathedral nave, the hand-carved linen-fold panelling, and all the greatest books in the world. Surely books deserved to be housed in a Gothic cathedral structure. A university was a repository of the world's culture accumulated through the ages. The average person cared less than nothing about abstract ideas. But here thought was god. Without the universities, past culture and historical knowledge would disappear from the earth. Would there be a university in Snowbound with which I could so closely identify as I had with Yale?

And New Haven was near New York, the center of contemporary American culture and life. Only an hour and a half away. My roots were still there in the city. Snowbound was at the other end of the world—probably provincial. Could I endure moving so far away from the city of cities? London and Paris did not compare. One friend had remarked, "Snowbound, is it? So you're moving out West into the snow belt. You're crazy."

I returned home feeling torn, undecided, forlorn, I climbed up the third floor, passing the door of the maids' room where so many cooks had lived and made life pleasanter for Thursty and me. I stood in the door of my writing room. This was the room where my glorious spiritual awakening had occurred. This was the place where I gladly forgot the world and plunged into the creative joy of writing my books. I burst into tears and ran back down the stairs.

I sought consolation with Margaret in the kitchen. She was weeping quietly. "Oh, Mrs. Owens, I thought I was going to take care of you the rest of your life."

I put my arms around her and we cried together. How could I live without her? She was a fine, truly noble woman. And who would do the cleaning and the laundry? I well knew that today only one servant in a thousand is satisfactory. And training a new one requires at least a year. I had been through it many times. And if I moved to Snowbound I must find and train new maids—if only part-time ones.

"But, my dear, dear Margaret, *if* I join the Zen Center I plan to live the simple life, do my own cooking, much as I hate it. Besides, you are not as well as you should be. And your son and grandchildren are here. They would never let you go. And there is no maid's room in those small apartments in Snowbound, I fear. And I could not allow you to go home alone at night on a bus in a strange town where rapes and muggings are commonplace. Besides, you'd die of loneliness. I can't bear to give you up but—but oh, do try to understand, my dear Margaret. You've been the most wonderful friend to me and seen me through all those difficult years of Mr. Owen's illness and everything and—" I ran from the room, sobbing.

"Dinner will be served in—fifteen minutes, Mrs. Owens," Margaret announced in a broken voice.

As I sat alone at the dinner table my two selves carried on an interior dialogue. Oh, I can't give it all up! I simply can't! And remember, Claire, you will be forced to find a new grocer, a new doctor, new dentist, new lawyer, new trust officer, new hairdresser. To say nothing of new friends. You know it's always been difficult for you to make changes. You are the stable type like your father, not a quick-change artist like your mother. And new strange streets in a strange city—you will have to find your way around them. Your sense of direction has always been poor. Thursty used to laugh at you about it all the time.

And Connecticut—despite your passion for New York, you have put roots down in this state too. I know, I know, I love this beautiful little state with its magnificent woodlands everywhere doing nothing but looking beautiful; its dreaming blue hills in the distance, and sparkling little brooks. Connecticut is my home. And now can I give up my friends of thirty years standing like Lucy and Ina and Louise and Julia? How can any woman of seventy-four pull herself up by the roots and make a whole new life for herself? Claire, you are a fool to throw away all the wonderful things you pres-

ently have for a very uncertain kind of future religious life. It can't be done, I tell you.

Should I stay or should I move to Snowbound? I wept, I prayed, I sat long hours in earnest meditation. What was the wisest course of action? My entire future life, my happiness, depended on this momentous decision.

But—but, I argued, I am so utterly alone. I long for a "flight of the alone to the Alone," as some mystic expressed it. In the mean time, I need some kind of family, some kind of group, as a focus to build my life around. If I don't join the Zen Center how is my spiritual life to develop? *I cannot do it alone!* And without it, my life will be an empty nothingness. If Zen can induce in me anything like the glory of those twelve beautiful years of my awakening, it is worth every sacrifice of everything and—I smiled slyly—I will be with my darling Dexter—I hope.

Finally I took the bit in my teeth and telephoned the real estate agent. The house was appraised and listed at $67,000. It was the summer of 1970.

Dexter wrote and inquired if I wished him to look at apartments for me. I said yes, tentatively. I was still hesitating. He investigated all the new high-rise apartment houses along West Avenue, sent me floor plans with measurements to scale, prices, photographs, services included—whether indoor heated garages, or garage attendants, or maid service. I wrote him he had executed his commission thoroughly and I was proud of him. He suggested that I come up in August to look at the apartments myself. And he added, "Then you can meet the girl I think I want to marry."

Oh God, I moaned, help me! It's come, sooner than I expected. But haven't you been urging him to marry? Yes, half-heartedly and as a matter of honor, not conviction. The reality is a knife straight to the heart. But you knew it was inevitable. If you really love Dexter as much as you claim, Claire, you would want him to live a normal natural happy life. I do. And I don't.

I flew to Snowbound this time. Dexter met me at the airport. His face was shining like the harvest moon. He flung his arms about me and kissed me soundly. He was trembling all over. Then he introduced me to a pretty blonde girl standing in the crowd. It was Hannah—*the* girl. At least I had the grace to feel sorry she had witnessed Dexter's ebullient welcome.

We were all staying in the house of someone's friend. That is the way the Zen people do things. I was sitting in the living room when Dexter announced he and Hannah would dash out and buy some ice cream for supper. They started off but he came running back into the living room and kissed me again. "I'm just so glad you are here."

At supper no one talked for some reason. The hostility between Hannah and me chilled the air for a radius of six feet at least. Afterward we all listened to a most illuminating tape recording by Ram Dass. He described his recent spiritual experiences in India. I was weary and went up to bed early. Shortly Dexter and Hannah came up to bid me goodnight. He sat on the edge of the bed. She soon left the room to attend to some domestic chore. Instantly Dexter caught me in his arms, pressed my breast fiercely against his chest, his heart pounding wildly, and kissed me full on the lips with pent-up passion again and again.

Such a wave of desire and love and unutterable sweetness flooded my body, my mind and heart, my whole being. I thought I should surely faint. This was exactly what we had been longing to do for a whole year. It seemed so right, so inevitable, the culmination of something, a fulfillment, the end of our affair? Our swan song? Renunciation?

Finally I drew away. "No, no, my dear darling Dexter, we mustn't. Not ever again. It's not fair to Hannah. But I'm glad. Just this once."

He rose from the bed and fled from the room as if it were on fire. I lay there and sobbed myself to sleep. Next morning after breakfast I said to Dexter, "If you must marry, then marry this one. She is far superior to any of the other girls you introduced me to in New Haven. They would have wrecked your life. You have a slightly messianic complex, my dear. You are not Jesus or Jung, remember. You can't go around saving everybody. Zen advises us to save ourselves before we try to help others, doesn't it? Hannah is a normal nice girl. So grab her while there's time."

But I went upstairs and cried for an hour loathing myself for being illogical, selfish and ridiculous. It did not lessen the pain one iota.

Hannah accompanied me on my tour of the apartment houses. Afterward, I took her to lunch. Dexter had chosen the most attractive apartment house on West Avenue, approximately fourteen blocks from the Center. It was the one I preferred also. A new high-rise of honey-colored brick with two fountains in front. Trees throughout the spacious well-kept grounds, pleasant managers and doormen, maid service, indoor garage, heated, with attendants to wash the car. The living room of the apartment and the bedroom were both unusually large and, more important, well-proportioned. I had learned that it is painful to live in a room that is not properly proportioned. A small kitchen and even smaller bathroom. It should be sufficient for my purpose and my new simple life style, I hoped, after an eleven room house with four baths and three servants. The entire east wall of the living room and bedroom was glass. This morning the sunshine flooded the whole apartment as it had never done in our colonial house. I signed the lease with a heavy heart. I knew it was the right thing to do, but Hannah had changed the situation.

I planned to move to Snowbound on October 1,1970. All the rest of the summer in New Haven strangers walked through my beloved house. It seemed like some kind of desecration. I strove to control my emotions by working to exhaustion every day—sorting, laying aside, throwing away, giving away, setting aside those items to be left for auction—a desecration in itself. I determined to take only the basic necessities. I felt almost like a nun entering a monastery, though my life in Snowbound would not be so severe and confined as that—I hoped.

The fatal day arrived. Dexter came down by bus—in order to drive us up in my car.

"I'm sorry you had that terrible twelve hour trip, dear." He laughed. "It was nothing. I did zazen most of the way." Never had I seen Dexter looking so ravishingly beautiful—not handsome—beautiful. Blue coat and blue tie that accentuated the blueness of his eyes, a white shirt and collar, thank heaven, and white trousers. His hair was washed and combed, his face well-shaven. I realized that high stiff collars were uncomfortable. Open collars could be very attractive. It was the bedraggled appearance that was offensive. I invited him to one of our clubs for dinner. And just to prove that I was not old-fashioned, I invited the rich homosexual in whose house Dexter had lived. We had a delightful evening. That night Dexter stayed in the guest room that had served as our zendo. Early next morning we sallied forth on the greatest adventure of our lives—of my life at any rate.

Chapter VII
THE MOVE

It was another memorable trip from New Haven to Snowbound with Dexter. The October day was as perfect as the Spring day had been when he and I drove up by way of Pennsylvania. This was one of those glorious Indian summer days—hot sun, cool dry air that acted like an elixir. The car flew along the road humming to itself like a happy bumble bee.

It was to be an all-day journey. There is something wonderfully intimate about a long automobile trip with a person for whom one cares. A warm private world is created inside the little glass house on wheels excluding everyone else. Time is suspended. All troubles are banished to the exterior, unable to penetrate the interior. Probably never again would Dexter and I be alone for a whole day like this. I relished every golden minute, longing for it never to end. Our silences were vibrant, only increasing the sweet awareness of his presence. Of course, Hannah was a shadow lurking in the offing. But, I repeatedly reminded myself, many sons love their mothers as much as their wives. So surely I need not worry too much.

In the late afternoon, we turned into West Avenue and approached the inn where I was to stay until my furniture arrived by moving van. After motoring for eight hours I was weary, hungry but blissfully happy. A whole new wonderful way of life lay before me with a delightful young man and Zen discipline.

Suddenly Dexter shattered my world as easily as if it had been a fragile red bauble on a Christmas tree. "I hope Hannah has come a day early. I hope she's already at my apartment now instead of waiting until tomorrow as we planned. I miss her already."

What a way to celebrate my arrival after an almost traumatic uprooting from my home in New Haven. I felt sick, selfish, wounded beyond words. My beautiful house of cards had come tumbling down about my head like a ton of bricks. Silently I chastised myself: it's natural, it's normal, it's right for him to want a young girl. And all young men need sex. You are a fool to grieve, Claire. Nothing I said lessened the pain one iota.

At the door of the inn I sent Dexter away abruptly, refusing dinner and even a goodnight kiss. He walked away looking hurt and bewildered. The poor young idiot, I said to myself, he doesn't realize how he's shattered my foolish dream.

I flung myself onto the bed fully clothed and burst into tears. My hands grasped the side of the mattress so convulsively, so fiercely, my nails all but tore the strong ticking. The roots of my new life in Snowbound were cut the very minute I arrived. It isn't fair, I moaned. He lured me up here and now this sudden rebuff.

Oh, Claire, you knew this would happen sooner or later. Later, yes, but not sooner. It's inevitable. You told him you *wanted* him to marry Hannah. A part of me does. Another part wants to keep him all to myself. How on earth do real mothers ever relinquish their real sons when they marry? To sever the silver cord is to lacerate one's self. If you really love him as you claim, you should be thinking of his happiness, not your own, all the time.

Oh, God, all I know is it hurts! It hurts unbearably! I should never have sold my house and at a $20,000 loss, too. Have I wrecked my life completely? Have I made an irretrievable mistake? I see nothing for me here in Snowbound but continual sorrow. Unless, Claire, another voice said, unless you can maintain yourself on a higher spiritual level than this, on a less selfish level. After all, your chief motive in moving to Snowbound was to enter Zen practice. Sometimes you forget this. And forgive Dexter, Claire. He is young and footloose. He does not realize what it means to own a home. He's not aware of the painful sacrifice you've made. He does not know what he did.

The next morning Dexter telephoned and asked me to have breakfast with him. No, I needed rest and did not wish to see him at all for several days. At dinner time that night he knocked on my bedroom door at the inn. He and Hannah had prepared a nice dinner. It was ready and he had come for me. I went meekly.

Hannah and I both struggled valiantly to become friends. She was really quite interesting—had studied pyschology and art. I realized that I was the one who should step out of the picture. But how could I so long as Dexter still loved me—and showed it? Yet I knew he loved Hannah too. I had seen him look at her tenderly.

I was glad he loved her. As a woman I did not want to see any woman marry without being loved by her husband. If Dexter had not loved her I should have felt angry with him. It was all very confusing. Zen couples, however, never acted as if they were in love.

He called me frequently on the phone and we carried on long conversations with a great deal of laughter. One day he said, "I reckon I always wanted a family and home, but no one seemed to click. Hannah and I clicked the first time we met."

I thought this would please Hannah so I called her immediately and told her. I was on both sides at once. I wanted them to be happily married. It was not only my sympathy for a woman but proof of my judgment in selecting Dexter as a superior type of man.

Hannah drove over from Massachusetts occasionally to stay in Dexter's apartment. He always insisted that the three of us dine together. Despite the radical change in his life—though he did not call it being "engaged"—he and I resumed our former delightful companionship and a second year of seeing each other several times a week.

Finally my furniture arrived and I moved into my apartment. Promptly half a dozen young people from the Center rushed to my assistance. They unpacked and placed my books in the shelves so logically it was never necessary to rearrange them. A pretty Canadian girl stored away my dishes, silver, and pans so conveniently in the kitchen cupboards it was impossible to improve on her system.

Almost immediately Roshi telephoned and suggested that I come to the Center the next day and begin a week's work full time. Every member was required to volunteer a certain amount of work for the Center.

I was stunned. "I'm sorry, Roshi, but it's impossible. I shall be glad to come later when I get settled. It's necessary for me to be here to receive long distance phone calls from my lawyer in New Haven, my trust officer and real estate agent. My husband's estate is not settled yet. Everything is in chaos. I must obtain a New York license for my car. And I don't even know how to get there. Find a new maid and laundress, new grocer. The man who is making my draperies is here every day. Why, my dresses are not even unpacked yet and—"

"Well, come as soon as you can."

I was very upset. Evidently he was not accustomed to dealing with householders. Only with young people who arrived with nothing but a suitcase and lived in one room. Did this mean the demands of the Center would always take precedence over my personal convenience? Was that good or bad?

Several weeks later I volunteered for work at the Center. If they assign me toilets to clean or cooking to do, I thought, I'm afraid I shall walk right out in spite of myself. They assigned me to office work. The atmosphere of the place seemed full of tension. Kolberg, the stern administrator, was entirely different from the spiritual teacher who spoke of serenity, love, the joys of kensho and satori.

After the sitting at the Center each night, Dexter waited for me outside, greeted me with a shining face, a smile and the same air of excitement he had displayed in New Haven. We went gaily off for ice cream in hot weather, hot cocoa in cold weather. We went out to dinner or cooked together, went to movies. Afterward, when alone I would dance about my apartment singing. He still loves me. And I love him. I can't help it. Love, love, what magic power it wields. It brightens my day, lifts my heart, fills me with joy and a sense of security. It makes me feel slightly intoxicated all the time, gay and animated. This is why Dexter says that in groups, "You always sparkle."

To be loved so intensely, I thought, so uncritically, to be accepted wholly for what one is, by a handsome attentive young man fills a woman with self-assurance. Love lends invulnerability. It is a shield that protects her against all the slings and arrows of fortune. Nothing can ever hurt her again—except of course her lover.

Snowbound weather fluctuated rapidly from one extreme to another. One night it turned unseasonably hot. In addition to the afternoon heat in the West room, there were sixty hot young bodies crowded into the zendo. It was overpowering. Heat, humidity, fatigue, and excitement brought me almost to the point of fainting or vomiting or both.

Breaking all the rules of the zendo I glanced about surreptitiously to find that tall figure with the beautiful blonde hair. He was not there.

When we walked in the kinhin line, I saw Dexter waiting in the foyer to join the second round of sitting. Instantly as I walked away, I began to swing my hips assuming his gaze was following me. My God, Claire, I admonished myself, what kind of woman are you! A grey-haired mature woman trying to lure a young man. Shame on you! But it was so spontaneous, so instinctive, so natural, I laughed and forgave myself. Never for a moment did I think of myself as old. I often laughed when I found myself automatically stepping back politely in the elevator to allow grey-haired women, who were probably much younger than I, to walk out of the elevator first. Something—was it love?—made me feel eternally young, vital, full of zest for life.

When I returned to my sitting cushion that night, my nausea had magically disappeared, the heat no longer suffocated me. So—the very presence of the beloved can heal like a miracle. I decided then and there that Claire was a hopeless case.

It was exactly as Susie had predicted in her letter. Bodhi-sattvas sprang up everywhere to help me. Seymour flew from Michigan to Snowbound in his private plane several times to meet with my new lawyer and new trust officer. He voluntarily left the management of his several factories, his positions as regent of the university, director of banks, board member of this and that—Red Cross, libraries, museums, civic organizations, just to arrange financial matters to my best advantage in my new setting.

When he left I drove him out to his plane. "Take care of Seymour. He is one of the pillars of the universe as far as I am concerned."

Who had ever heard of anyone being so kind? My friends called him "the fabulous Mr. T". What could one do to show one's appreciation of such kindness besides send him $100 art books?

Everywhere I went strangers rushed forward to do unexpected favors. When I was sick with the flu, Blanch, Dexter and Hannah all rushed to the rescue with soup and fruit juices. The sangha indeed became my family. The young people were always bringing me flowers and books like solicitous sons and daughters. Yet I am anything but the maternal type. I did not understand it at all. I never indulged in those motherly admonitions about wrapping up warm and all that. It was all a great mystery to me, but I loved it.

One day I was unable to find the post office. A stranger volunteered to drive there—about ten blocks away. She asked me to follow her car. She did not look like a humanitarian. Her face was sharp as a hatchet, her hair dyed the color of brass. Mr. Arna, the manager of the apartment house, drove me to lunch one grey day because he said I looked too weak after the flu. He helped me hang pictures, move furniture. He was tirelessly and cheerfully helpful. The dozen attendants in the building were ready, willing and able to assist me in getting settled. Bodhisattvas everywhere—except my maids. Each was worse than the last. I missed my dear faithful Margaret more sorely every day.

Later a woman I had met only twice in my life telephoned. "This is Edith May, remember me? Mrs. Owens, I think you work too hard. Why don't I come over and do whatever is necessary. And I don't want any pay for it."

"Oh, Mrs. May, how very kind of you. I most certainly do need some help but I'll pay you, of course. We simply won't argue about that point. I have absolutely no time for any of my personal affairs. I don't have time to pay my bills, balance my checkbook, sew on buttons, go shopping or anything."

She came and we removed all the things I had thrown helter-skelter into the various closets to tidy up the rooms. We worked for many hours rearranging, laughed at ourselves and each other and thoroughly enjoyed an onerous chore.

"Edith, you are so at one with your work and so enjoy being helpful to others, I believe you are a born Zen Buddhist."

"Oh no! Oh, no! Mrs. Owens, I'm a staunch Congregationalist."

Edith found me another woman, Helena, who incredibly enough liked to clean and wash and iron. Helena was also a treasure—they both still are.

I questioned Roshi concerning all these Bodhisattvas springing up everywhere. "It must be Zen."

"No. It's beyond Zen. They sense something in you."

"But what? I'm not aware of anything."

"It's better that you are not aware," and he gave me one of those enigmatic Zen smiles that could be interpreted in two entirely different ways.

No wonderful Bodhisattvas, however, appeared to cook my meals. Zen taught us that no work is menial if we become one with it. Then it becomes a pleasure and a vehicle for enlightment. But who could become one with cooking?

I was striving to live the simple natural life. The minute I walked into the kitchen, however, my body bristled like a cat confronted by an enemy. Could I never free myself of the tradition of the old South that a lady should not perform menial work, but sit on a cushion and eat strawberries and cream? Cooking, I reminded myself, is a fine art and a science. Try to be one with it. But the prejudice was in the very marrow of my bones. When young people came to dinner we prepared it together and laughed so much it took the curse off it.

Neither Bodhisattvas nor love was able to overcome the snow problem. It began in October. The winter in Snowbound lasts fully five months of the year, is twice as long and twice as severe as in New Haven. I had always considered snow one of nature's mistakes. Snowbound driving was hazardous, walking dangerous. Battling with winter weather was a new experience. My husband and I had usually vacationed in the Bahamas, Puerto Rico, or Florida in the coldest months.

It was painful to rise at six every Sunday morning in winter to drive through the snow to hear Roshi's teisho. (Often, however, they contained enough food for thought for a whole week.) But extremely low blood pressure made early morning my least energetic time physically. Several nights a week I also drove to the Center alone through the snow and ice, rain and fog, lightning storms and the gloom of night holding the threat of mugging and rape. Seventy-four, I reflected, is a fine time for a woman to commence such a strenuous new regime. It was spiritually rewarding, even necessary, but nervously such a strain that it kept me awake at night.

One night when I had dined out at the Women's University Club, I found the entire surface of West Avenue had become a sheet of ice. Cars ahead of me, completely out of control, spun around and around striking trees and other cars. I inched my way home at five miles an hour. When I walked into the house, my legs were trembling.

Later Dexter admonished me, "You should have phoned me. I would have come and gotten you."

"But it was late at night. I didn't want to wake you up."

"What of it? Next time call me, you hear?"

Blanch made the same offer. But how could I impose on the kindness of my friends? It seemed to me an excellent way to lose them. But what remarkable kindness these Zen people showed. Perhaps it would imbue me with sufficient courage to brave it alone next time.

Chapter VIII
ZEN AND THE COUNTERCULTURE

Despite my preoccupation with Dexter I plunged wholeheartedly into training at the Zen Center. Roshi Kolberg's word was law. We all feared his displeasure, respected his Zen learning, reverenced the enlightenment he had experienced in Japan years ago. Many members unconsciously regarded him as a father figure, a symbol of authority. They loved or hated him or felt ambivalent. They feared or worshipped him, or both. One man, expecting our spiritual teacher to be superhuman, was shocked to discover that Roshi was human enough to catch a cold like other people. Unconsciously I expected him to be a saint.

The zendo or meditation hall was open every night. I went to sit several nights every week. On Sunday mornings at eight we sat in zazen for an hour. The Roshi delivered a talk (teisho) for an hour or more. He discussed Zen masters—Dogen and Hakuin and others, or the various Mahayana scriptures (sutras) or the principles of Zen and Buddhism. This required on the part of the trainees a whole new approach to life. It actually produced so real an interior wrench that it felt physical.

On some Sundays while Kolberg talked I was filled with resistance, other times with confusion. Occasionally his teisho would leave me in a state of exaltation. I would float home on a cloud of purification, eager to remain on that high spiritual plane, to forget men, love, sex, food, my aches and pains and other trivia.

The Roshi often read Zen stories that were upsetting. There was an aspirant who knocked on the door of a Zen master, asking him to accept him as a disciple. The master slammed the door in his face. The third time he applied, the master slammed the door and broke the applicant's leg. At that moment, however, the supplicant came to enlightenment.

Was this the spiritual life? This kind of cruelty horrified me. I protested to one of my men friends. He laughed. "I would be willing to have my leg broken if I could come to enlightenment."

Men and women were different, I realized, in more ways than one. I reluctantly admitted that the master broke the other man's leg only when he sensed that the aspirant was on the verge of a breakthrough. The shock precipitated it. Nevertheless such cruelty disturbed me. Roshi frequently spoke extemporaneously during the dokusan break on the difficulties of practicing zazen. Each one of us was convinced that his talk was directed at us personally. He discussed the practical details, clarified, encouraged, and informed in concise and pertinent phrases. I urged Roshi to publish them in pamphlet form for our daily reference. Everything about Zen and Buddhism was so new and strange it was necessary to hear the same statements repeated over and over again: the necessity of quieting the discursive intellect, the joy of becoming one with one's work until it became effortless play, the delicious experience of buoyancy, the danger to others of our own rampant egos. Everything in Roshi's talks I accepted with reservation because I did not yet fully understand them, but I was eager to learn and to experience—everything if possible.

In dokusan, the brief private interview with our teacher, students were allowed to discuss problems concerning their zazen practice—nothing else. Never anything of our personal life. I related to Roshi the beautiful experiences that were beginning to happen to me as a result of zazen: the joy that bubbled up in my chest periodically like a small fountain, a feeling of greater muscular coordination, kinship with the sangha, the strong sense of direction and purpose in my life with which Zen imbued me.

It was also a deep satisfaction to know that whatever aspect of zazen or Zen I might mention, the Roshi would understand and clarify it as no one else I knew was capable of doing. This creates a strong bond with one's teacher.

The Roshi gave me my first koan to solve, "Who am I?" I repeated it thousands of times during zazen practice. A koan is an enigma, a puzzle, that defies solution by the rational mind. Zen never explains the process or purpose of a koan. The meditator must experience the process, then he sees the purpose. This is to so frustrate the rational mind that it is defeated and surrenders its dominance. This permits the shy, weaker True-self to function.

I struggled to solve my koan first with my conscious mind—a solution which Roshi would not accept. Finally one day while in Connecticut and *not* in the zendo, I beheld the image of an enormous circle of brown wood suspended in space. I realized it was a symbol of the universe. One small segment was missing. I saw myself replacing it in the circle. The segment was I. I was an integral part of the universe—that's who I was! I did not think it, I did not imagine it; I saw it, I experienced it, consequently I knew it was true. A truth beyond logic, beyond thought.

Weeks after this incident occurred, I reported it to Roshi expecting him to be very pleased. He tested me in the Rinzai Zen way. He thrust out his hand. "Why is this called a hand?"

"I can't understand Zen techniques," I said.

"What is so technical about that?"

He would not sanction my understanding of this koan. Usually members report such insights during dokusan while attending sesshin in the zendo. So I consoled myself by concluding that if I had reported my experience immediately, instead of weeks afterward, I would have still been in a high mindstate that would have enabled me to meet his Rinzai test. But I felt it was not politic to divulge this to my teacher.

I urged him to give me a new koan. He reluctantly gave me "What is Mu?" The very word "Mu" was meaningless to me. It annoyed me to no end. Why couldn't Americans be given American words? I worked on it a long time thinking I would never achieve a breakthrough. Why could not a religion as wonderful as Zen Buddhism be Americanized for Americans? What is Mu? I was striking my head on a stone wall. No answer came. It was extremely frustrating. I worked on it for a long time until months later I believed the answer came in the form of imagery while I was in Virginia on vacation. Later my teacher did not agree with me.

Rinzai Zen is the severest sect of Buddhism. Discipline is rigorous. Severity is considered conducive to enlightenment. Always I had valued gentleness, kindness and love above everything. Sometimes I wondered why I had strayed into this severe discipline. Members informed me that when Roshi had returned from the workshop in Bucke's County, he remarked to them, "There is a beautiful little old lady in New Haven. It is just a matter of time until she moves to Snowbound." I wasn't beautiful, I wasn't little, and did not consider myself old, though I was a lady. How did he know my intentions? I did not know them myself a year ago. Later Roshi informed me that, "It was your karma to come to Snowbound." Was it? Were events in our lives caused by the unfathomable past over which we presently had no control? Was that fair or unfair?

Apparently because I was the oldest person at the Center, or had had much life experience or perhaps because of my spiritual awakening years ago, the young members came to me frequently for counselling. Later I was appointed an official counselor. They came with personal, family and sex problems.

It was a shock but a relief to find that these modern young people called the sex organs by their names without a qualm, especially the men. Some of them asked about solutions for premature ejaculations and the inability of girls to achieve orgasms. I distributed the pamphlets on understanding sex written by Doctors Masters and Johnson.

I explained the difficulties—physical and psychological—of women in achieving a happy climax with a man. I recommended to them the method the great birth control pioneer, Margaret Sanger, had suggested to me years ago. A man should play with a woman's breasts a long time before he attempts anything else. I assured them that with honesty, knowledge, love and reciprocal effort a woman could become radiant, blossom like a flower. No more nerves, no irritability, no nagging. I knew. I had experienced it.

Several members who came for counselling asked if they should become nuns or monks. I seldom gave advice, never criticized. I listened. I asked questions. Verbalization often threw so much light on their own problems that they themselves became aware of the best solution.

Often someone would say to me in great distress, "My parents are coming. They hate my being in Zen. I will bring all the food and do all the cooking if only you will invite them to dinner and explain Zen to them." I attempted to show the Christian parents that despite the employment of different methods and means, the three basic principles of the higher religions were similar: the awakening of the self with its innate good, union with one's source, and the integration of one's religious principles into daily life. I assured them that different terminologies caused different religious systems to seem more dissimilar than they actually were. We always parted good friends and often corresponded afterward. One woman even established a "Claire Club" using Awakening to the Good as a guidebook, for which it is not at all adequate.

There was one all-too-frequent problem, however, that was beyond my competence—their neurotic relationships with one or both of their parents, or with their siblings. My heart ached for some of these exceptionally fine young men and girls. I observed their parents sitting for several hours at a dinner table and never once looking at, or speaking to, their sons or daughters.

Some of the Zen members were terrified when childhood memories activated by zazen, after being long-suppressed in their unconscious, suddenly rose into consciousness. In desperation I attempted to allay their fears by resorting to psychology. For example, Ingrid was utterly overwhelmed during zazen when confronted with painful memories of lack of mother love when she was a child and the divorce that also deprived her of her father's affection.

I described to her the four levels of the unconscious mind that it is necessary to penetrate during the self-realization process. I explained the discoveries of Masters and Houston, Stanislav Grof and Jung (though Jung mentioned only three levels, omitting the first). First, the level of imagery. Second, the neurotic level. Third, the historic-symbolic. Fourth, the deepest level where the religious experience occurs. Jung found it necessary to penetrate all levels, especially the neurotic level, before one can arrive at the deepest level, the collective unconscious. He stated that his patients had "returned to their source" only after they had successfully lived through and understood their neurosis.

To convince Ingrid, I pocketed my pride and confessed that only my spontaneous religious awakening cured my neurosis caused by my mother's lack of love of me as a child. I had been an unwanted child from the moment of conception—for good reasons.

I warned Ingrid and other frightened and bewildered young members to welcome the emergence during meditation of painful childhood memories and to live through them thoroughly if they sincerely wished to attain enlightenment. A neurosis was like an abcessed tooth. No one can be healthy until he or she removes it, however painful the process.

I stated that all religions are therapeutic according to Jung, that they should be eternally grateful to have found zazen and Zen. I encouraged them further by revealing that the Roshi had informed me he planned to invite a psychiatrist who was a Zen member to move to the Center. Serious neurotic problems were beyond my amateur therapy.

There were cases where zazen had so improved the sons and daughters that their parents gratefully made donations to the Center. Roshi contended that a neurosis was a strong incentive to spiritual practice.

Was it primarily creative people who were drawn to Zen? Or did zazen awaken the dormant creativity in meditators? The Center was filled with painters, sculptors, wood carvers, cabinet makers, weavers, potters, writers and musicians. A group formed an excellent small orchestra, another produced puppet plays to celebrate various events in the Buddha's life. Most of the members were college graduates and there was a sprinkling of Ph.D.'s.

Despite their serious dedication, their sense of humor spontaneously flashed forth during the weekly dharma dialogues. The quick laughter of the audience was like a healthy wind that blew away the tensions. First, one member sat on the dais, spoke on a Zen subject then was attacked from all sides by questions sharp and pointed as arrows. The purpose was to expose the speaker's Zen errors. Some young speakers, however, became terrified.

My impulse was to comfort them. Roshi had asked me to sit in the front row. But I literally could not bring myself to ask questions that hurt or frightened these vulnerable young people who were obviously already suffering. I asked gentle constructive questions. This was against the rules of the game. Yet I always wished to help not hinder Roshi's highly successful work. This left me in a quandary.

Later this attitude was to cause Roshi to admonish me with a laugh that ill-concealed his serious intent, "Claire, you are always undermining my good work. You want me to be kind and gentle with everyone. But it is necessary to be rough with some of these members."

I fully realized that cessation of conceptual thinking is essential if enlightenment is ever to be attained. It was difficult to accept the severe means necessary to accomplish spiritual ends. Novels and autobiographies reported similar severities of training in Catholic monasteries.

Many Zen students appeared to be so ignorant of the world, of the vagaries and hidden motives of human nature (including their own), so vulnerable, so full of ideals that their very youth was endearing. As in the case of the Yale students I felt intense compassion for all and a deep love for several. I believed I saw their faults with new clarity because zazen clarifies one's insights. But they were suffering from their own weaknesses and faults. And they were striving valiantly for inner spiritual development. It seemed to me that all this would fill any older woman with the urge never to criticize, but to encourage, to strengthen their self-esteem and sense of security which appeared to me inordinately low, to emphasize their virtues—potential and actual.

Over our weekly luncheons of green salad and cottage cheese (which I loathed but dutifully ate), Marian and I talked endlessly of Zen and self-realization from all angles.

"The greatest virtues of these counterculture people," she said, "lies in the fact that no one forces them to enter this strict Zen training. No one forces them to sit for long hours daily in meditation. No one forces them to go to the Center daily through all kinds of inclement weather. But they go."

"Why?" I asked, "Is it evolution? Is it their karma? They appear to be there voluntarily as a result of free will and usually against the wishes of their parents. Whatever the reason, in my estimation they deserve respect and encouragement."

Marian agreed. "Yet sometimes the staff members are not very friendly."

"Don't you think," I asked, "they feel they *should* be serious and severe while on duty? The way trained nurses are. Socially they all seem very affable outside the Center."

"Be that as it may," Marian said, "how many other people in the world today are practicing self-discipline to transform themselves into spiritual beings, into loving, selfless, generous persons without rampant ego?"

"Exactly. It's truly an amazing and inspiring spectacle. It offers hope for the salvation of the human race that is plunging us daily into more crime and corruption."

But it was not all sweetness and light in the counterculture. As a person fresh from conventional society I was confronted with a complete reversal of values in almost every area. I agreed with the younger generation's values—moral, ethical and spiritual—but it was a little difficult to adjust to some of their social values. To plunge abruptly from a world of formal dinner parties, exquisite evening gowns, good manners and good grooming, and helpful servants into the milieu of the casual counterculture required much silent adjustment.

They maintained that they wished to live simply, naturally, and honestly. They did—sometimes to the point of rudeness. After all, I thought, what are good manners but consideration for others? All social amenities, however, had been tossed out the window indiscriminately, the good with the bad.

A hostess might work for hours preparing a fine dinner for them, (as I did several times). They would arrive thirty minutes late or twenty minutes early before she was even dressed and leave without so much as a thank you. Next day or next week, however, they might bring flowers or books. Evidently, I reflected, they had different ways of saying thank you to which I was not yet accustomed. I examined my own standards. Formerly in my social circle we laid too much emphasis on courtesy and too little—or none—on spiritual development. But must one preclude the other?

When the young Zen people invited me to dinner or a party I bathed and dressed in my party clothes as I had always done in deference to my host and hostess. On arrival I observed that often most of them were in dirty blue jeans, the dirtier the better, and if torn that was considered a mark of merit.

It kept me busy reminding myself that their life style was to them only an external symbol of important principles. And one could observe them admirably striving to integrate their Zen principles into their daily lives, but did not the excesses of the counterculture sometimes mislead them?

When I dined in the apartments of young members it was often in the kitchen on a bare wooden table. I had never eaten in a kitchen in my life. It is impossible if one has servants. But they never discovered my secret. There were no chairs except in the kitchen. They preferred to sit on the bare floor. And all floors are dusty; gravity sees to that. It was never necessary for me to demure, for someone always quickly brought out a kitchen chair for me. They took off their shoes—Japanese style, went barefoot in their homes—and even on the street—which was not Japanese style. They claimed it was natural and healthy. It was also dirty.

They believed in keeping their material possessions at a minimum. Their bedrooms were furnished with a mattress (no springs) thrown on the floor—that was all. I realized they were protesting against the dangerous worship of material things of their parents' generation—and mine—but was there not a sensible middle ground?

It was admirable to see them help strangers, other races, other drivers in automobile accidents, and clean up neighborhoods. Zen admonishes us never to make value judgements, to accept all people as they are because all people possess a True-self or Buddha-nature, replete with virtues—at least potentially. All this left me in a state of inner conflict.

It was extremely difficult to become accustomed to all the customs of the rebellious counterculture. Naturalness and simplicity were their aim—admirable, theoretically. The length of men's hair has varied through the centuries. It was not the length of the hair and beards that was disturbing—it was their unwashed wild condition.

Pretty young girls I had always regarded as one of life's most charming sights. It saddened me to see girls dressing like pioneer women with long mud-colored skirts and shapeless blouses and rags tied over their heads. They looked like peasant farm women—and they were not either. Their long straight stringy hair fell into the food, into their eyes, and concealed their sweet young faces.

One night every week Blanch would call me on the phone and as mature women we would discuss the virtues and faults of the counterculture, of Zen and the world. "You know, Blanch," I said, "I believe I have analyzed why the way the girls dress and wear their hair upsets me so much."

She laughed. "Why? Some fine psychological reason I have no doubt."

"No," I answered, "philosophical this time. I believe in Hegel's definition of beauty, 'Beauty is infinity manifesting itself as the sensuous.'"

"Oh, Claire, that's excellent. Mind if I copy it down? I can use it in my art lecture."

"Go right ahead. If ugliness is deliberately cultivated, why doesn't it distress the young too? And what of all those sentient beings they daily vow to liberate? Other beings may consider beauty, as I do, a means toward spiritual liberation. Aristotle maintained that the function of beauty is purification and—"

Blanch interrupted. "That's what you said in one of your nature poems."

"Yes, I feel many people experience this purification, perhaps without always realizing it."

"Have you read Govinda's *The Way of the White Clouds?*" Blanch asked. "Never heard of it."

"Oh Claire, you would love it. It is a beautiful book about his experiences and spiritual development in Tibet. He says—wait, I have a copy right here. He says 'Beauty is the greatest... messenger of truth.' He's quoting someone else. Buddha, I think, 'Had I not expressed the eternal Dharma,... had I not appealed to humanity through beauty, my teaching would never have moved the hearts of men.'"

"Exactly! Beauty is a vital part of all religions. Why do the dignitaries of all religions wear beautiful colorful vestments? Why do we have gold statues at the—"

"Figures, Roshi always calls them," Blanch said.

"All right, figures, though they are statues too." We both laughed. "Oh, well," I concluded, "the way the youngsters of this generation dress is none of my immediate business so I am careful to remain quiet, but I suffer. I feel cheated by youth, deprived of the natural beauty of youth."

There was another custom that raised doubts. At the Center everyone was addressed by his or her first name. Surnames had died a premature death. I was literally shocked to hear a strange young boy or girl in slovenly clothes with unwashed hair, of whom I knew absolutely nothing, address me as "Claire."

I had been brought up to consider that the use of one's given name was a privilege conferred only on one's most intimate friends. At the Center I always referred to myself as "Mrs. Owens." It had absolutely no effect.

I considered a certain formality in human relationships was only digni-
fied. And yet if I believed in the Zen principle that we were all one—as I had
experienced it during my great awakening years ago—then Zen was right and
I was wrong. Age, sex, social status did not matter. Nevertheless it was still
difficult to accept too much familiarity. Politicians endeavored to create
equality by legislation but in Zen it just happened naturally—apparently.

And one could observe the equality of the sexes in its early stages. Most
of the young couples lived together before they married. Many of the wives,
or otherwise, worked outside the home. The young husbands, or otherwise,
learned to cook, clean house, wash clothes, bathe and feed the baby. The girls
had a tacit agreement to dispense with special feminine privileges. The men
never opened heavy doors for them, never helped them into the cars, never
assisted them with their coats or drew out their chairs at the dinner table.
They automatically offered me all these little social amenities. I loved it. I
refused even to analyze whether it was wise or unwise.

Zenites, which I laughingly called them to their horror, honestly did not
value money. They sought jobs where they would be of service to the community not where they would draw a high salary. They worked in children's
orphanages, the laundry of insane asylums, on garbage trucks. They chose
part-time jobs of housecleaning, babysitting or janitoring in order to leave
ample time to practice and work at the Center.

Probably my young counterculture friends silently tolerated my fashion-
able clothes (the shops sold no other kind), my coiffure, my independent
income, large shiny car and linen table cloths as merely regrettable relics of
a by-gone era. They were never reluctant, however, to accept checks on their
birthdays and weddings. I honestly believe, however, I derived more pleasure from giving than they did from receiving. To many of them all money
was tainted. To me it meant freedom to give without accounting to some man
for my questionable actions.

Zen and the counterculture taught me a very helpful lesson. Nothing is all
good or all evil. Everybody and everything in life is a mixture of good and
bad. I had abandoned Christianity because it seemed to offer no acceptable
solution to the ever-pressing problem of evil. The answer offered by
Buddhism I did not yet entirely understand except that it involved karma,
reincarnation, and ignorance, in the Buddhist sense—whatever that means.
Familiar words had unfamiliar meanings that must be learned.

The young Zen members purchased my books, read them, mailed them to
their parents, sought my counsel, listened with respect to my ideas and invited me to their social festivities. Our serious but humorous discussions of Zen
and Buddha, of the Center, and the effects of zazen and sesshin were always
animated and brought us a sense of kinship.

It was an exceedingly strenuous life for me—too strenuous for my health.
I loved these spiritually-minded young people, enjoyed their laughter—it
was laughter rather than wit. Everything was amusing to them. With the addition of Dexter's love and attention and the joy that was beginning to accrue
from the practice of zazen, I was happy—ecstatically happy, during the
first year.

For the first time in my life I was able to be myself, naturally, simply. No more keeping up with all the Joneses of the world, no striving after the latest fashions, no wearing of false masks that conventional society demanded, no pretense. For the first time the pressures that society exerts on everyone was lifted from my shoulders. I felt a glorious sense of freedom. Alone in New Haven I had been unable to throw off the unwanted, unapproved constraints of a largely false society.

When others occasionally became disgruntled and threatened to leave the Center I would say, "But look at the shining goal we have to strive for—enlightenment; at the guide on our spiritual path—expert though severe—the Roshi. The whole world may think we are idiots but we have the sangha behind us—hundreds in Snowbound and more hundreds in the affiliate groups all over the United States."

Chapter IX
SESSHIN AND IMAGES

"No one knows what Zen is all about," Roshi said to me one Spring night in dokusan, "until one has been to a sesshin. I think you are ready now. You should apply for the May sesshin. The weather will be nice then and that will make it easier for you."

I applied, sent in my fee, and was accepted. I felt very apprehensive. I might be a complete failure. Perhaps nothing would happen to me or worse yet, too much might happen, something terrible and I would be disgraced. And did I, at seventy-five, have the stamina to endure rising at 4:30, sitting motionless on the floor with erect spine without any back support for nine hours every day for four days with little food and less sleep?

While waiting for the crucial date to arrive, I wrote a long letter to my cousin Laura in California. She had long been urging me to tell her more about Zen.

Darling Laura:
Here it is. You asked for it.

As you know from my other letters I long to come to enlightenment again—permanently this time, I hope. In the meantime I deeply desire to be *spontaneously* good, and selfless, compassionate and helpful to others—and joyous. On many days zazen leaves me feeling this way. On other days my old ego is rampant and I do not feel so virtuous.

I know zazen can release my True-self if I practice long enough at home and at the Center. At home, however, there are always a dozen pressing chores that must be done at a given time to ensure the smooth running of one's daily life. So I jump up from my zazen cushion to make that urgent telephone call I forgot, or put the bean sprouts to soak—or whatever.

I know Zen is wonderful, our teacher is wonderful—but—but it is all too easy to be aware of the difficulties. For instance, the zendo is kept very cold. That is considered a spur to our practice. The bare floors are like ice and we are supposed to go barefooted—why, no one explains. The floors are waxed and shiney clean but the soles of the feet of some of those young men are obviously not. I simply cannot bring myself to step where dirty feet have walked. Also I am afraid of taking cold which for my susceptible constitution always entails three weeks in bed with fever. So I wear stockings. Evidently there are concessions made for age.

The place is always over-crowded. The monitors are most solicitous in many ways. They always reserve a seat for me in the corner out of the fiercely cold drafts. Roshi said to me, "If you come there will always be a good seat for you." I do not find physical hardships conducive to better practice. And the blows of the keosaku stick on one's shoulders is a shock initially to one's dignity, especially if one was brought up in the old South, as you know I was, where no one ever strikes a lady under *any* circumstances.

We had been wearing regular street clothes of subdued colors. Recently the Roshi announced that we must all wear Japanese robes—all alike, all brown. My old ego screamed in protest, silently, of course. It objected violently to losing its identity. I did not want to look exactly like everyone else. But now that we all wear identical robes in the meditation hall it reduces distractions wonderfully. Again, Zen was right and I was wrong, as frequently happens.

The greatest adjustment of all is required by the nature of zazen itself. Its express purpose is liberation of the True-self or one's Original-nature by quieting the discursive intellect. But it is that very intellect on which one has prided oneself for a lifetime. This (temporary) rejection of the rational mind often causes it to raise merry hell. At least mine does.

The deliberate deflation of the ego by the whole system of Zen training is extremely painful until the benefits begin to accrue. If one is mature it is doubly so. One has been directing one's life for years—even if not entirely satifactorily. Then suddenly to be reduced to an obedient ignorant schoolgirl again is humiliating. Prostrations before the gold figures of the Buddha and one's spiritual teacher is against all concepts acceptable in the West—even though the Roshi assures us Buddha figures are but a representation of enlightenment.

To renounce parties, television, cocktails, pretty clothes, bright colors, perfume and jewelry seem—at least in the beginning—unnecessary deprivation even to attain spiritual development.

The greatest problem of all, however—is self-discipline. It is unbelievably difficult to train oneself to go to that pillow—at home or in the zendo—for several uninterrupted hours every day. The body rebels against sitting motionless. The mind is like a beehive with thoughts flying in and out continuously. Yet Aldous Huxley said that self-realization is the only process devised by man which changes his character, behavior and hierarchy of values, so—I hang in there, as the young people say. And it pays off.

Zen is designed to diminish the ego. But I found it doubly effective because of my wild expectations of myself. After I had been a member for only three months, I indulged in the foolish fantasy that I would come to enlightenment immediately in a blaze of glory. I visualized it as occurring in the zendo. My body would emanate great rays of light such as I have seen in pictures of Ramakrishna. And I was very generous. I daydreamed that half a dozen others in the zendo would come to spontaneous self-realization at the same time I did. It has not happened that way at all. I struggled arduously, painfully every day for a long time before I began to feel the benefits zazen brings. I will write you about those when I accumulate a few more.

Gassho, as Zen people say, though I don't quite know what it means. And love to you and your husband. I know what that means.

Claire

P.S. The difficulty is that at first all the benefits of zazen are fleeting, transient, lasting a few hours or a day or two. They must all be reawakened again every day. That is the reason we are urged to meditate regularly at home and in the zendo every day of our lives.

You're a concert pianist so you know how you must practice the same piece of music everyday—to say nothing of the scales. This is the way it is with zazen.

P. P.S. You asked if I am not grateful to have a warm mink coat in this bitterly cold city. You will laugh. I dare not wear it to the Zen Center. Buddhists consider it wrong to kill any living thing—even a mosquito. So my fur coat remains in storage while I freeze. I would send it to you if you didn't live in that desert.

At sesshin sixty people from Snowbound and various states of America were present in the main zendo. At ordinary times the overflow sits in the dining room, the library, the basement, so eager are people in their search for truth, peace and happiness. We lived, ate, slept, practiced zazen, went to dokusan, and listened to Roshi's admonishments all in the same building without going outdoors for four exciting, exhausting days.

We were told to sit two hours before breakfast. Never in my life had I gone without my breakfast. I expected to become so faint I would collapse on the floor. To my amazement I did not even feel hungry. Only later did I learn that scientific research has discovered that during meditation the rate of metabolism and oxygen consumption decreases and that deep meditation is more rejuvenating than sleep. As usual Zen was right and I was wrong. It was a humiliating discovery but wonderful.

In sesshin we all sat facing a blank wall, as usual. But the zendo was charged with unusual electric vibrations of a large group of people concentrating on the hara with extraordinary vigor. Roshi walked between the rows of brown robed aspirants exhorting us to greater endeavor, encouraging us. He even resorted to a Biblical phrase, "Knock and it shall be opened to you."

We broke for a light breakfast and later for a heavier lunch of bean sprouts, cottage cheese and other strange vegetarian dishes. No dinner, except a piece of fruit and herb tea. I laughed to think that for years I had been accustomed to a five course dinner of soup, roast beef or steak, vegetables, salad and dessert followed by a demitass of coffee—and often a liquor. We were alloted bathing hours and certain chores in cleaning the Center. I trembled for fear they might assign me chores I could not force myself to perform—like cleaning toilets. Watering the innumerable plants on three floors was my very pleasant work while I strove desperately to "be one with it" but did not succeed.

The first afternoon, I suddenly became intensely aware of Dexter. He's thinking of me now, I thought. I must remember to ask him about it. I did so later and he said, yes, that afternoon he had turned to Hannah and remarked, "This is Claire's first sesshin. I wonder how she's getting along." (Often when my phone rang I would say immediately, "Hello Dexter," and it would be he).

From 5:00 in the morning until 9:30 at night we sat in zazen. The strong souls sat up all night and meditated. Nothing seemed to be happening to me until the third day. As I settled myself quickly and silently on my cushion at 5:00 A.M. I beheld projected before my eyes an endless parade of colored images. They passed across the blank wall before me like continuous motion pictures. It began with green wall paper with a beautiful pink floral design on it. I saw a figure of Buddha, then a Buddha with the Roshi's face, the Virgin Mary with the infant Jesus in her arms. A green forest with monkeys cavorting about, many buildings, a stage with actors on it. A light like a small flashlight played across all these scenes. And once I beheld a small golden dragon.

No one had prepared me for this phenomenon. I was not frightened but astounded. My body shook uncontrollably and I was wracked with deep continuous sobs—for what reason I had no idea. Every time I attempted to take a kleenex paper out of the long sleeve of my Japanese robe one of the monitors would mutter, "No moving." But what was I supposed to do with all that mucuous flowing from my nose across my upper lip? I refused to swallow it. So I defied the rules and wiped my nose. The whole procedure might have been terrifying except that Roshi was keeping his eagle eye on me and on all the others as were the experienced monitors, Milda and Pat.

The parade of images continued for twelve hours, from five in the morning until five in the afternoon except that finally there was a change. I beheld a group of ancient Egyptians and Jews dressed in Biblical garb—long striped gowns and striped headdresses. They were walking around and around a well gazing at me intently with a strange expression in their eyes which I was unable to interpret. Unfortunately at five o'clock in the afternoon the bell rang for supper and all imagery disappeared. Could this have been the Historic-Symbolic level emerging as described by Jung, Masters and Houston, and Grof?

That evening in great excitement I attempted to relate these startling happenings to Roshi in dokusan. He dismissed them. "*Makyo!* Not to be clung to. They can become obstacles to your progress on the path."

At the end of the fourth day the members streamed out of the zendo laughing, crying, kissing, throwing their arms around each other. We felt overwhelmed with love, joy, and an unexpected energy. I felt I possessed the strength to move a house. Roshi warned us that although we had built up a surplus of *joriki* (tremendous energy) we should go home and rest for several days. I recalled that Jung said when the unconscious is released, the energy hitherto consumed in conflicts now becomes available.

Immediately on returning home I was confronted by my rational mind, waiting at the door like a neglected husband to demand explanation of such non-rational activities carried on without his presence or permission. Promptly, for what reason I did not know, I turned to Aldous Huxley's little book, *Heaven and Hell*, of which I had understood nothing years ago when I first purchased it. This time my hair all but stood on end. It offered explanations. Reasons are almost as exciting as experiences. And everything has a reason. I must find it.

Huxley maintained that the visionary world one sees is the mind's antipodes. It can be induced by various means—fasting, fatigue, illness, drugs, hypnosis, asceticism. (He omitted meditation for some strange reason.) It occurs in all countries in all ages.

The scientific explanation is that the lowering of the "biological efficiency of the brain permits into consciousness mental events normally excluded because they have no survival value." The sugar in the brain is reduced and the "nicotinic acid, a known inhibitor of visions," is removed from the blood. The examples he cited of images beheld were those described in *Temptations of St. Anthony* and by Milarepa and by the poet AE.

This imagery all follows a pattern. These "images of the *archetypal* world are symbolic." They arise from the collective unconscious. Color is a hallmark of the given. One sees patterned things—carpets, carvings (I saw pink wall paper with green designs), heroic and fabled figures (I saw Buddha and a dragon), landscapes and so forth.

Visionary experience can be terrible, Huxley warns us. Faith "... guarantees that the visionary experience shall be blissful." (Roshi repeatedly admonished trainees that we must have faith that Buddha actually experienced enlightenment and also that we ourselves are capable of it. Having experienced self-realization years ago, I found my faith ready-made). Huxley explained that fear, hate, anger guarantee that the visionary experience shall be appalling.

Biologically useless material seems to derive from Mind-at-Large. Huxley himself believed that "visionary experiences enter into our own consciousness from somewhere 'out there' in the infinity of Mind-at-Large.... Mortification of the body opens the door into a transcendental world of Being." (Is that, I wondered, the reason for the whacks with the keosaku stick?) Singing concentrates "the carbon dioxide in one's lungs." This lowers the efficiency of the cerebral reducing valve, making visionary experiences possible. (So that's why we chant and repeat and repeat the same words). "This will admit biologically useless material from Mind-at-Large."

I closed Huxley's small illuminating book. Without breathing, with closed eyes, I sat motionless, overcome by a feeling of awe. Awe at his prodigious knowledge, awe at the profound truths he disclosed, at the wonders of the human mind, and awe that Zen had given me so beautiful an experience. And Huxley's explanations brought deep satisfaction to my thinking rational mind. My conscious mind and my unconscious, reason and intuition, the masculine principle and the feminine principle, were functioning together harmoniously. I felt whole, beautifully whole as nature intends us to be. So the strange, incomprehensible, incredible claims of the greatest mystics were biologically possible and scientifically explicable. I looked forward eagerly to my next sesshin of seven days.

Chapter X
LANCE AND PLATO

One day Lois Triffin phoned me from New Haven. "There's a Yale student who's joined the Zen Center and he knows no one in Snowbound. He's unbelievably handsome and unbelievably shy. Name's Lance Mead. From a wealthy prominent family in Boston. Why don't you invite him to dinner? You can make him feel like a million dollars the way you do all your young men."

At the next sitting I relayed Lois' message to Lance—part of it. He was another young man who was "tall, dark and handsome." His hair was brown and wavy, his eyes dark blue, fringed with long curling black lashes, his nose slightly too large, small even teeth like the kernels of young corn, and well shaped lips. He was, as Lois said, unbelievably handsome and apparently oblivious to the fact. He had no beard, thank goodness.

He was exceedingly quiet and reserved even for a Bostonian. I invited him to dinner and he declined. This was quite disconcerting. A week later, however, he asked if he might come to call. I asked him to tell me about his courses in philosophy in which he majored at Yale, his family in Boston, his present job at the Paper Company and his progress in Zen. After much encouragement he talked freely and interestingly. He found everything full of humor. He was twenty-three. Soon we were dining together two or three evenings a week.

He invited me to small Chinese and vegetarian restaurants. They usually made me sick. It did not seem to matter. We often cooked dinner at my apartment, he performing most of the work. We laughed and talked until we forgot to watch our boiling pots. Occasionally when I longed for a really good, five-course dinner I treated us to the New Yorker, the best restaurant in Snowbound in my estimation.

Occasionally Lance would ask if he might bring Haig to dinner, the man who shared his apartment. Haig was a strong broad-shouldered former football player from a Midwestern university. He had dark reddish hair cut short, very fair skin, was always noticeably immaculate and was seriously dedicated to the practice of Zen. Lance now talked freely when he and I were alone, but even with his friend Haig he said very little, unless I asked him questions to draw him out. Haig and I discussed the wonders and confusions of Zen Buddhism, with great animation.

At the Zen Center there are many ceremonies—weddings and special events celebrating Buddha's birthday and his day of enlightenment. Dexter's and Hannah's wedding was scheduled to be performed in the zendo at the end of the summer of 1971.

Dexter said, "I want you to sit right on the front row."

I laughed to restrain my tears. "I'll be there with rings on my fingers and bells on my toes."

71

"Well, be sure you also wear that passionate pink dress you look so snazzy in."

At the wedding I wore a long rosy pink evening gown I had purchased during the first winter I had been in Palm Beach with Thurston. At the Breakers Hotel everyone dressed up every night. The gown closely fitted my tall slender figure. It was very decollete with beads and sparkling things around the neck and sleeves of the long diaphanous coat. The entire dress was made more alluring by a transparent rose chiffon coat with long loose sleeves that served to conceal my thin ugly arms. I loved it because as I walked it fluttered in the breeze behind me like the wings of a butterfly. The young people often asked me to wear it at their weddings. I appeared in the only pair of high heel shoes that ever desecrated the Center. In my excitement at Dexter's wedding I forgot to remove them in the zendo. But could anyone imagine anything so incongruous as a woman in a formal evening gown with bare feet?

During the ceremony I strove desperately to display a happy face. Everyone at the Center was aware of the warm friendship Dexter and I had enjoyed for two years. Lance sitting at my side was a great moral support. But did not many a mother watch her older son getting married with her younger son sitting by her side?

Dexter looked unusually handsome with his freshly shampooed hair, his blue peasant blouse which Hannah had made for him accentuating the blueness of his eyes. The lights glinted on his blond beard that he had recently grown. He and Hannah, like all the other Zen couples, repeated their marriage lines with what seemed shocking absence of emotion. How calm these young people were nowadays. None of the couples, except Susie and Bob, ever revealed the slightest signs of being in love. At my wedding I had been agitated to the depths of my being. I had repeated my vows in a whisper, overwhelmed by the enormity of the event.

I gazed at the beautiful face of Dexter as he kneeled before the Roshi at the altar with the golden image of Buddha behind him. Suddenly I began to feel sick. I felt as if my child was being physically, violently torn from my womb. The pain was unbelievable. I clenched my hands and pressed them fiercely over my abdomen restraining the tears I was determined not to shed even if the world came to an end.

Then a vividly clear image appeared before my eyes. A large long white cord binding Dexter and me together physically—an umbilical cord. I prayed even at that moment that his wedding ceremony would sever the cord. It did not.

Without the supportive presence of Lance I could never have endured that painful day. I asked him to accompany me to the wedding breakfast at Dexter's apartment which we had ordered from a caterer. My gift to the bride and groom.

After their marriage Dexter continued to invite me to frequent dinners at their apartment. I reciprocated by taking them out to restaurants. Dexter's feeling for me seemed unabated, and mine for him. I realized that I was the one who should step out of the picture. Hostility sometimes chilled the apartment like a cold draft. My next sesshin, however, altered this situation.

One day at some celebration at the Center—I forget just what it was—refreshments were served. I stood in one corner of the dining room. First Lance, then Haig, then Dexter came rushing over bringing me punch and cookies and sweet breads. The four of us stood laughing and talking. Silently I was thinking, it's lovely for me but they really should be more attentive to the young girls.

A visiting mother walked by with her daughter who was a member of the Zen Center. She commented to her daughter, in a loud voice, "Why should *she* have three of the best looking men in this whole place dancing attendance on her?"

I smiled at her. "Karma."

"Touche," the girl murmured as they walked away.

In leaving I tripped on the stairs and might have fallen if a young man, whom I did not even know, had not caught my arm. The same woman said, "That's one way of getting attention."

I had long ceased to seek for a cause of my warm wonderful friendships with young men. I merely enjoyed them while they lasted. It appeared, however, that each fulfilled the other's strong need for love. I was convinced I could not live without having a man *in love* with me. It was more essential than the air I breathed, the food I ate.

One night over dinner in a small tea room Lance said, "I can tell you are happy tonight. Your eyes are as bright as two stars."

"I didn't know stars were ever green."

He laughed. "Of course they are."

"And what do you think *yours* are like, Mister? Like black pools shining with light."

He tossed his head. "Oh, well, that's different."

Often when he called me on the phone he would say, "Claire, Claire", in a warm soft voice. "It's such a beautiful name I just love to say it." And I loved to hear it.

Once when he came to my apartment I stepped out into the hall to receive him. "As I got out of the elevator, Claire, and saw you standing there in your pretty red dress you looked about thirty-five years old."

He always looked a beautiful twenty-three.

On a certain Sunday morning when Lance and Haig and I met after the teisho, the autumn weather was so incredibly warm and sunny we decided to go on a picnic to the country land the Center owned. It was about an hour's drive from the city. We collected food and they both changed into very short shorts. All three of us sat on the front seat, I in the middle. As we bounced along our thighs would touch occasionally and each of us would move away quickly as if in danger of being scorched. Once the female devil that lurks in every woman prompted me *not* to move my thigh, I was shocked to see how I reveled in being female, delighting in luring men on without the slightest intention of satisfying them. I chastized myself but dismissed it all blithely by thinking, it's the way nature made women—so—. Was it merely the healthy sex urge of youth or did zazen arouse erotic desires in all ages?

After lunch we sat on the side of a hill looking over a distant lake. We fell into an unaccustomed silence, letting the warmth and beauty of the day and the scene sink into our very flesh. The sun was warm on my bare arms, a vagrant little breeze ran its fingers through my hair, the woods were still in green leaf, the distant view was enchanting. And there were two handsome affectionate young men sitting on either side of me. I had everything. I wanted for nothing at this moment. Love and nature, companionship and a good lunch fulfilled all my needs. As I gazed into empty space suddenly everything physical, personal, material faded away. Time ceased to exist. I was faintly aware of a living presence hovering over that blue lake. It was a rare vibrant moment, free of all dross. It vanished so soon as someone spoke.

Haig was careful to remain in the background and not trespass on Lance's preserves. But the three of us often cooked dinner together at my apartment or went out to dinner. And I imagined Lance and I were being very correct and circumspect at the Center but everyone was well aware of our warm friendship.

Sometimes, however, Lance would withdraw completely from me, from life. He remained silent as an iceberg. At first I interpreted it as an affront to me. I felt hurt and disconcerted. The minute I forgot my old ego long enough to concern myself with him, I realized he was suffering from some cause beyond my comprehension. I then longed to help him, to wish I had deeper knowledge of psychology. This mood lasted all day. Then next time we met he was cordial, charming and solicitous.

One night Lance took me to a small Chinese restaurant for dinner. He always drove my car—opening the door, helping me out solicitously. He could not have been more attentive if I had been his mother, grandmother and sweetheart rolled into one. We sat drinking endless cups of Chinese tea, laughing and talking vivaciously as we always did. A lock of his dark hair fell across his forehead. Without thinking I reached over and smoothed his hair back. Such a flood of tenderness, gratitude and love poured from his shining black eyes, his face, his whole being it revealed too much. It forced me to turn my eyes away.

Somehow my simple gesture seemed a symbol of all mothers' love for all sons. His response seemed to contain all the yearning, the tenderness and love of all sons for all mothers everywhere. It was so poignant a moment I knew I would never forget it so long as I lived. But it saddened me to see such a revelation of hunger for love. Did he disclose the secret history of his life in that one revealing look?

Why, oh why, were all human beings created with an insatiable yearning for love? If Lance had been my own darling son, I felt I could not have loved him more. Surely the mother-son relationship is the closest on earth, closer than the wife-husband, daughter-father, daughter-mother relation. In all mother-son relationships there is an element of man-woman, too. And more often than is admitted there may be passion, conventionally restrained, lurking behind the scenes eager to emerge. I recalled reading Dexter the passage in Jung on the deeper psychological meaning of incest. Jung explained that the desire to unite with one's source sometimes appears disguised as a desire to unite with another person.

Mothers are required to love many children. One evening Lance bid me a particularly tender good night at my door. He seldom kissed my cheek as Dexter always had but his eyes glowed with shining warmth. His steady gaze filled my whole body, my whole being with a delicious golden glow. It constricted my heart with love. I longed to protect him from myself, from himself. Yet the experience of any kind of love—full, deep, selfless—possesses a purity that is at moments incredible. I found that meditation intensifies all one's faculties.

I closed the door softly, overwhelmed by a flood of emotion greater than my heart and body could contain. I flung myself down on to the bed fully clothed. I could not think. I simply drifted in the sea of love like a piece of will-less seaweed abandoning myself to the ebb and flow—blindly, blissfully. The warm caressing waves of emotion lifted me up, washed over me, carrying me this way and that. Not thinking, not wanting, I had no worries, no doubts, no problems. I surrendered to some force far stronger than I.

Gradually as I lay there drifting deliciously in Lance's love for me and my love for this one handsome young man, I felt my love begin to expand within me physically. It was as if it were the ever-widening circles in a pond when a pebble has been dropped in it. Then it burst through its physical limitations—expanding, ever expanding until it was as wide as the sea! *I loved not merely one young man but everyman!* It felt warm, selfless, all-embracing, too vast, too wonderful to believe.

Finally I leapt off the bed and rushed to the bookcase in the living room. First I turned hastily to Plato's *Phaedrus* then to the *Symposium*. Socrates described the transformation of love from the particular to the universal.

Socrates understood love as a kind of divine madness filled with beauty and goodness. It was a path that led to truth, to philosophy, to a search for the beyond. The first impulse toward seeking something higher originates in falling in love. I did not believe a word of it when I had first read these dialogues years ago. I now hungrily read my notes written in the margins of the *Symposium* describing the rungs of the "ladder to perfection" as conceived by Socrates.

The first rung was the love of the beauty of, and passion for, one beautiful youth. This could be an elevating, purifying experience without sex, Socrates maintained. Was it because it was without sex? Socrates, though a husband and father of sons, loved the young Alcibiades but it was never consummated physically. The philosopher was many years older than the beautiful youth. Did the disparity of ages have a bearing?

Socrates stated that such love was able to elevate him (the lover) to the high plane of dialectic. I had never understood the connection before. Nor had I met anyone else who did. Certainly Lance and I had not achieved that height but we did discuss Zen and Buddhism, zazen and enlightenment with passionate intensity. That Lance was in his 20's and I in my 70's did not seem to matter—or was the beauty of our relationship due to this?

To enumerate accurately the different rungs of Socrates' ladder to perfection was not simple even though I had puzzled over it for days when I first read Plato. At that time I was in the hospital with a broken leg. Plato's *Dialogues* had virtually saved my life and brought me to a second enlightenment—almost.

The first rung is love for one individual. This appears to lead to the second rung—love of the beauty of all beautiful bodies. Next, love of "spiritual loveliness" that "quickens in his (the lover's) heart a longing for such discourse as tends toward the building of a noble nature."

The fourth rung is the love of the beauty of laws, institutions and the sciences, "so that he may know the beauty of every kind of knowledge.... He will find the seeds of the most fruitful discourse and the loftiest thought and the golden harvest of philosophy."

The highest rung of the ladder is "the final revelation.... There bursts upon him that wonderous vision which is the very soul of the beauty he has toiled so long for. It is an everlasting loveliness which neither comes nor goes, which neither flowers nor fades.... It will be neither words nor knowledge... but subsisting by itself... in eternal oneness.... Starting from individual beauties, the quest from universal beauty must find him mounting the heavenly ladder stepping from rung to rung.... [Then] he shall be called a friend of god and if ever it is given man to put on immortality, it shall be given to him."

Slowly, reverently, incredulously, I returned the large, heavy book to its shelf. I stood there weeping quietly, feeling unworthy, grateful, and quietly ecstatic. It was all too wonderful. I scarcely dared think of it. Was it possibly possible that such a glorious transformation could happen to me? Even briefly? To find that the love of one person could expand into love for all people! Love of all mankind was certainly one of the goals of Zen. Had not my inner being been awakened by zazen to prepare it for this momentous experience?

Perhaps I was not following the proper sequence of steps in climbing the Buddha's spiritual path or Socrates' ladder. Similar goals were arrived at by different means, were they not? The laws of the human psyche are universal. Had not Emerson said, you can feel what Plato felt?

Certainly I felt love for Lance individually, then it expanded to love of all people and concern for the "spiritual loveliness" of the young people at the Zen Center. And never in my life had my intellect been so stimulated by thought, by the sciences, especially psychology and physics, as it was now during my discipline in Zen. Now—in the near future would there come the "love of Absolute Beauty, simple, separate and everlasting," as Jowett translated it? I was ready, willing and eager. Whether I was able remained to be seen.

My friend Blanch and I disagreed on many things—but amicably. She was like the sister I never had and longed for as were Robbie and Ruth in high school, Clare Ousley in college, Francis Fox in New York, Lucy, Ina and Marion and Louise in Connecticut. I always found that an intimate, understanding, appreciative, tolerant woman friend is a necessity to a woman. Woman talk is different from talk with men. Both are essential.

Blanch and I carried on long, long, satisfying telephone conversations about Zen and the Center, the weather, the Roshi and his teishos, poetry, clothes, recipes for cooking bulghur the best way and every other conceivable subject.

"Isn't it exciting," I asked her one day, "that the religious experience has at last come into the respectable limelight? Every week new evidence emerges that psychologists, neurologists, physiologists and other scientists, are engaged in research into the scientific facts of spiritual growth and states. They call it altered states of consciousness. I snatch up every new scholarly journal the minute it arrives and devour it immediately like a hungry beggar."

"Like what?"

"Oh, the *Journal of Transpersonal Psychology*, *Journal of Humanistic Psychology*, Rindge's *Human Dimensions*, *Journal of Altered States of Consciousness*, Prince's *Newsletter of the Bucke Society* in Montreal."

"Oh, dear," Blanch sighed, "I don't have time to read such things. My Japanese classes at the U. of S. keep my nose to the grindstone. Though I am learning all kinds of new things about Buddhism in it. Besides I have to cook and keep house for my family and—"

"And an extremely nice intelligent family it is, too. Three wonderful children."

"I think so. You said, Claire, that you receive a flood of brochures and announcements from centers for self-realization from all across this country and Canada. Have you received the catalogs of the Tibetan Institute, Naropa, in Colorado and Nyingam in California?"

"Yes, fascinating. With beautiful delicate illustrations. And many booklets from Hindu ashrams."

"Do you ever get brochures from the other Zen Centers in California and New York?"

"California, yes, never New York."

She laughed. "So maybe the world need not go down to ruin after all with all these people learning to actualize their noblest potentials."

I exchanged with other members the relevant books, old and new. Tart's *Altered States of Consciousness*, Lilly's *Center of the Cyclone*, Capra's *Tao of Physics*, White's *What Is Meditation?*, Durckheim's *Hara*, Dean's *Psychiatry and Mysticism*, Pearce's *The Crack in the Cosmic Egg*, and *Zen and the Art of Motorcycle Maintainance* by Robert Pirsig.

Blanch was an ardent member of the Woman's Liberation Movement. Intellectually I knew men had exploited women from the beginning of time but I found them so interesting that emotionally I forgave them—almost.

Several of us often sat in zazen in my apartment before lunch or dinner—Marian, or Dexter and Hannah, or Lance and Haig and other members of the Zen Center. Afterwards we drank gallons of herb tea and discussed the twin revolutions that were occurring in America. Not only the spiritual revolution in which we were all deeply involved but the scientific revolution. It was difficult to understand why they did not all wax as rapturously excited as I did.

Haig sometimes gently reminded me that the purpose of Zen was to quiet the discursive intellect and awaken the True-self that seemed to dwell in the unconscious, not the conscious, mind.

My conscious and unconscious, however, plunged ahead like a pair of unruly horses in fierce rivalry—sometimes working separately, sometimes together. How could anyone be calm and quiet? Historic events were happening right under our noses. A vital half of the human mind was being awakened and investigated, the half which the Western world had neglected with the exception of Jung and lesser figures of psychology in Europe. Maslow had been the pioneer in America. A whole fascinating new area of the human brain was being discovered like an unexplored territory of fabulous riches.

Not only was science beginning to verify the claims of religion or rather, of the religious *experience*, but this new human potential movement indicated that the battle of the century was being joined—the reconciliation of science and religion. No longer was the mystical experience condemned by psychiatrists as pathological. Even scientists were beginning to regard it as the most beautiful and desirable of all human experiences. Naturally it was an important change to me. After my spontaneous mystical experience in New Haven, many of my friends had looked at me askance. No one enjoys that. Many skeptics still regarded Zen as outre. Some inquisitive college professors, whom I met at conferences and corresponded with, felt too impatient to spend years in achieving results through meditation. So they resorted to psychedelics—experimentally. This allowed them to write of states of consciousness not only theoretically but experientially.

Dexter and Hannah gave many interesting dinner parties in their new home. Dexter had purchased a house in a black neighborhood to show his racial sympathy. Usually Thomas, a musician from Harvard, and Hale, a scientist from Massachusetts Institute of Technology, were present. They were both devoted to Hannah.

"All of us training in spiritual centers of whatever kind are in the very center of the storm," Thomas remarked.

"Yes," I said. "I read recently that Toynbee, you know the famous English historian, stated that the major event of the Twentieth Century would be recorded by history not as the World Wars but as the introduction of Buddhism into the West."

"Isn't it thrilling to think," Hannah asked as she served the pizza, "that we at the Zen Center might contribute one small fragment to the movement that might be the salvation of the world?

"I long to think that," I answered. "But what practical influence can spiritual figures exert on society at large—politically, economically and most important of all militarily?"

"But the Buddhist monks and nuns immolated themselves in Vietnam in protest against the war," Hannah said.

"Did it prevent the Communists," I asked, "from taking over South Vietnam? That sort of sacrifice has no effect on conquerors, as you saw. They destroyed the Buddhist religion there."

"We had no business going to war in Vietnam in the first place," Dexter murmured.

"And look at Tibet," Hale said, "thousands of monasteries and monks and a highly spiritual populace were conquered by the Chinese Communists. They destroyed all that and took over the country."

"But," Thomas argued, "in Japan, Zen has influenced every aspect of life."

"Even the political, economic and military?" I asked. "What about Pearl Harbor?" I failed to remember that these young people had not been born then or were babies. "That was when the Japanese Air Force destroyed the American Fleet one quiet Sunday morning and forced President Roosevelt to enter World War II against Japan and Germany."

"Well," Hannah said, "many Zen members after several years of training at the Center become public school teachers. They can pass on the principles of religion they learn to their students."

"I may teach when I get my degree," Hale said.

"So long as you don't call it Zen," Thomas murmured.

"Yes," I agreed, "maybe that is the answer, Hannah. This present generation of spiritual young people may not change the political and economic climate but they may be able to train the next generation to meditate, and awaken the virtues in the True-self of their pupils and children so they may change the world. I know several college professors who are now introducing meditation and the ideal of self-realization in their classes to the—"

Thomas laughed. "To the horror of their colleagues usually."

I shrugged. "So they tell me."

Every day the feeling of one's own inner growth was exciting, the affectionate companionship of unusual young men and women was exciting, Zen was exciting, life itself was unbearably exciting. So I went singing down the days—and developed a fine case of insomnia from over stimulation. Always that fly in every precious ointment. Perfection is not permitted us—except for fleeting moments. I wonder why.

Someday I feared my task might become the development not only of a beautiful inner spiritual life, but of a healthier body. But not yet. Until my body rebelled completely I knew I would continue at my delightfully mad pace of overstimulation.

Often when I would rise from my hour of meditation before breakfast I would close my eyes, hold my breath, lay my hands on the head of the Buddha figure Susie had given me. I stood waiting until the little fountains of joy bubbling up in my chest subsided. Whenever this happened I would remain on this high plane all day.

At the end of such a day when everything in life had functioned harmoniously I would say to myself, see what zazen can do for you, Claire? Never, never forget that there is a plane, a plateau on the spiritual path that is attainable by zazen long before one arrives at the highest peak. A plateau where all one's acts are performed with ease and skill, problems are clarified, where one's encounter with others is a warm harmonious encounter, where one's mind and insight are stimulated to greater activity.

I know, I know, I murmured, and to attain and maintain this high plane is my daily effort. If only it weren't so difficult. If only I, if only everyone in the world, could experience this elevated plateau continuously, what a glorious place the world would be.

Even so I am eternally grateful that these inner mind states have been granted me intermittently at least. If only I can make them permanent. And if only I could help others toward them. What am I good for otherwise?

But remember, Claire, Kolberg repeatedly admonishes us that one is not able to help others wisely until one has first helped oneself—that is, advanced on the Buddha's Way.

Chapter XI
SESSHIN, REMORSE AND JEWELS

In October I was scheduled to attend my first seven-day sesshin. I *felt* I wanted to go. Yet three days before the crucial day, my rational mind staged an unexpected and vociferous battle to maintain its own supremacy.

I don't understand you, Claire, it protested. All your life you have fought for your freedom. Look at your record. In college you abandoned all the parties of commencement week to rush over to Alabama and obtain a position just so you could be financially independent. You wanted so much to be free of family domination you didn't care if your father disinherited you. You said you could not bear to be told what to do, what to think, what to say, how to dress by someone else all the time. You even considered it a point of honor in college to break any rules you regarded as designed for children.

You struggled painfully for years to free yourself from your mother's fundamentalist Christian church—its repressions and puritanism. You moved to New York City primarily because you assumed it would permit you complete freedom.

You went swimming naked in the ocean just to prove you were free to be natural—scandalous behavior for a nice girl in those backward days. You deceived your men friends. You told them you had an engagement every Wednesday night just so you would be free to sit at home in sweet solitude and let your own self unfold. You forfeited good jobs in two large social service organizations because large institutions considered they had the right to interfere with your freedom and private personal life after hours.

You dared risk disgrace when you lived in that "companionate marriage" in Virginia just because you wanted to be free of the conventions and restrictions of marriage. I honestly thought that for seventy-five years you had devoted all your efforts to obtaining freedom—not only as a woman but as a human being.

And now at long last you *are* free. You have your own money. You have no husband or family to dominate you. You can spend your money and your life as you wish. You live alone and like it. You feel no need for a husband. You are free to do exactly what you like when you like. You can work on your manuscript all night if you wish with no one to admonish you. You're free at long last. Don't you realize that, for heaven's sake?

And now you're throwing it all away. You have deliberately committed yourself to an institution with the strictest rules you ever encountered. Even when you're not *in* the Center you allow Zen to interfere with everything in your life. During sesshin Zen even tells you when to rise, when to bathe, what to eat, what to wear, what to do, not to talk, not to think. My God, woman, you thought those were the reasons you left home as a girl! What are you? An ignorant obedient school girl again? Honestly, Claire Myers Owens, you are a fool. A fool to submit to such tyranny as Zen training—especially in sesshin.

Besides, how can you wish to suppress your intellect? All your life you've reveled in it. Even in high school, chemistry class excited you. And in college physics, the discovery that there was a reason for everything made you nearly die of joy. Later when you read Northrop, Sheldon, Jung and Plato you were elated for weeks. But in sesshin you strain every nerve to transcend your discursive intellect. It's an outrage!

This violent protest of my rational mind almost paralyzed me. In desperation I sought support in every book in sight. What could reassure me of the value and beauty of self-realization? It was shocking to find how few books there are that describe the joys of the immediate personal experience. I plunged into Yogananda's *Autobiography of a Yogi*, Bucke's *Cosmic Consciousness*, Whitman's *Leaves of Grass*, Millay's *Renascence*, the Paradisio of Dante's *Divine Comedy*, Kolberg's enlightenment account in *Introduction to Zen*, and for final reassurance even resorted to my own *Awakening to the Good*.

Nothing diminished the rebellion of my rational mind. Yet I was *committed* to this discipline as an aspirant of enlightenment. This was my purpose in moving to Snowbound, my purpose in life. I arrived at sesshin in a distressingly agitated, negative state of mind. At the end of the first three days I said to Roshi in dokusan, "I might as well pack my bag and go home. My rational mind is completely blocking any zazen. Reason is in the saddle and riding me mercilessly."

"This often happens," Roshi said calmly. "The ego is so strong in the Western mind. You return to your mat and concentrate on your *hara* with every ounce of energy of your being." He held up a stiff card and struck it repeatedly with the end of a pencil. "Concentration is like a battering ram. Strike and strike again against the closed door of your unconscious and it will open."

I did not believe a word of it. I returned to the zendo, however, and concentrated as never before. Finally, a breakthrough! Before my mind's eye I beheld a row of people—life-size and real: my mother, father, grandmother, brother—all dead, and Hannah—very much alive. They were all looking at me with accusing eyes. The implication was that I had hurt them.

Such violent remorse arose in me it seemed to pull my ego up by the roots. It destroyed the illusion of my own goodness. My body shook, I sobbed uncontrollably hour after hour.

By noon my body felt so abnormally heavy, my legs so weak it was impossible for me to rise to walk in the kinhing line. Two of the ever vigilant monitors, Pat and Jeff, carried me upstairs and laid me on the bed. Pat kissed me gently and they silently withdrew. As I lay there I saw a vision of the primordial earth millions of years ago—bare, brown, dry, cracked, desolate, no green vegetation, no human beings, no living thing anywhere as far as ever the eye could see.

I seemed to see myself in the midst of this desolation on a treadmill getting nowhere fast. Then suddenly I beheld suspended in distant space a beautiful city of light—glowing, radiant. Was this the future of mankind, a golden age, or a symbol of light for me? Milda brought me some fruit for lunch. Eating was unthinkable.

That evening when I went to dokusan I presented the expiation scene to Roshi, he pronounced expiation as highly desirable. But, I protested, surely I had never hurt anyone so badly that I should suffer so excruciatingly?

"Probably expiation for unkindnesses you committed in your past lives," he explained.

(None of this was meaningful to me until months afterward. One Sunday Roshi gave a very moving teisho on the "taking of the ten precepts." Kolberg explained that in Buddhism there is no sin as in Christianity. One did not repent because one had sinned against a god. One repented at having done wrong by becoming separated from one's True-self. That was a principle I could accept. At twenty-five I had found it impossible to accept a wrathful, vengeful God. Godliness excluded anger in my mind. Zen, however, was a logical, mature approach to one's reprehensible behavior.)

The next morning at the sesshin when I returned to sitting in the zendo there appeared before my astonished eyes a detached black hand with all the fingers outlined in light. Then there appeared a fern leaf on a long stem detached from its bush. It was enameled in white and studded with jewels— amethysts, which are said to be my birth stone—whatever that means.

Then suddenly the brown wooden divider wall in front of me changed to beautiful unearthly ice with an underglow of blue, then to a luminous blue with lights—source unseen—flickering across the bottom and green fern leaves hanging over the top of the four foot high wall. Then it turned to brown gauze. I could distinctly see the coarse threads that composed it. *Suddenly I saw right through this gauze wall!* I beheld two men sitting on cushions on the other side and the legs of Pat, the monitor, as he walked down the aisle with the kyosaku stick. It was impossible to believe my own eyes even while it was happening.

I had read accounts of Hindu yogis who claimed they possessed the power to see through walls, walk barefooted on hotcoals and perform all kinds of prodigous impossible feats. I had never believed a word of it. Now I myself was seeing through a solid wooden wall! It was impossible but true.

I related all these phenomena to Roshi in dokusan. His eyes shone and he looked so excited I thought he was going to experience another enlightenment then and there. But he didn't and I didn't and I felt he was disappointed that I hadn't. "Makyo. Psychic power. It comes unbidden but you must not cling to it," he admonished me.

Nevertheless it was deeply impressive to experience the extension of one's normal faculties. When the sitting ended for the day I placed my hand on the gauze partition. It was a wall of solid wood. The image of gauze vanished.

Snowbound weather indulged in its usual fluctuations with a vengeance. It had been almost 90 degrees when we began the sesshin. On the fifth day the thermometer went down to 40. I was sitting in the cold draft between the open windows and the open door. I caught a cold, developed a fever and was in bed for the last two days of the sesshin. Later my doctor forbade me ever to participate in another sesshin. I had developed palpitations of the heart. This was a bitter disappointment. Did it mean I must struggle toward enlightenment without sesshin? Was it possible? It would be ten times more difficult.

When I conveyed the doctor's verdict to Roshi, he remarked, "It may be a blessing in disguise."

The minute I returned home from sesshin my rational mind lay in wait for me at the door ready to leap out at me like a jealous husband. (Just the way my husband used to meet me at the door with suspicious eyes after I had attended a movie alone. He would demand, "What picture did you see? Tell me all about it." To verify my statements he would consult the motion picture ads in the afternoon paper.)

Now it was necessary to attend first to my cold. It was worse and my fever higher. I drank three cups of hot camomile tea, placed bottles of fruit juice on the night table and fell into bed. I hoped to discover rational reasons in my own mind for my astounding experiences during sesshin that would pacify my rebellious thinking mind.

Of course it could all be dismissed as makyo as Zen Master Yasutani advises. But did not makyo itself contain meanings? Would rational analysis, however, be an obstacle to advancement on the spiritual path or would it lend support and incentive? I really had no choice. I felt the way Bertrand Russell did when he said, "One must understand or die."

Why does one see those extraordinary images in sesshin? What do they mean? Why jewels of all things? They seem so worldly and irrelevant. For that matter, why are the figures of the Buddha gold? What is the purpose of placing flowers and lighted incense on the altar before the many Buddha figures? Why the striking of the shoulders with a stick?

Zen says that the purpose of flower offerings is to express the gratitude of Buddha's followers. True enough. But why not place other offerings there— money, for instance? No one ever heard of money being placed on any altar. Why not?

All my cogitation was of no avail. I brought on chill and much sneezing by dashing out into the living room for a certain book. Then I piled the pillows high behind me and once again sought clarification of man's world of Visionary Experiences. The only book that analyzes such phenomena in a meaningful scientific way as far as I was aware was Huxley's *Heaven and Hell*.

He explains that flowers, lighted tapers, shining gold images, lights, primary colors, jewels, great art and stained glass windows possess the power to *transport us to another world*, to the antipodes of the human mind, a kind of heaven, the ideal world, to the Other Earth of Platonic dialogues. Once again rational explanation stopped my reading, stopped my breathing. Excitement raced through my blood.

Huxley explains the purpose of many mysterious religious customs. Now I understood the reason that during sesshin, Zen discipline necessitates little sleep, less food, nine hours of zazen, silence and the blows of the kyosaku stick. For the first time my fierce emotional resistance against the physical hardships of Zen melted away now that my reasoning mind was able to comprehend and consequently consent.

It was simply impossible for me to obey blindly without question the way many of the very young members apparently could. As Yasutani remarked, Western aspirants insisted on being given a map to show where they are going before they are willing to commence their spiritual journey.

Intellectually I finally accepted even the pain and indignity of the whacks on the shoulders.

"Every paradise abounds in gems." Even in the Christian Bible "Ezekiel's version of the Garden of Eden describes the topaz, diamond ... sapphire, emerald and gold.... The Buddhist paradises are adorned with 'stones of fire'.... 'The Western paradise of the Pure Land Sect is walled with silver, gold and beryl.'" As I read this cold chills ran down my back. Was this the reason that as a Christian child I was assured that heaven was paved with streets of gold and had pearly gates? Ideas at which I had laughed in ignorance I now understood at long last.

Even Socrates informs us in the *Phaedo* that there exists an ideal world above and beyond the world of matter filled with precious gems. "In other words," Huxley states, "precious stones are precious because they bear a faint resemblance to the glowing marvels seen with the inner eye of the visionary." So, I thought, perhaps I should not have given all my diamond rings to my brother after all. But when I first entered Zen I assumed that all jewelry was too worldly. (Besides I had arthritis in my fingers). I used to gaze for long periods at those diamonds sparkling in the light, fascinated by the mystery of their fascination. How good it was to understand.

"'The view of that world,' Plato says, 'is a vision of blessed beholders *(for to see things) as they are in themselves* is bliss unalloyed and inexpressible.'"

I closed my eyes. Deep sobs of sheer joy rose from my very hara. (Of course, crying filled my painful sinuses with more mucus.) That was the identical phrase used continually in Buddhism. Skeptical intellects which doubted the religious experience surely could not doubt Plato. Philosophy lent greater credibility to Zen and all Buddhism.

"When worshippers offer flowers at the altar they are returning to the gods things which they know, or (if they are not visionaries—obscurely feel) to be indigenous to heaven."

"Flowers indigenous to heaven"—how wonderful! Why hadn't I thought of that? All my life I had been puzzled by the irresitible attraction which flowers exerted on everyone. Other brightly colored inanimate objects did not exert the same mysterious allure. I had assumed the mystery of flowers was due not only to the color but to the fact that they are living. Yet a living animal did not affect us the same way as flowers. This explanation was itself a precious jewel I would secrete in a corner of my mind.

This would also explain the reason that extraordinary light from those stained glass windows in St. Chappelle had induced in me a feeling of a presence descending in the light that memorable day in Paris.

"The more than human personages of visionary experience never do anything (similarly the blessed never do anything in heaven). They are content to merely exist.... To be busy is the law of *our* being. The law of *theirs* is to do nothing.... And that accounts for the overwhelming impression made upon the beholder by the great static masterpieces of religious art" such as the figures of the Buddha in his profound stillness. Already zazen had taught me the enrichment derived from sitting motionless. The Bible says, "Be still and know I am God." All my life I had wondered what that beautiful statement meant. Never had I met anyone who knew. Not even ministers.

Such simple words. Yet such complexity and profundity in the human experience that occurred behind the words.

In Chinese paintings "this revelation of the wilderness living according to the laws of its own being, transports the mind toward its antipodes for primeval Nature bears a strange resemblance to that inner world where no account is taken of our personal wishes."

"In the nuptial embrace personality is melted down, the individual ceases to be himself and becomes a part of the vast impersonal universe." Ah, yes, I sighed, I had experienced this once or twice. It explains what D. H. Lawrence was attempting to convey in his novels and poems. His critics dismissed his ideas as nothing but dirty sex.

"For the healthy visionary, the perception of the infinite in finite particular is a revelation of divine immanance." I closed my eyes and allowed the wonder of this to flow through me like a river of light until the emotion gradually subsided.

"The nature of the mind is such that the sinner who repents and makes an act of faith in a higher power is more likely to have a blissful visionary experience (was my remorse the cause of my seeing through the wall?) than is the self-satisfied pillar of society.... Hence the enormous importance attached in all the great religious traditions, to the state of mind at the moment of death."

Huxley's rational explanations caused me to clasp his little book against my breast till the waves of excitement died down. Oh, oh, I murmured, the learning process of the conscious mind is almost as exciting as the awakening of the unconscious. But can the former carry me all the way to enlightenment as the latter can?

Dexter and Hannah, eager to hear all about my sesshin, invited me to dinner. I described to Hannah the expiation scene and my remorse for having hurt her. It abolished my hostile feeling toward her forever after. I laughed. "Sesshin accomplished for me what I was not strong enough to accomplish by myself." She and I became good friends after this. It cooled Dexter's ardor and mine. We have remained good friends for the last six years but the magic is gone—as it should—alas.

Lance and Haig, also eager to hear all about the sesshin, took me out to dinner. They were very excited about my actual experiences. When I related Huxley's explanations, however, Haig looked quite upset.

"Roshi cautions us about the danger of the intellectual approach. It's an obstacle to practice."

Lance spoke up. "Only for beginners like you and me, Haig. You forget Claire had a tremendous enlightenment experience before she ever came into Zen. Roshi says it's safe once one has attained self-realization."

I patted his hand. Thank you, dear, for coming to my rescue. I've arrived at a stage where my rational mind refuses to remain in the background. But the wonderful thing is, logical reasons for the experiences from my unconscious lend support and validity to them."

Chapter XII
ROSHI AND ONENESS

One night I entered the dokusan room for the usual private interview. I gasshoed and prostrated before the Roshi. Then he immediately violated all the rules of the order.

His eyes were shining as he said, "I'm going to give a lecture at the museum in Montreal in two weeks. On 'Art in Zen and Zen in Art.' I wish you could hear me. I shall need all the help I can get."

"Why, I should like to hear you."

"Then how would you like to fly up to Montreal with me for three days? The Center will bear part of your expenses."

I was almost speechless. "Why, why, I don't know how I could help you but—but yes, I'd love to go. Thank you."

He was a collector and connoisseur of far Eastern art, that I knew. I doubted if he needed me or anyone. Then why? The Roshi was a very shrewd operator. There was usually a purpose behind his every action.

That night—pleased but puzzled—I lay awake wondering and worrying. Was this trip to be part of my Zen discipline? He was a mysterious man. Please, I murmured, don't let him be too severe with me. These have been the three most strenuous years of my entire life. Never have I worked so hard with such concentration and dedication or been so humbled.

Night and day, year after year, I have struggled to adjust myself to this ancient Japanese-Chinese-Indian religion. I know it contains the profoundest truths I have ever encountered but—it's such a severe discipline—Rinzai Zen. It's such an austere institution—our Center. He's such a formidable teacher—our Roshi. All those endless rules he enforces with uncompromising vigor. All those hundreds of recalcitrant aspirants he is training on the steep and stony path to spiritual self-realization.

But Claire, I chastised myself, all your whole wonderful way of life at present is created by Zen (and by my own arduous efforts too, I interjected). You have a shining goal to work toward, expert guidance on the path and a community of aspiring companions in the sangha. You know you are happier than you ever have been in your whole life. So you should be grateful to the system—though strenuous, to the Roshi—though strict, to the Buddha—though distant. They have lifted you from a directionless, fragmented life, from uncertainty toward direction, toward wholeness, and certitude to a plane of spiritual yearning sweet beyond belief.

I know, I know, but don't forget all my pain and work and hardship. Or is it because of them? That is the question:

Is Zen wise when it ignores cold and drafty meditation halls, when it considers flu and coughs excellent opportunity to practice detachment from the body? Are pain and even neuroses conducive to greater spiritual incentive? Why must Zen always ignore or belittle everyone's finest accomplishments? Does it fear that giving compliments might inflate the ego? Personally I've always found positive appreciation an incentive to greater endeavor.

Must Zen demand total involvement, subordinating every personal interest to insignificance? Must the monitors whack us so fiercely on the shoulders with that kyosaku stick? Is it true that it changes the body chemistry releasing adrenalin and histamine—beneficial to spiritual growth?

The Roshi says Zen inflicts pain in order to help, insults in order to praise, shows disrespectful respect. I simply don't understand such an inverted process.

When anyone complains about the severity of Zen, Roshi laughs. He maintains that his methods are child's play compared to the discipline in the Japanese monastery where he trained so long and painfully. All windows open in the winter, while it was snowing, open to the mosquitoes in the summer. And the sitters were not allowed to brush them off and certainly not to kill them.

Are these hardships what brought him to the enlightenment he describes in his *Introduction*? But we are Americans and laymen, not monks, not Japanese, not trained to subservience, asceticism and mortification. This is a Protestant country. It is not in our tradition.

But, Claire, all this severity is designed to bring you to selflessness, joy and creativity and it already has to a limited extent. It is designed to bring you *eventually* to wisdom and compassion, to enlightenment. *You*, of all people, should know that enlightenment is worth any ordeal.

I do, I do, but couldn't the same result be achieved by gentler methods than Rinzai? Soto Zen perhaps? Well, Claire, one thing is certain. You should be honored that the Roshi has invited you to accompany him to Canada.

Oh, I am but I am a little frightened too. How shall I act? If he is an ordained monk and my spiritual teacher, and I am his pupil, should I open doors for him and help him on with his coat? Or should he help me? Is he too spiritual to cope efficiently with practical matters? He is usually accompanied by a disciple who takes responsibility for all practical details. Must I manage the tickets and customs and see that we always catch the right plane?

One of the students drove us to the airport to commence our trip to Canada. Roshi quietly assumed the lead, played the customary role of the man, opened doors for me, held my coat. He acted simply and naturally. He appeared to feel a calm oneness with the practicalities of travel, with the complexities of customs. He had brought many art objects with him to illustrate his lecture. No effort, no commotion, no friction.

He also seemed at one with me. All our movements coordinated as if we were veterans of years of traveling together as my husband and I had once been. At first, however, I felt constrained and uncertain, aware of many dualities.

Never had I seen Roshi Kolberg so calm and relaxed, so gentle and considerate. He was simply a different man. In the Toronto air terminal while waiting for our connection to Montreal we ate lunch and discussed art. We talked of its purpose, meaning and influence.

In a sudden burst of courage I voiced my views. "For years I assumed that the greatest art possessed the power to bring one to enlightenment. Then I discovered that it could prepare one, bring an altered state of consciousness as the psychologists call it, but not the highest state of consciousness. I realized that the greatest art was the greatest as a result of the artist's own enlightenment which preceded and precipitated his art."

Roshi laughed. "That's exactly what I plan to tell the audience tonight at the museum. They won't like it."

He listened to me respectfully for the first time after I had listened to him in respectful silence for three years on all subjects. He had refused to read my books, refused to listen to my description of my awakening that day in Pennsylvania. All that while I had felt hurt and resentful that in spite of my advanced age and experience I had been treated like an ignorant child. Today, however, it was no longer a teacher-student relationship. He treated me like an equal at long last. Of course I would never know as much about Zen Buddhism as he did. His knowledge of Zen was prodigious. But I had had a glorious enlightenment experience that lasted twelve years, published books about it, lectured on art, traveled and knew a few things myself. I felt entitled to a little recognition.

"But," I continued, "Aristotle said the function of art is purification. I've had that happen many times as I am sure you have, too." I described the cleansing process I underwent the first time I saw Titian's *Pope Paul*.

We talked on and on. It was the first real conversation we had ever had. We sat wrapped in a warm atmosphere of effortless rapport that was infinitely sweet.

Nothing is ever perfect. Nature, fate, karma or whatever always arranges matters so that there is a fly in the precious ointment. After we boarded the plane to Montreal he delivered a lecture against psychology in general. Zen did not need psychology, he maintained. I listened but answered never a word. Why spoil our trip when it was beginning so auspiciously?

He was well aware from my writings that I believed scientific research proved the validity of Zen's spiritual claims. I felt deeply that rational support strengthened one's faith in Zen. After all, zazen and enlightenment were both psychological processes, in my estimation. I wrote on Zen but I also wrote on other methods of actualizing man's noblest potentials. I had lectured on Jung and Houston and Masters. I would be false to myself if I omitted the psychological facts and rational analyses.

That night in Montreal when our Zen group arrived at the museum, I asked the Roshi, "Where do you want me to sit?"

"On the front seat. I need all the inspiration I can get."

I did not believe a word of it. Soon his lecture proved he needed no one. It was profound in thought, dynamic in force. He played with large ideas as easily as a juggler tosses small balls in the air. He held the audience motionless and silent for an hour and a half. At the end I asked the curator his opinion, "Superb! Inspiring!"

All the Zen people who were to conduct a workshop were staying at the same hotel. The following morning Roshi phoned me. "I'd like to have you accompany me to the museum to see their fine loan exhibit of Far Eastern art."

We strolled among very un-Western paintings and sculptures. We stood before a strangely moving black and white scroll of a single bamboo branch, each delicate leaf significant by itself, like a declaration of independence from all human control, an assertion of its cosmic connection. Yet the bold black slash across the top left me cold, but aroused Roshi's excitement.

"I like that unique Japanese combination of fierceness and delicacy."

So this was why Zen appealed to him so strongly. "I like the delicacy," I murmured, "but not the fierceness."

Next we stood silent, wrapped, before the portrait of a homely old Chinese mandarin. His elaborate silken garments were painted in colors that still glowed like jewels after all these centuries. The lyrical grace of those intricately flowing robes somehow seemed to speak of something—beyond analysis—beyond man almost. An inexplicable inner turmoil arose within me. Only once before in my life had draperies so deeply affected me. That was the Greek marble group of the Three Fates in London. I had stared incredulously, almost frightened, at the provocative lines of those draperies of marble. They had seemed to carry me to another world.

Roshi's response to the sensuous beauty of this painting before us was as palpable as physical pressure. His voice was low and vibrant, his eyes glowed. This intensified my own reactions.

As if in a temple he whispered, "In the West men think they must be masculine, aggressive and somatotonic. In the East delicacy is highly prized."

Suddenly something began to vibrate in my chest, something broke—moved—melted. I felt as if I had become disembodied. I felt as if our bodies had disappeared, that my personality and Roshi's flowed into each other in a oneness that left me dazed with delight.

Striving to keep my feet on firm ground I asked him, "Can this delicacy be because the Chinese cultivated the deepest level of the unconscious, source of creativity and spirituality and seat of the feminine principle?"

"Why do you have to conceptualize and psychologize every experience, Claire?"

We strolled into the next room. Our steps were abruptly arrested by a figure of painted wood. It was a Zen master of the 13th Century, Roshi said. It was almost life-size.

This figure struck me motionless like a physical blow. This had happened to me only once before. Venus de Milo in the Louvre. This Zen man with his long robe still swirling about him with animation after 600 years—surely he was the embodiment of indestructibility, from everlasting to everlasting. The mouth of the figure was slightly open. Was he caught in the moment of spiritual ecstasy as Bellini had caught St. Theresa? But his eyes! They were incredible! They were nothing but two black holes in the wood. So how could they leave me hypnotized?

"Interesting, isn't it," Roshi whispered, "that the vertical line of the robe leads one's eyes to his folded hands. And the flowing lines of his torso direct one's attention to the focal point—those incredible eyes."

Roshi's words were casual but his body emanated electrical vibrations. His oneness with this great ancient spiritual sculpture was evident. I could feel a charge of energy flowing from him. The impact of this extraordinary man of living flesh standing beside me, the impact of this extraordinary man of living wood standing in front of me dissolved all barriers between us, banished the boundaries of the self. A flood of feeling all but carried me away.

Slowly we walked away in silence only to return immediately by tacit agreement. Again struck motionless, I stood there staring at this Buddhist figure. The artist's apparent awareness of the eternal awakened my awareness of it. I had read that artists in the ancient Orient never commenced their work until they were completely one with their object, until subject and object became one.

I stood there literally rooted to the spot. My entire being was undergoing a rigorous process of purification. Doubts and defilements were being washed utterly away. I felt elevated to another plane of consciousness. I was drawn deeper and deeper into a blissful state of oneness—with the work of art, with Zen Buddhism, with my companion, with mankind in general, with the unknown, the uncreated, the unborn. It was a vibrant moment—breathless—timeless.

Finally in a slight daze I followed Roshi as he led me up one of those interminable flights of stairs which museum architects delight in inflicting on their foot-sore spectators. Roshi, who was not famous for his patience, was wonderfully patient as I was obliged to ascend each step with both feet because of heart palpitations. He guided me to a bronze bust of the Buddha. It was not in the special loan exhibit but in the museum's permanent collection.

This is it! I silently exclaimed. This is the truly enlightened Buddha face I have been seeking in vain for years. Surely it was created by an artist himself enlightened. Here at last is the face of a man obviously spiritual, wise and compassionate with that little enigmatic smile characteristic of the fully realized. It is all writ there plain to see. But pleasure so intense, so prolonged became painful. It was too much. I was unable to endure any more joyous agitation this day. I turned away without a word.

During our homeward flight the stewardess asked me my preference of sandwiches for lunch. Then she said, "And what will your husband have?"

Roshi and I laughed but left her in happy ignorance. A car from the Center met us at the airport. "We can all three sit on the front seat," Roshi suggested.

I saw it would be very crowded. "Oh, Roshi, I'm sorry but I'll have to put my arm around back of you to make enough room. Do you mind?"

He laughed. "It's all right. I'm your husband now, remember?"

I said goodbye in a glow of happy incredulity. I had glimpsed the very essence of my spiritual teacher. This journey to Montreal had established a new relationship, forged an indestructible bond with the Roshi that might serve, I hoped, as a bridge between our differences forever after—despite my penchant for psychology and scientific rational supports for Zen experiences.

Sunday morning Roshi suggested that I might like to share my Canadian experience with the whole sangha. I stood before a hundred members crowded into the zendo and painted a verbal picture of a different Roshi. A Roshi never seen by them perhaps and never seen before by me—never—ever.

I concluded by saying, "Here at the Center every day, we see the highly efficient administrator of a large institution and a stern but successful teacher.

But in Montreal I saw the other Roshi—calm, relaxed, gentle—at one with all things and all people. One aspect that fascinated me was that the

practical, the physical, the sensuous, the intellectual and intuitive, the aesthetic and the spiritual, were all united harmoniously. Must not the *whole* man of tomorrow be instrumental in creating the golden age about which I hear you all talk so much?

"You know how in his teisho Roshi is always urging us to feel at one with whatever we're engaged in. Although I have occasionally experienced that joyous sense of oneness, frankly I never understood the significance of it until Montreal. Our *complete* oneness with anything obliterates our enemy, the old ego. It can bring joy, selflessness, and love of others. It can bring harmony with the Tao, with ultimate reality—faintly—briefly or otherwise. I reckon the greatest value of oneness is the obliteration of duality—the cause of all man's troubles.

"In short, the Roshi I saw in Montreal reminds me of something I read recently. Blofeld describes the Tibetan lamas as men 'possessing an inner stillness, a sweetness, a gentle gaiety, an oblivion to physical discomfort.'"

I sat down amid loud applause—very unorthodox in a religious hall. After all the zendo is a temple. Roshi rose and, smiling deprecatingly, murmured, "To the pure, all things are pure."

During the next few days the glow of my experience of oneness faded somewhat. As usual my rational mind questioned the scientific possibility of man's oneness with inanimate things, with other people or the cosmos. Eagerly I turned to *Frontiers of Consciousness* edited by my friend, John. I reread the chapter, "Energy Fields and the Human Body," by William Tiller, professor of material science at Stanford University and consultant to the government in solid state physics. Tiller said that every person's body was surrounded by an electromagnetic energy field that has been photographed. Also, at times the human body can tap energy from the cosmos through the endocrine glands, energy centers or chakras. Imagine a scientist admitting this!

In great excitement I phoned Blanch and told her what Tiller said. She was so immersed in her course in Japanese that she had little time to see anyone. Each year, however, she invited me to be part of her family at Thanksgiving and Christmas. It was comforting to be in the midst of a family in a real house, sitting before a real wood fireplace as I had done most of my life. In between celebrations we talked on the phone by the hour.

"But," Blanch countered, "Eastern religions have always known all that about drawing on cosmic power. If people knew it intuitively and experientially, it's bound to be true."

"Oh, but, my dear that's just the point! Is it? People have dreams and fantasies, visions and hallucinations which are not true *literally*. Oh, wait, you'll like this. Tiller also says man's free will creates mental patterns that are not consistent with those initially set and this causes disease."

"That," Blanch said, "is the reason Roshi and Buddhism discourages our reliance on the intellect."

"I know. And Tiller also hypothesizes that the body is composed of seven levels of substance that do not interact very strongly. Interaction can be caused by the *mind*. So you see it's all a little confusing but very exciting coming from a physicist, isn't it?"

When we hung up I went to the bookcase. As so often and mysteriously happens my hand seemed guided to the particular book I needed at this particular moment, *Man and His Symbols* by Jung and his associates.

In the chapter on "Science and the Unconscious," von Franz says that the "parallelisms in psychology and physics suggest a possible ultimate *one-ness* of both fields of reality... a one-ness of all life phenomena."

And I was certain that in one of his numerous books on my shelves, Jung said that self-realized man harmoniously unites the four functions of the mind—thinking, intuition, sensation and feeling.

And somewhere, but where I had forgot, I thought Niels Bohr said that quantum mechanics reveals the basic one-ness of the universe.

Chapter XIII
"YOUR WORK CAN BE YOUR PRACTICE"

"Your work can be your practice," Roshi said to me in answer to my unspoken question. I did not believe a word of it.

The Roshi had conferred another unexpected honor on me. Dr. Charles Tart, psychologist at the University of California, asked Roshi Kolberg to write a chapter on the psychology of Zen Buddhism for the book he was planning, *Transpersonal Psychologies*. Each chapter was to be written by a different person on a different religion. Roshi assigned the Zen chapter to me. It was a prestigious company—Tart, Lilly, Goleman, Ornstein and others.

It was an interesting challenge but presented one danger. Would all that prolonged intellectual research damage my practice now that my zazen was yielding such beneficial results? Joy, concern for others, certitude.

Roshi then answered my unspoken question. "Your work can be your practice." But I did not believe a word of it.

Roshi presented me with a list of twenty books on Zen that were authentic. He warned against writers who gave a distorted or untrue account of Zen. Lance offered to beg, borrow or buy all these books for me and to type my manuscript. He was the only living mortal who was able to decipher my execrable handwriting.

I sat in my writing chair and gazed at the high stack of books with real hunger. To my chagrin, however, I soon realized I possessed very little accurate theoretical knowledge of Zen or Buddhism. Mine was limited experiential knowledge derived from three years of zazen practice at the Center. Roshi always discouraged beginning practitioners from reading books on Zen. The intellectual approach was an obstacle on the path to enlightenment. This assignment, however, afforded a legitimate excuse for me to study Zen and Buddhist literature—something I had been longing to do because my rational mind still hesitated to accept certain principles and was ignorant of others.

Before writing my 100 pages on Zen I determined to plunge, if possible, right down to the very bedrock of Zen and Buddhism. I wished to reassure myself that I was not wasting my life, energy and money on a fallacious system of religion and that my paper for Tart would be accurate. Primarily, however, I wished to learn, to satisfy my doubting conscious mind.

Tart had furnished all his contributors with an outline to follow. At first I resented this, preferring complete freedom. Later I was grateful for it. It served as a restraint. I am inclined to be too emotional, too lyrical, and to soar off into the stratosphere. My paper would not be scientific but it was being written for a scientist. And, thank heaven, it would be permissible to introduce psychology into it to my mind's content.

Before even commencing to write, however, I, as an Occidental must thoroughly understand Zen Buddhism in my own way in all its aspects—

experiential and religious, psychological and philosophical. Was it valid in every way and for everyone? Also, did Zen meet an urgent need in America today? Many thoughtful Americans felt that everything they believed in had failed them in the last few years. Their hierarchy of values had somehow betrayed them—political and economic, aesthetic and religious, cognitive and ethical.

Liberals and radicals had found that politics did not fulfill all their needs nor solve their personal problems as they had expected.

Who could forget the Wall street crash of 1929? The cry of "God is dead" was heard in a supposedly Christian land; Art, whose function Aristotle says is purification, today revealed the neuroses of the artists; reason, and its off-spring, science, once the supreme value of the Western world, now found that its adherents were afraid in a world they themselves had made; ethics was an obsolete word. The youth of the nation were becoming drug addicts. They threw bombs, committed burglary, murder and rape as daily events.

Many people felt lost—frightened—bewildered. They did not know where to turn for help, truth or direction. In desperation they unconsciously or consciously were seeking ultimate answers to ultimate questions of life: Who am I? Why am I here? Why was I born? What is the purpose of life—if any? What is the meaning of life—if any? What is the secret of human happiness? Am I innately good or innately evil? Can I become good? If so, how?

Is there an ultimate reality? Can the individual communicate or unite with it? If so, how? What is the nature of the universe? What is truth? How does one explain the problem of evil? Why is there so much suffering in life? Why all the crime and corruption, violence, hate, war, and injustice in society? What is the ideal society? Did Zen Buddhism answer all these basic questions satisfactorily?

And more important, the question was, did the knowledge gained through zazen and enlightenment answer these questions *experientially* and therefore convincingly?

I read volume after volume, thought strenuously, asked myself unanswerable questions and practiced zazen at home and at the zendo with renewed vigor every day. I proceeded however, in the wrong sequence. First I read books by or about the Japanese Zen masters, Dogen, Hakuin, Suzuki and others. But Zen evolved from Chinese Ch'an which incorporated Taoism, so I read *Tao Teh Ching* by Lao-Tsu and also Hui-neng's *Platform Scripture* and Chugang-Tsu.

But Chinese Buddhism was brought into China from India in the Sixth Century by Bodhidharma. Consequently I pored over excerpts from a few of the 10,000 Indian sutras translated from Pali and Sanskrit. They were written hundreds of years after Buddha's death in 483 B.C. Like Jesus, Buddha never wrote a word. The Way was transmitted orally by Buddhist monks for centuries, later transcribed by scholars into their scriptures, the Prajna Paramita, the Lankavatara, Awakening of the Faith, Sutra of the Wonderful Law, the Surangama and others.

In China the nature of the Buddhist religion changed. The Indians were poetic, imaginative, speculative, whereas the Chinese were sensible, matter of fact, direct, down to earth. They incorporated their national Chinese characteristics into the imported Indian Buddhism. Buddhism moved from China to Japan without too many changes, although it appears as if Zen had permeated many aspects of its daily life for nearly a thousand years, not only religion but behavior, the arts, even flower arrangement and the tea ceremony.

The enormity of my task stunned me. Buddhism embraced the profoundest questions of human life. It deserved the study of a lifetime by a dedicated scholar. What could I do in six months (the deadline) and in only 100 pages?

Unforeseen difficulties arose. The English translations from Eastern languages were often made by Christian ministers or missionaries. Their viewpoint was biased, their terminology still Christian. Eastern phraseology and terms were used without defining their terms. The ambiguities, the negativisms, the paradoxes in Zen writing drove me wild. They seemed to my simple American mind unnecessary. The profundity, the universal truths, the inordinate nobility of Zen Buddhism seemed to me to deserve a simple, lucid, positive presentation in modem Western language for modern Western people. I would attempt to accomplish this in my limited way for myself, if not for others.

First I strove to simplify the basic principles of Zen Buddhism as I understood them:

—that every sentient being possesses a True-self or Buddha-mind;
—that the True-self contains innumerable virtues that are inherent in all people;
—that zazen or meditation is a way to discover or uncover the True-self by quieting the discursive intellect and liberating the self;
—that the True-self awakened by meditation can lead to enlightenment, though later the self itself is transcended;
—that enlightenment is the most important experience in life of which man is capable; it is satori or realization of Mind;
—that self realization is not the final goal of Zen;
—that the final goal is the integration of spiritual principles into daily life.

The validity of these principles was provided by observation of the aspirants training at the Center, my own experiences, as well as written accounts. They seemed to prove that meditation relaxes the body, quiets the mind and nerves, alleviates pain, resolves tension, diminishes or extinguishes the ego, liberates the True-self affording the body-mind opportunity to heal itself as nature apparently intended. It transforms character and behavior and one's hierarchy of values, freeing one from attachment to material possessions and the values of the relative world.

Zazen, or meditation, awakens innumerable other virtues we are not aware we possess: an honesty of which we did not know ourselves capable, a concern for others we can scarcely believe, joy like no other, energy that is latent, an ability to cope with problems that surprises us, a new muscular coordination, greater harmony with things and people.

Meditation awakens these qualities only partially, occasionally and briefly. Enlightenment awakens them fully, continuously and permanently—eventually. Zazen is a daily rehearsal for life's greatest drama—the actualization of our finest potentials.

Zazen may also activate our neuroses—if any, bringing understanding and alleviation or fear and terror. Sometimes a professional Zen psychiatrist is required.

Often the spiritual awakening is precipitated by suffering. Frequently the aspirant is confronted by a problem insoluble by the conscious, reasoning mind. It strives to solve it, is defeated, surrenders its life-time dominance.

Then the ego dies. Death of the ego is essential to attainment of the highest state of consciousness. The Buddhists call it, "the great death." Meditation merely diminishes the ego. In enlightenment it is annihilated. Usually a great subjective light, that seems cosmic, appears. Its origin has never been explained, at least scientifically. One merges with it, feels oneself being purified, purged of defilements, faults, and weaknesses. One feels born again. The ectasy is ineffable.

Then come intuitive insights into one's own nature and that of others, into the nature of the universe and one finds them all good. (Zen maintains that to see into one's own nature is enlightenment). One experiences a sense of oneness with all things, love of all people regardless of sex or age, race or social status. One sees into the past and future, sometimes into past reincarnations.

The transformation is cataclysmic as an earthquake. All the old ways of acting, thinking, and feeling disappear. New ones spring into being as if by magic. One may feel it physically, as if a stream of cosmic energy—first immanent, then transcendent and then one and the same—directs one's every thought, emotion and action.

After the enlightenment *event* we live in the enlightened *state*. This brings a selflessness of which we did not know ourselves capable, the creativity for which we long, the certitude we have been seeking all our lives, a compassion we thought possible only to Buddha.

The actualization of our noblest potentials increases the clarity of the thinking mind (usually), heals or transcends ailments. It brings greater rapport with nature, deeper response to the arts. Old prejudices fall away like empty husks. It awakens the inherent urge to sacrifice oneself for others.

The realized person is unable to feel anger, hate or jealousy. He loves his enemies to his own great astonishment exactly as Jesus taught but for which he offered no adequate method of attainment. After realizing the self all fear of old age, illness and death disappear. One feels secure as an integral part of the universal scheme of things.

The highest state of consciousness induces a joy that surpasses that conferred by youth or beauty, love or passion, fame or wealth. It reveals the secret of happiness, the meaning of life.

The validity of this *experiential* and *religious* aspect of Zen Buddhism I felt was unassailable. Even if one has personally experienced many of these glorious transformations of character, behavior and feelings one's rational mind may refuse to accept them. Mine refused. Did other traditions offer intellectual support?

Spontaneous spiritual awakening is described in other religious literature, in the Bible and the writing of the great Christian mystics—St. Theresa, St. John of the Cross, Eckhart, Ruysbroeck and others. They offer little psychological explanation. In the *induced* variety, for example, the Hindu's *Bhagavad Gita* and the *Tao Teh Ching*, there is little rational analysis.

What explanation do the poets who experienced the highest state of consciousness have to offer in validation? Edna Millay's *Renascence* describes with deep emotion how she died, was buried under the earth and then reborn when she smelled the fragrance of the spring blossoms. The experience filled her with compassion for the suffering of all mankind. I was living in New York when that wonderful poem was published. No one understood it then— I least of all. Nor has anyone analyzed it properly yet.

Whitman's *Leaves of Grass* was a hundred years before its time. Many readers hate that poem because they do not understand it. And never once have I read an adequate appraisal—even to this day—of the experiences or their meaning. America was not yet ready for self-realization in 1885, but I see the book as one long paean of praise of the joy and love that one feels after being spiritually awakened.

Dante's *Divine Comedy*, which many critics consider the greatest poem ever written, contains a description of the various stages through which one passes before arriving in paradise, that is, the state of enlightenment.

The poets' account of the spontaneous variety of spiritual awakening are more lyrical, more impassioned, more joyous than accounts by those whose awakening was induced by external means, though it may be more transitory. No one has ever taken the trouble to investigate this matter—but I do not doubt that they will soon.

One very confusing aspect of enlightenment is that there are various kinds. The shallow and the full. If one practices concentrative meditation the ego may disappear. But if provocative situations arise again it springs into life again. If insight meditation is practiced the ego may be permanently annihilated, according to Goleman's account of Buddhism.

Neither the religious nor the poetic descriptions, however beautiful, satisfy doubting reason. How then do the psychologists analyze Zen Buddhism? Or rather zazen and enlightenment? After all, Tart asked me to explain the psychology of Zen, did he not? Do meditation and self-realization obey the universal laws of the human psyche? If so, what are they?

Where are the books on this subject? There are none so far as I could discover. But surely zazen and enlightenment are psychological processes of the unconscious mind, aren't they? As such, undoubtedly they are legitimate subjects for psychological investigation that might satisfy the skeptical, rational mind.

Most orthodox psychologists in academia have always been concerned almost exclusively with the functions of the conscious mind, not the unconscious. Freud and Jung are often not taught in universities today in their courses in psychology though the public at large has accepted them. And who are the psychologists, professional and otherwise who have studied the unconscious? The Freudians study only the second level—the neurotic. They seem unaware of the religious level; consequently they still consider the mystical awakening pathological. (I had published an article attempting to refute this idea). James, Bucke, Maslow and Underhill conducted research primarily into the *spontaneous* variety, not the *induced*. Masters and Houston, Stanislav Grof, and Jung were concerned with the induced variety—employing different means. Unless distinction is made between the two varieties of realizing the self—spontaneous and induced—confusion is likely to arise. Methods, means and sequence of inner events may vary but the final results in both varieties are similar in kind, if not degree, duration and value.

In *Varieties of Religious Experience*, James primarily studied the results of the spontaneous variety, not the psychological *process* involved. He stated that there exists an unseen order in the universe and that our supreme good lies in attaining harmony with it. This adds a new zest to life and even enchantment. It involves "dying to be born again," but it seems he committed one minor error. He said that the once-born are the healthy individuals and those who must be twice-born are sick. The opposite seems to be true. Most of us, except small children, are spiritually "sick" until we are "reborn" spiritually. As Christians we were brought up on the maxim of Jesus that unless we die and are born again we cannot see the kingdom of heaven— meaning enlightenment. Had James misunderstood his Bible?

Bucke did not analyze the psychological *process* of attaining spontaneous cosmic consciousness. He interpreted it as the next step in evolution. He listed the cases of those with full cosmic sense: Buddha, Jesus, Paul, Mohammed, Dante, Blake and Whitman—all spontaneous cases except Buddha who attained it after six years of meditation. The characteristics listed were subjective light, moral elevation, loss of fear of death and charisma.

Maslow also studied the *results* of spontaneous self-actualization rather than the *process*. In *Toward a Psychology of Being* he states that man's basic needs must be met first: safety, belongingness, love, respect, and self-esteem before the person is ready or able to enjoy a peak experience—or at least a major one. The characteristics of the self-actualized individual he enumerated as spontaneity, detachment, identification with the human species, creativeness, playfulness and at least forty-five more.

Underhill studied primarily the great Christian mystics whose initial experience was spontaneous. She found that they passed through five fairly definite psychological stages: Awakening, Purgation, Illumination, Dark Night of the Soul, and the Unitive life. Many religious people and artists attained the third stage but few the fourth and even fewer the fifth, the Unitive life. The Unitive life is full permanent enlightenment, the state I was now striving to induce through Zen meditation after my spontaneous, but transient, awakening of twelve years duration.

What scientific explanations of the induction process did the psychologist offer? Masters and Houston, Stanislav Grof, and Jung researched the experience of reality induced by external means. Masters and Houston experimented with 200 subjects. They administered psychedelic drugs to them under their own expert guidance. In *Varieties of Psychedelic Experience* they describe their discovery of the four levels of the unconscious: 1) the Sensory, where the subjects see innumerable images—probably meaningless; 2) the Recollective-Analytical level where the subject confronts and sometimes understands his neurosis and even may see a solution for it; 3) the Historic-Symbolic level where an actual historical event is chosen unconsciously and seen by the subject but which aids him in the solution of his own psychological problems; 4) the Integral level—the deepest layer of the unconscious in which the religious awakening occurs—in some people.

Stanislav Grof, a professional psychiatrist, experimented with 2,000 subjects who were administered psychedelics, usually LSD, under his experienced guidance. His account of self-realization is given in more detail than that of Masters and Houston, but the levels he discovered in the unconscious are very similar to those found by Masters and Houston.

Jung, in his psychoanalytical therapy, administered therapeutic treatment to thousands of patients—neurotic and normal. He encountered three levels in the unconscious. He omitted the first, the Sensory—where meaningless images may occur—if they are meaningless. He began with the neurotic level, then aided his patients to penetrate the Historic-Symbolic level of which many patients drew or painted the meaningful images they beheld. He then guided them to penetration of what he considered the deepest level, the Collective unconscious, where the religious experience transpires. This level he found to be universal—source of the idea of the universal brotherhood of man.Usually his patients were not cured of their neuroses until they underwent the religious experience. (I could well believe that, for certainly my neurosis connected with my mother was cured by my spontaneous spiritual awakening.) Jung defined self-realization as the discovery of the self, return to one's source and identity with mankind.

Did these principles and stages of the psychologists apply to zazen and Zen enlightenment? Did the meditator penetrate the same levels of the unconscious and in the same order as those encountered by the subjects of Jung, Masters and Houston, and Grof? What of all those bewildering images the Zen trainee beholds in early sesshin? What of the painful arousal of the neurotic level and later meaningful images such as I saw?

Yasutani in his introductory lectures terms all these makyo. To him everything that is not enlightenment is makyo. True, but even makyo can be analyzed. Were Zen stages similar to the levels awakened by Jungian therapy and psychedelics under proper guidance? What of the kensho, the mild form of awakening? What of the deepest stage, satori, the great final spiritual enlightenment? Were the levels penetrated in Zen similar to those in Jungian therapy and those sometimes awakened by drugs?

Empirically both observation and experience suggested to me at this time the conclusion that the psychological *process* and *stages* in awakening the unconscious mind seemed similar in some ways in the induced methods of Zen, Jungian therapy and the ingestion of psychedelic drugs under the most expert guidance. The *means* differ radically in zazen, therapy and drugs. And it must be added that meditation and therapy benefit mind and body, whereas drugs are injurious to both. Masters and Houston and Grof employed them as tools essential to their experiments.

In the *induced* variety the means and methods and sequence of events differ from the spontaneous variety, but what of the all-important *results*? On the surface they may appear similar to the layman. The crucial difference seems in value, intensity, duration and especially the transformed life style that follows after the Zen enlightenment. The trainee brought to enlightenment through a religious system seems filled with greater joy, love, strength and selflessness than the analysands or those who ingest drugs, of whom few

attain a spiritual awakening. To an impartial investigator, however, each system strengthens and supports the validity of the other at a time when the world is full of skeptics who discourage all forms of inner development. Later when Ken Wilber's brilliant and original paper appeared, "Psychologia

Perennis: The Spectrum of Consciousness", I was inclined to agree with him that "Jung is an... example of a Transpersonal Band therapist... he explicitly denied the existence of a purely non-dual Consciousness." In short, his system did not penetrate to the deepest spiritual level that Wilber terms the "Level of the Mind", as do Mahayana Buddhism, Taoism, Vedanta, Sufism and Christian Mysticism.

Scientific explanation of the physiological basis for man's intuitive and spiritual faculties has been offered by Dr. Bogen of California. As a neurosurgeon he was called on to operate on the injured brains of soldiers returning from the Vietnamese, or was it Korean, war? He discovered that the two hemispheres of the brain perform entirely different functions.

The left hemisphere is concerned with reason, language, mathematics and analysis. The right hemisphere is concerned with intuition, imagery, creativity, the spiritual experience and synthesis. Since the right hemisphere and its functions are an observable fact, those scientists who have long ignored everything intuitive and spiritual are now obliged to accept the scientific evidence.

The scientific materialistic West appears to be in urgent need of a system to awaken what Dr. Bogen sees as the right hemisphere and Zen terms the True-self. The Zen Buddhist master, Roshi Kolberg, has stated in a recent *Zen Voice* that Zen must gradually become Americanized for Americans as Indian Buddhism was altered by and for the Chinese and Japanese. Will this involve embracing scientific analyses of zazen and enlightenment to make it acceptable to Western scientists and others so oriented? Will it also involve changes in Japanese and Sanskrit terminology and certain very ancient rituals?

Recently it was very gratifying to hear the comments on my Zen poems by a scientist—Joel Elkes, chief psychiatrist of Johns Hopkins Medical School. I wrote on the top of my poems, "Not science but true." He replied, "I believe there is a phase-change in the structure of science. As new methods for inner observation develop, much of our view of the outer world is bound to change and, as you say,... we must go on discarding our most cherished errors. Very hard at times."

Every day when I sat down to write, it was incredible, but my old ego flew out the window exactly as it did when I practiced deep zazen. Later when I rose from my writing chair I felt strangely purified and strengthened exactly as I did after a good session of meditation. So Roshi was right, as usual, and I was wrong. "Your work can be your practice." This was a joyous discovery. Also, between writings my conscious mind was stimulated, my thinking clarified. I marveled repeatedly at the wonders of the human mind of which we in the West know so little but are striving to understand through meditation and enlightenment, the new psychology of self-realization, psychiatry and even physiology, chemistry and neurology.

When half of my manuscript for Dr. Tart was half finished Roshi asked to see it. It was a very rough draft, not ready for anyone to read. He glanced over it and appeared not too enthusiastic.

Later he phoned me. "Keep the psychology to a minimum, Claire."

"Oh, Roshi, I can't do that. Dr. Tart would never accept it. This chapter is not only about Zen the religion, but also about the psychology of Zen. After all, the religious experience is a psychological process."

"It is much more than that," Roshi replied.

I was very distressed. I wrote him a letter:

> Dear Roshi:
> If the Roshi is going to be disturbed I would rather give up the Tart paper altogether, though I very much enjoy writing it. I sold my home and pulled up all my roots in New Haven to rebuild my life around the Zen Center. I cannot train there, however, unless my relations with my teacher are harmonious. I'd rather abandon the Zen chapter altogether.
> Gassho,
> Claire

Later he phoned me and said he had worded his remark very awkwardly. Forget it. Carry on.

My correspondence with Dr. Tart proved he was an excellent editor—tactful, humorous, but meticulous. Every phrase must mean exactly what it said and say exactly what it meant. Every statement must be accurate down to the most infinitesimal detail. The necessity for clarity, logic, accuracy, comprehensiveness, and continuity filled me with joy. The reason many brilliant minds worship science was obvious. There was a purity, a finality, a deep satisfaction about it. Yet did science ever awaken one to the good, or to discovery of the self and reality, or produce a more ethical life style?

As I consulted various books and journals, one elusive half-truth after another would flash before my mind's eye. The pursuit of ultimate truth became as exhilerating as a fox hunt. To pursue my quarry over unfamiliar terrain, fight my way through the brambles and thickets of other people's ideas, demanded a clear eye, persistence and an intense zest for the chase.

Then came the most difficult task of all. Dr. Tart wished his contributing authors to compare, and distinguish between, orthodox Western psychology and spiritual psychology. The former studies the conscious mind primarily—personality, emotion, motivation, memory, cognitive powers, and perception; whereas the latter is concerned with the unconscious, its various levels, their functions and contents.

I purchased the textbook on orthodox psychology currently being used at the University of Snowbound, of which Tart thoroughly approved, and gave myself a refresher course. The task of distinguishing between, and comparing the processes of, the conscious mind and the unconscious under each category nearly pulled my brains out by the roots. I do not believe it has ever been done before.

It was all very fine if I wrote only three hours in the morning. But if the writing was progressing well the urge to continue writing in the afternoon or even evening was irrestible. I recalled Somerset Maugham's remark. "If anyone says he writes more than three hours a day, he is a liar!" If I succumbed to the temptation of overwork I paid for it with a sleepless night. My whole body protested. All sorts of ailments attacked me during the night, making my bed a battlefield. Often I did not turn out my light till five in the morning, sometimes reading a whole book but awakening promptly at eight. After many such nights I looked pale and haggard from lack of sleep and rest.

Why all my life had I expected my body to meet all demands on it? Even in high school my father often scolded me for studying too long, saying, "Pink cheeks are more important than good grades." In college by senior year I grew so exhausted from extracurricular work it was impossible to go down to lunch until I rested on the bed for half an hour. When I lived in New York, before I could dress to go out on my nightly engagement with some interesting man, I was obliged to sit down at the basin to wash my face. I was too weary to stand.

And here I was, now wrecking my health by lack of selfdiscipline, by lack of moderation. Even vanity was no deterrant. I knew the essence of Buddhism is self-discipline and the Middle Way—no excesses—no attachments. The magnetic attraction of writing, however, was as strong as that of a lover. In fact, I fell in love with my manuscript. I wanted to be with it, touch it, work on it every minute of the day to the neglect of everything else. Fortunately Edith came to my rescue—sewed on buttons, paid my bills, balanced my checkbook. Also, if I received invitations to dinner for three successive evenings, like an idiot, I accepted. Then too much stimulation meant sleepless nights. People stimulated me—especially men—conversation stimulated me. I loved to talk. And Zen was a subject so intriguing, so complicated, it offered irresistible fascination to us. Also of course, I drove to the Zen Center for sitting several nights a week.

Lance came often and we reviewed the illegible manuscript that he was to type. We talked about Zen and self-realization in various forms. Although we were discussing some of the profoundest subjects in human life, we laughed frequently. Youth sees humor everywhere.

One morning I made an announcement. "Well, Lance, I think I am able to explain the experiential and religious aspects of Zen Buddhism for Tart's paper and also make a few original suggestions, I hope, concerning the psychology of Zen and the levels of the unconscious. Now I've arrived at the place in Dr. Tart's outline where I disagree with him. He asks me to describe Buddha's philosophy out of which his psychology grew. I must tell Dr. Tart it was the reverse. Buddha's enlightenment experiences when he sat all night under the Bo tree occurred in his unconscious and were psychological, but not philosophical—if philosophy is defined in Western terms."

"Yes," Lance said, "and afterward *his* philosophy derived from his intuitive insights when they rose up into his consciousness. Philosophy in the West is a product of conscious logical reasoning—not experience."

"Exactly. Now, Lance dear, you majored in philosophy at Yale. So you can be of great assistance to me in this area." "If I haven't forgotten more than I learned."

"You read the new Webster there on the coffee table. I'll read the old definition of philosophy."

Lance read aloud, "'Philosophy: Pursuit of wisdom, search for truth through logical reasoning rather than factual observation; a discipline comprising logic, aesthetics, ethics, metaphysics and epistemology.'"

"What's that?" I asked. "I once knew but—"

"The theory of the nature of knowledge, its validity and limits. And Buddhism believes rational knowledge is *very* limited. It considers that wisdom derives only from intuition and *experiential* knowledge—which Mr. Webster does not even mention."

I read from my old, faded, dog-eared edition of Webster, "'The love of wisdom.' That was Socrates' definition of philosophy, remember?" I continued, "'In actual usage the science which investigates the facts and principles of reality and of human nature and conduct... the science which comprises ethics, logic, aesthetics, metaphysics and the theory of knowledge.' But philosophy is *not* a science."

"And," Lance protested, "Buddhism repeatedly insists it is not a philosophy."

"Yet if philosophy is the love and pursuit of wisdom, then Buddhism *is* a philosophy. Meditation and enlightenment both are the pursuit of wisdom."

"All right, Claire, you win—theoretically. The dictionaries give contradictory definitions of philosophy if we take into account the Buddhist definition of wisdom."

"Well, that's a pretty how-do-you-do, isn't it? We shall have to unscramble this tangle."

Lance smiled. "I thought eggs were scrambled and tangles were untangled."

I laughed. "Touché."

"Well," Lance said, "if I remember Yale correctly it taught us that philosophy consists of—" he closed his eyes and counted them off on his fingers— "logic—the study of ideal methods of thought; ethics—the study of ideal conduct; politics—the study of ideal society; aesthetics—the study of ideal form or beauty; and metaphysics—a study of ultimate reality, the nature of matter and mind, and their interrelation in the process of perception and knowledge.'"

I laughed. "Oh, my! Sounds very much like Durant. I thought popular philosophy was beneath academia."

"Oh, no, he was assigned to our reading list."

"See that volume in the bookcase there with the spine hanging loose? That's Durant. I wore it to a frazzle. I remember he said philosophy dealt with subjects not yet open to science—good and evil, beauty and ugliness, order and freedom, life and death. Buddhism does just that, yet it's not a study of theories. It is an experience."

"Perhaps," Lance suggested, "we should see how Buddhist philosophy compares with Western philosophy."

"All right. Now, I'm not asserting anything. I am merely thinking aloud. Is Buddhist philosophy established on this premise: that once enlightenment and wisdom are attained through the unconscious, the problems of the conscious mind will be solved automatically?—that logic and ideal methods of thought will be awakened?—ethical conduct will be so spontaneous that theories of ideal conduct can easily be deduced and that—"

"And," Lance continued, "that an ideal society will emerge when all men are enlightened and the study of ideal conduct will be unnecessary; that ideal form or beauty will be produced by enlightened artists, and therefore its principle known to all; that ultimate reality, the nature of matter, mind and man—being known intuitively—can be translated into rational terms? I have never seen these ideas expressed in any books—have you, Claire?"

"No, but it's fun to play with such ideas." Suddenly something stopped me cold. "Oh, I see one of my own fallacies. *Is* logic invariably awakened by the arousal of the unconscious and intuitive insights?"

"If so," Lance said, his eyes shining, his voice excited, "then why did the Eastern world fail to develop science, technology, industry and affluence as the rational West did? As a consequence of neglecting the rational hemisphere of the brain, the spiritual aesthetic East even today suffers from poverty, famine, disease and illiteracy and overpopulation."

"Good point. Another thing that puzzles me. Enlightenment seems to activate the intellects of *some* men like Buddha and Jung, Dante and Leonardo, Socrates and Plato, but not others like Whitman and Beethoven. Why is that?"

"Goodness, Claire, are you going to include all this in your chapter on Zen?"

I laughed. "Don't worry, I am simply exploring."

"Don't you think, Claire, you should explain things like karma, for instance? And hara?"

"Oh, yes, indeed. Karma, the law of cause and effect. As I understand it, it means our life today is conditioned by our thoughts and actions in our past lives. We are paying in this life for mistakes we made in our previous lives on earth. Zen seems to believe that the hara is the physical center of vital energy and is connected with something ultimate."

"Dharma?" Lance quizzed me like a schoolmaster.

"The law of the universe."

"Nirvana?"

"Isn't that the pure state of eternal bliss and peace?"

"Reincarnation?"

"The return repeatedly to physical life and death until one has perfected oneself. It offers man many chances."

Lance looked very serious. "Buddha says we are perfect and that universe is perfect. Do you believe that?"

"No. I believe the universe and mankind are both evolving. As witness the search for the religious experience in the United States today."

"How will you explain the concept of the void and emptiness, Claire?"

"Well, dear, it's more than a concept. That is exactly what one *experiences* in the moment of awakening—a nothingness that yet contains everything. Tibetan Buddhists call the void—'the Inexpressible Reality'."

"What of the Four Noble Truths and the Eight-fold Noble Path?" Lance inquired, "though they're not emphasized much in Mahayana."

"Yes," I replied, "to me those are fundamental to Buddhism. But of course Zen does not depend on the Hinayana sutras. But I think I must quote these." I opened the *Buddhist Bible* lying beside my chair. "Majjhina-Nikaya, the Digha-Nikaya and the Samyutta-Nikaya. Because in the Majjhina Buddha was purported to have said that he was not even certain he had attained enlightenment until the Four Noble Truths became clear to him: that life is suffering, that suffering is caused by desire, that there is a way to extinguish suffering, that it can be extinguished by following the Eight-fold Noble Path."

"Wait," Lance said, "let's see if I can quote them correctly: 'Right understanding, right mindfulness, right speech, right action, right living, right effort, right attentiveness and right concentration'."

"Good! You have a better memory than I have. Then arises the next difficulty—interpreting Buddha's meaning of the word 'suffering,' 'desire' and 'right.' They do not mean what we mean in English. I have toiled many a long hour over all that. That's why I am struggling to write of Zen in English that does not necessitate re-translation of English."

"But, Claire, if a man is enlightened, surely he follows these paths spontaneously, doesn't he?"

"Of course, but how many are enlightened in any country? Apparently it means we must also use our will power until we become enlightened." Suddenly a hunger pang struck me in the stomach. "Oh, goodness, but I'm starving!"

Lance laughed. "I was starving an hour ago."

"Oh, my dear boy, why didn't you say so an hour ago? Come, let's have pancakes for lunch."

"But I used up all your flour last time."

"Ah, wait till you see my new organic buckwheat. Lighter than the lightest feather."

When we rose Lance said, "As a philosophy major I must come to the defense of reason. It has given man abstract thought, science, technology, medicine, education, sanitation, cured plagues and most contagious diseases and invented uncounted labor-saving machines for his comfort and convenience."

"And," I added, "atomic bombs—to say nothing of subjecting all of us to the continual fear of nuclear annihilation from the face of the earth. And deluding the whole Western civilization into worshipping materialism. *And* to say nothing of science poisoning us and our environment with all sorts of deadly chemicals."

He shrugged as we walked out to the kitchen. "I'll toss the tossed salad if you'll make the pancakes, Lance dear. You are an expert on that."

"Well nobody makes green salad as marvelous as yours."

"Hey, hey, young fella. What is this? A mutual admiration society?"

He looked at me seriously, tenderly. "I certainly hope so."

I laid my hand on his arm. "My dear Lance, never doubt it for an instant."

I continued to read and study, think and write, week after week. One night I came upon a passage in the Buddhist Bible edited by Goddard that literally stopped my breathing until the wave of excitement subsided. If philosophy was the pursuit of wisdom, this was philosophy. All my life I had won- dered why there was so much unhappiness in the world. If Christianity offered an answer, I had never been able to understand it. Buddha explained that men were unhappy because they were in conflict with the laws of life and of the Dharma, the law of the universe. Men desired *not* to grow old, *not* to die, *not* to become ill. But those are the laws of life. They are inevitable. Old age, one learns in Buddhism, seems the natural time of life for an intensive spiritual discipline preparatory to death. And death is but a transition to another form of consciousness if one believes in reincarnation. One returns to earth in another body many times until one has perfected oneself spiritually. Then one may attain Nirvana and the cycle of physical death and rebirth is terminated. Illness, if not cured, can be alleviated or transcended by meditation and enlightenment.

People are also unhappy because they do not live in harmony with the laws of the Dharma. They expect permanent happiness from transient things such as wealth, power, fame, youth and beauty, love and passion, marriage and motherhood (he might have added). Only permanent things are able to bring permanent happiness. If one enters the stream and flows with the natural flow of the universe one is at one with Tao and all is well.

In great excitement I rose and walked the floor, pounding one fist into the palm of the other hand. I knew, I knew, all this was true. Meditation had brought me to the experience of these truths more forcibly and more frequently through the months and years—though only intermittently, not permanently. Everything beautiful slips away and one must practice zazen to find it again.

The truth of these universals could be tested by applying them to the particular and personal. I, for example, no longer grieved because I had gray hair and lines in my face. Aging was a law of life. It could be joyous. The deep intuitive and insightful understanding of Zen maturity, the sweet com- panionship of my Zen friends and the small ecstasies induced by meditation— all were beginning to compensate for loss of youth and beauty.

Death did not frighten me when I was in a high mind-state but did so when I was in an ordinary state. As to illness—time and time again I felt an attack of illness commencing, sat down and concentrated in zazen. It disappeared. Once my eyes and nose began to run like four little rivers. The doctor said it was hayfever. I had never had hayfever in my life and did not intend to have it now, thank you. So I came home and practiced meditation more arduously than ever before. It disappeared forever.

Time and time again I prayed—I beseeched—I grasped the Buddha figure passionately in my hands, longing to surrender my total being, my whole life, to Zen Buddhism. But always something still restrained me like an invisible rein on an eager horse. Was it the world, my ego, my intellect?

But why, why is man created so that he is so easily misled in the first place? And, oh why, is it so difficult to perfect oneself, to come to full enlightenment? Is this the reason the true aspirant withdraws to a monastery? Severe self-discipline is a little too difficult while living in the world with its 10,000 distractions. But why does karma, or whatever, make inner development so difficult?

One night something guided my hand to the Surangama sutra. It discussed the true nature of mind and the reality of absolute mind. Then I read the teachings of the Zen Master Hsi Yun, concerning the doctrine that universal mind alone is real, that one must abandon seeking for anything and realize it by cessation of all effort and allow it to happen.

Of course Roshi had said these same things to us a hundred times—but in Zen words must be repeated over and over. Later I wrote Roshi a letter before he went for his winter of writing and work with affiliate Zen groups in Mexico. I reported my inner progress and asked, "What shall I do now?"

He replied, "Do nothing. Just be. As Lao Tzu said, 'Do nothing. But be sure nothing is left undone.'"

This I realized was the most difficult thing in life to do—to be—just to be.

In writing my chapter on Zen I was determined not to fall easy prey to the fascination of Eastern religious terminology. I refused to employ it because I did not understand it. I found few Westerners (except the Roshi) who did—however glibly they tossed the impressive Sanskrit and Japanese terms about. Consequently, I resorted to reliable Western writers like Huston Smith and his *Religions of Man*, Govinda and his *Psychological Attitude of Early Buddhist Philosophy*. I read Durkheim's *Hara* and *Tao of Physics* by Capra, and of course, Kolberg's *Introduction to Zen* until my paperback copy of Kolberg fell apart.

Last of all I read for the third time and understood for the first time *The Meeting of East and West* by Northrop, the Yale philosopher who had responded so warmly and understandingly to my book, *Awakening to the Good*. I was beside myself with excitement. I had never been able to understand Northrop until after I experienced Zen. And Northrop clarified my conceptual understanding of Zen.

When Lance returned from a visit to his family in Boston, I said, "While you were galavanting around having a merry ole time, I took a graduate course in philosophy."

He laughed. "In one week?"

"Yes." I exhibited the faded red volume of East and West that was also falling apart. Every blank page, front and back, was filled with my notations in black ink, red ink and blue pencil.

"You see, Lance, dear, I appear to have been born in the form of a question mark. All my life I have wondered why no one could devise a good life and a good society that worked for everyone. I thought I had found it when I read Plato but—"

"But," Lance interjected, "the dialectic method of Socrates and the ideal Republic of Plato are too difficult for most people to put into practice; was that it?"

"Exactly. And also I have virtually worn holes in my poor brain wondering why different countries and races have developed such different cultures and hierarchy of values. What is considered good in one country or period of history is considered evil in another. How can that be? Surely there must be *one* truth. To find it—this is the purpose of my present study of Zen Buddhism. But to understand the value of Zen Buddhism I felt it necessary to measure it against Western cultures such as Greek and German, French and Russian, British and American, but my knowledge was inadequate."

Lance smiled. "Necessary *and* thrilling. You're all starry-eyed right now."

Often at twenty-three he seemed the calm indulgent father and I at seventy-six the enthusiastic child.

"But learning is so exciting. Lance!"

"More than the spiritual experience?"

"Oh Lance, no! Nothing in the world equals that. Not even love, though it runs it a close second." I clasped the faded red Northrop book against my breasts. "This explains everything and is highly approving of Buddhism, incidentally. Reading it is equivalent to a graduate course in philosophy. Did you study under him at Yale?"

"No, I'm sorry to say. But of course we read him."

"The most exciting thing is—he explains that the differences in various cultures are caused by their different concepts of the nature of man and the nature of things and ideas of the good—all of which are derived from the philosophy of the time which in turn is derived largely from the science of the time."

Lance shook his head. "That's true of Western civilization but there was little science when Buddhism was established and no philosophy in the Western sense. Indian culture grew out of the Upanishads and the Vedas, Hinduism and Buddhism."

"All right, all right, young fella. But I nearly fainted with joy when I realized that the philosophies trickled down to the general public through the years and actually determined the political and economic systems, ethics and art and sometimes even the religion of each culture. Isn't that illuminating!!"

"I question some of that—"

"Forgive me, Lance dear, but I must tell you something this minute or I shall explode. For years I had vaguely believed Greek civilization was perfect. I was struck dumb with horror when this book pointed out the inadequacies in the philosophy of the great Socrates and Plato on which Greek culture was largely founded. And also the inadequacies in—"

Lance interrupted. "I know, the inadequacies of Aristotle and Aquinas in Christianity."

"You do have an excellent memory, Lance. And in Britain and America our philosophy of life, our politics, were founded on the philosophy of Locke and Hume, Bentham and Mills, which derived from the science of Newton and Galileo. Jefferson's noble Declaration of Independence was based on Locke. And our economic system was based on Adam Smith and other British economists. Ideas apparently do not just float around in the air but derive from men's minds and books. So you see why our business culture today believes that the good for both man and the state is economic, that man should conform to society's laws, written and unwritten. That's the way we lost the habit of being ourselves. And yet our noble concept of freedom in America and Britain also derived from these same philosophers. In America we interpreted them to mean social *equality*. In England they interpreted them to mean a *class* system. A system in which each person was given equal opportunity to find his proper level in society according to his abilities."

"Most Americans," Lance said, "don't understand that, except maybe Southerners and Bostonians. So many of them descend from the British."

"When I was a girl, my Virginia grandmother advocated the class system like the British which, I noticed when last in England, has not disappeared there yet. Remember Thomas Wolfe's *You Can't Go Home Again*? His encounter in London with a char woman who did not object to being a char woman and who upheld the caste system which Wolfe could not understand. I used to know Wolfe in New York."

"So you told me. To continue—as I recall it, Northrop's *East and West* says that in France many of the difficulties in their culture were due largely to the inadequacies in Descartes and Voltaire, despite their many brilliant concepts. And in Germany, Kant, Fitche and Hegel's philosophies, despite their many eternal verities, actually made the emergence of a Hitler almost inevitable. And he points out the error of Marx's philosophy. Marx identified the nature of man and the good with the theoretical component *only*. So he made the mistake of postulating that man's primary value in life is economic."

I leaned forward eagerly in my chair. "Isn't it all the more tragic that it was out of ignorance, not evil intent, that the West's most brilliant scientists and philosophers committed such egregious errors? In America it is only today that we are beginning to understand these mistakes in the various cultures. All our Western philosophies and Christianity (based on Aristotle) made the mistake of postulating that the theoretic component in things *alone* is primary and ultimate. They all denigrated the immediately apprehended aesthetic continuum which is also primary and ultimate. And therefore they stimulated our ego, competition, materialism and produced our present crisis."

Lance said, "Buddhism, Hinduism and Taoism identified the nature of man and the nature of things with the immediately apprehended aesthetic component *only*. They, in their turn neglected the theoretic component and consequently the cultivation of the intellect; this caused their failure to develop science and technology, industry, affluence, birth control and so lost the means of abolishing the appalling poverty, disease and illiteracy of the East."

"So my dear, with all their virtues neither Western nor Eastern civilization is adequate because neither is complete. Isn't it tragic that the whole human race should suffer from ignorance? But I suppose it's all a matter of the slow evolution of the human mind. You know, of course, Lance, that Teilhard and Sinnott both maintained that the physical evolution of man has reached its ceiling? And that from now on man's evolution will be mental and spiritual. And that it may not even occur unless man assists in the process. Listen." I opened Northrop at a book mark. "He says that 'The tragic ills of [Western] civilization. . . [are due to] the pursuit of philosophy grounded upon scientific knowledge. . . [and] neglect of moral philosophy.'"

"I see Buddhism as a way of life that involves a moral philosophy that will balance our Western overemphasis on things."

"I forget one point," Lance said. "Why does Northrop say that the theoretic component and the aesthetic component are both ultimate?"

"Because neither can be derived from anything else—consequently they are irreducible, primary and ultimate."

"Though I think he also says the theoretic is *inferred* from the existence of the immediately apprehended aethestic continuum, but not vice-versa."

"Oh, Lance, that's the whole point of *East and West*—that the two components must be recognized as equal and so must be combined in man, culture, philosophy, and religion."

"In everything," Lance added, "especially in politics and economics."

"One thing, Lance, which Northrop says that puzzles me. I must ask Roshi to explain it."

"If he will."

"I know he dislikes explaining things—in words, at least. Northrop says Buddhism, Hinduism and Taoism are not theistic nor pantheistic. They do not identify the divine with the differentiated aesthetic continuum, which is the totality of the immediately apprehended, but merely with the indeterminate, undifferentiated aesthetic continuum *within the totality*. Frankly, I don't understand that."

"Neither do I, Claire, but that might explain why Buddha said the universe is perfect. Maybe the translation of the word 'universe' is not exactly correct."

"It's like when I read Plato, I longed passionately to read him in the original and now I long to read the sutras in Sanskrit. This helped me to. Northrop says that, 'Self does not project out of itself the emotionally moving, aesthetically vivid, immediately apprehended aesthetic continuum. Self and object are constituted of the irreducible aesthetic continuum.' It requires time to experience this, I found. At first it feels like a projection out of oneself. Of course, Roshi tells us this repeatedly in his teisho in Zen terms."

Lance stretched his arms and legs. "Oh, Claire, my throat's parched, isn't yours? Mind if I pour us each a glass of pineapple juice?"

"Good idea. You know where everything is."

We sat in unaccustomed silence and sipped our drinks. Then I plunged eagerly into the discussion again. "And another thing, Northrop says that the four theistic religions—Christianity, Judaism, Islam and even Shintoism—identify the divine with the theoretic component and neglect the aesthetic component. Haven't you always been puzzled by the Catholics maintaining that God can be known by reason? Have you ever met anyone who has?"

"Not Catholics. But what of Socrates and Plato?"

"But *was* it reason alone in their case? This may be heresy, but I have always held the theory that in Socratic dialectic, the conscious mind had so thoroughly been activated that it activated the unconscious. Because we know religious experience—or 'love of beauty Absolute, and everlasting' occurs in the *unconscious*. And love and passion for a beautiful youth does not occur in the rational mind either. Remember the ladder to perfection in *Phaedrus*?"

Then we discussed the problem of values derived from our own current philosophy. Lance related the struggle he encountered with the prevailing social values of traditional Boston and how even today his parents and friends there objected to his new Zen values.

"I'm sure I've told you, Lance—probably ten times already—about my Virginia grandmother. She taught me that social status based on breeding and ancestery, good family and good manners, constituted the highest value. Not until recently did I realize that her teaching concerning the importance of being ladies and gentlemen was fundamentally moral and ethical—a matter of honor, honesty, integrity, and all that."

Lance shrugged. "Those words are not in the vocabulary of the younger generation. They are obsolete. I mean lady and gentleman, not honor and honesty."

"Words, my dear, run the fashion gamut the same as clothes. Your generation embody many of the same ideas in other terms. Everything in Zen involves honor, honesty and integrity. Those are the ideals that have disappeared from the world of today and perhaps one cause of our present tragedy. Where was I? Oh, yes, and then when I lived in New York City, the group I associated with considered the aesthetic the highest value. They lived only for the best plays, concerts, exhibits and books. So did I."

"But don't most of us accept the hierarchy of values of the society in which we live?"

"Yes, unfortunately. My husband was descended from old New York Dutch ancestry and I from old Virginia, yet when we married and bought a house in Connecticut we found people were judged primarily by their wealth and material possessions. Women were slaves of fashion. They thought that to wear the latest style dress somehow made them superior to others. Not to appear in the latest shade of nail polish was a disgrace. How silly can women get? I blush to think of what a fool I was. But when I took all those courses at Yale, the professors easily convinced me that the cognitive value, the intellectual, was primary, although political value ran neck and neck with it among the socialists and pro-communists."

"Philosophers," Lance said, "tell us there are six values by which men live. Certainly in America until the counterculture emerged, the metaphysical or the spiritual experience was not the lowest value—it was almost nonexistent."

"Don't I know. My point is that I seemed to have lived under all six of the value systems, the last being the spiritual as I found it in Zen. But unconsciously all those years I was seeking for the highest value. I did not know how to find it."

"Not even," Lance asked, "when you had your great self-realization experience in 1950?"

"Ah, you even remember the year."

He smiled. "I remember everything you have ever told me about yourself."

I reached over and grasped his hand. "I'm ashamed to admit it, but in those days I lacked the courage to live outwardly by a value different from that of people around me. Not until I came to the Center did I have the courage to do so. With the help from Zen and Roshi and all you nice young Zenites."

Lance made a grimace. "That awful word."

Suddenly a mysterious change occurred in both of us. Words commenced to flow from our mouths of their own accord without ratiocination. Thinking became effortless. It was no longer work. It was play—joyful play.

"Lance, there still remains another major problem if we are going to make the world over nearer our heart's desire. Zen shows us how to activate intuition and spirituality. How can the intellect be activated without also activating the dangerous ego? Is it impossible?"

"Buddha certainly did and Socrates and Plato. The question is—is it a matter of intellectual people becoming enlightened or of enlightenment activating the intellect?"

"I just don't know, yet I *do* know that the writing of this chapter on Zen has awakened my True-self the way deep zazen does and yet at the same time, never in my life has my inquiring intellect been so—so inquiring."

"Dear Claire," Lance murmured.

"Oh, goodness, I'm always going off on a personal tangent. Is that merely because I am a woman? Anyway, all my reasoning is inductive—from the particular to the general. The point is, judging from my own experience, zazen may quiet the discursive intellect *during* meditation, but it may stimulate the intellect *between* sittings, especially *after* advancement on the spiritual path."

"You mean, Claire, that if the intellect is awakened as the consequence of the enlightenment process, the ego is then no longer a problem because the ego died in order to make enlightenment possible?"

I clapped my hands with delight. "That's it! You have answered our $64 question. Granted that man's first effort should be to create good men, that is, enlightened men. Now the vital problem is—does it inevitably follow that they would create a good society—a peaceful, prosperous, just and happy world? Would any enlightened man, for example, wish to be President, a ruler over other men, a lawyer, or even a scientist?"

"Teilhard was a scientist, a paleonthologist and a mystic. But his own church refused to accept the earth's evidence of evolution."

"True," I said, "but perhaps Plato was wise. He knew the 'true philosopher', as he called the man who was both enlightened *and* intellectual, would not care to rule others. Don't you think that's the reason in the *Republic* the 'philosopher king' and the 'guardians' had no choice but to serve the state for a period of time?"

"But," Lance protested, "neither Washington nor Jefferson wished to be president of the United States in the early days of our Republic. They preferred to be country gentlemen and enjoy their country estates. They voluntarily sacrificed their personal lives to serve their country. John, and John Quincy Adams, too. Because there were simply no other men qualified to save the colonies from disintegration. Most men were concerned with their egos, not with the country."

I sighed. "So there is still hope. Granted that meditation and enlightenment can solve the immediate personal problems of the individual. What if he is imprisoned or lives in a tyrannical oppressive society?"

"You mean like the dissidents in Stalin's Communist Russia?" Lance asked.

"Yes. How effective can a reformer or spiritual person be under such adverse circumstances? You remember in Vietnam the way the Buddhist monks and nuns immolated themselves? Did it save their country or their religion from being conquered by the Communists of the North?"

Lance clasped his hands together with great enthusiasm. "Well, don't you see? That's it! It just proves that government, politics and economics, science, industry and medicine require reason and thought—that is, the theoretic component to be honored and exercised but—"

"But," I added, "tempered by the religious principles that have been deeply *experienced* through meditation, not merely read about."

"In Japan today Zen men are members of parliament and successful business men," Lance said.

"You know, Lance, all this study and discussion with you clarifies for me at last Buddha's differentiation between the permanent and the transitory, the absolute and the relative world of phenomena. Reports from our intellect and senses are continually changing but the reports from our intuition and experiential wisdom are changeless and eternal. Why, oh why, has it required so many years for this truth to penetrate my thick skull? Roshi has told us all this a hundred times. I seem to be subject to a delayed reaction."

"Maybe, Claire, you simply were not ready to receive it till this moment. But surely the reason meditation and Buddhism are so vitally important today in the West, here and now, is because we honor only the transitory which inevitably brings us suffering."

"So," I said, "the creation of the ideal society today seems to require: first, that the True-self dormant in every man must be awakened by meditation or other methods; second, that many men must attain enlightenment; third, their intellects must be activated; if not as a result of meditation, other ways should be found perhaps (though everyone does not need to be intellectual); fourth, intuition and reason should be united and should function harmoniously together."

"Don't forget the fifth goal of Zen is to integrate spiritual principles into one's daily life style. And this all means the ancient enemies—religion and science—will be reconciled—or at least the religious experience."

"Oh, Lance, it is happening already, judging by all these scholarly journals." I laid my hand fondly on the high stack of magazines beside my chair, ready to cascade onto the floor. "To say nothing of all the revolutionary books on all aspects of self-realization issuing from the universities nowadays. There is a marvelous but quiet revolution in progress in America that may save the world—I hope."

"But Claire, there is still strong opposition to this union in religion and science."

"Yet didn't Buddha say Nirvana is a reconciliation and transcendence of all opposites? And what is so opposite as feeling and thought, experience and theory, religion and science?"

While we talked it was as if gradually a river of purification was flowing through us. As if certain ideas possessed a cleansing power. It was as if Lance and I were two innocent children walking in the morning of the world. There was something young, pristine, elemental, pure, but profound about our relationship more than I had ever been aware of heretofore. I did not understand it. It was infinitely sweet, mysteriously beautiful, more exhilarating than any cocktail party.

We talked on and on, brilliantly, it seemed to us. Never before had we seemed to think so deeply, express our ideas with such crystal clarity. We felt that every word was a precious sparkling jewel to flash at each other. It filled us with inexplicable pleasure. Thinking was not *work*. It was effortless, joyous *play*.

When Lance left I walked about the apartment feeling as buoyant as if I were levitating to the ceiling—though I am sure I was not. In his teishos or more often in his extemporaneous talks, Roshi referred repeatedly to buoyancy. So this was what he meant! The exalted mind-state lasted for several days, affecting everything I did, thought, felt and wrote. I was elevated to another plane of existence.

I mentioned this experience of work becoming play to the Roshi. It is a deep satisfaction that one's teacher is always able to explain one's every experience. No wonder it is a rule that a teacher must himself be enlightened. No wonder a teacher is necessary to the novice on the spiritual path. Roshi loaned me his copy of Sorokin's book, *Forms and Techniques of Altruistic and Spiritual Growth*. He suggested that I read the chapter on 'How Altruism Is Cultivated in Zen' by Kita and Nagaya, one a member of parliament, the other in business in Japan. They said, "When the utilitarian ideas of advantage and disadvantage have been transcended, every activity naturally accords with the law (dharma) and there is what is known as *Yukezammi*, the samadhi in which all activity is play."

I laid down the book with tears of joy in my eyes. I swallowed hard, clasped my hands tightly together and smiled and smiled and smiled. What a glorious discovery! Was there no end to the wonders of the human mind that Zen could awaken?

The next step in my research in the rational realm seemed to be a comparison of Buddha with other great men. I looked back over my own recent intellectual life. Jung and Socrates (or Plato) and Buddha each successively had burst suddenly, unexpectedly across my mental landscape like dazzling comets.

At fifty-four my spontaneous awakening had overwhelmed me with ecstasy and riotous emotions. Intellectually, however, it had left me wandering lost in a wilderness of doubt and ignorance. I had sought light on this cataclysm that had shaken me like an inner earthquake.

Then I met Jung—in print—later in person. His books came to my rescue. They offered the first explanation I had ever heard that self-realization was a natural function of the healthy unconscious mind. Jung was a world-renowned psychological authority and his books assured me that my awakening was not pathological or even queer, but that I was extremely fortunate, sane and healthy. What a relief! I felt indebted, grateful and filled with wild admiration.

At that point I thought Jung surely must be the greatest man the world had ever produced. That is, if the criteria for greatness are the discovery of profound universal truths, keenness of intellect, creativity, productivity, goodness, and service to others. He was self-realized *and* intellectual.

Jung stated that self-realization united the four functions of the mind—intuition and thinking, feeling and sensation—to create the whole man. Evidently he included the spiritual in intuition and feeling, did he not? The chief drawback to his system of realizing the self was that it necessitated a Jungian therapist, a great expense of time and money. Also I had never heard of analysands going about the world as joyous humanitarians or religious models selflessly serving others or living pure, beautiful inspiring lives. Doubtless they existed, but where were they?

Then I met Socrates. In 1963 I had been lying in the hospital for four months with a broken leg, sunk in depression. I was plunged into the Dark Night of the Soul after twelve happy years that followed my great mystical experience. Plato's *Dialogues*, purported to be those of Socrates and his pupils, had saved my life and sanity. Socrates induced a second enlightenment in me—almost. The nobility, the selflessness, the wisdom, the irony and spirituality of Socrates were overwhelming. He discovered and enunciated universal truths, possessed keenness of intellect, was creative, productive, selflessly good and spent his life serving others by teaching them how to become a "true philosopher." He himself was a true philosopher, that is, an enlightened man and he possessed an incredibly brilliant intellect.

Socrates employed reason as the means and dialectic as the method to create the "true philosopher." On the ladder to perfection he believed it necessary to develop personal love and passion, the love of all people, the intellectual understanding of science and government. The highest rung of the ladder, however, was the religious experience, love of Absolute beauty. This always occurs not in the conscious mind but in the deepest level of the unconscious. So he united the conscious mind and the unconscious, the theoretical component and the feeling-intuitive-aesthetic. And activation of the conscious mind appeared to activate the unconscious.

The drawback to the Socratic method was that a Socrates was necessary to lead the dialectic and where is the Socrates of today? And besides, ironically enough, his means and methods converted none of his pupils into true philosophers, not even his beloved Alcibiades. My admiration of, and gratitude to, Socrates was unbounded. Surely he was the greatest man who ever lived. He had lifted me from the Dark Night of the Soul and literally inspired me to seek the fifth stage of inner development, the Unitive life. But where? Not in philosophy.

Then I met Buddha. He discovered and enunciated universal truths, possessed a brilliant intellect, was skilled in dialectic, produced a wonderful workable world system for spiritual development, and spent forty selfless years walking over India teaching his system to thousands of followers. He was both enlightened *and* intellectual.

Buddhism and Zen taught me the magic of meditation, awakened the True-self, filled my days with happiness, with Zen friends, creativity, and concern for others. It gave my life purpose, direction and a shining goal to strive for. It revealed brief but radiant glimpses of the shining realm of enlightenment. Surely Buddha was the greatest man who ever lived.

Or rather, Jung and Socrates and Buddha were surely the greatest men the human race had ever produced. All three were enlightened *and* intellectual. Which was the greatest? Obviously what the world needed was a great psychologist, like Jung, who included Freudian principles within limits *and* a great philosopher like Socrates (or Plato), and a great religious leader like Buddha. This conclusion appeared to me so momentous it prompted me to dance about the apartment, to skip and sing and laugh aloud. Was this not an answer to one of life's most difficult problems?

After dancing about too happy to contain my joy, I stopped at the Buddha figure sitting in eternal smiling serenity on the chest of drawers. Suddenly I seemed to see Zen Buddhism plain. Like a wind storm, tremendous emotion swept through my whole being—body, mind and heart, carrying all the dust and debris of doubt before it. I seemed to be granted a new crystal clear perspective of Zen that revealed its inordinate power, beauty and profundity as a whole system heretofore viewed only in its fragmented parts.

I saw that Zen Buddhism offers a way for any man, for everyman, to awaken his own inherent good through zazen, to be happy and kind, compassionate and wise by his own efforts at little cost and little direction, but with strenuous work and self-discipline.

It offers a way to attain the most beautiful experience possible to a human being—the actualization of his own noblest potentials. It shows every man a way to go singing down the streets of life, a way to free himself from hate and envy, ignorance and avarice, and compulsive attachment to material possessions.

Merely by practicing zazen several hours every day and more intensively at sesshins, any individual can learn to be creative, to release his dormant desire to help others, to intensify all his sensuous enjoyment until every insignificant commonplace in life becomes a thing of beauty and a manifestation of reality. The aspirant can bring "the delight and wonder of satori" into every minute of every day. With the aid of Zen he can bring the eternal into the now. That means perfection, joy, harmony and love.

Also, I saw that Zen Buddhism teaches a method of self-discipline, a way to abstain willingly from self-indulgence of the senses—like overeating, over-drinking, over-indolence. It teaches a method of controlling the mind which itself is the wonder of the ages. It teaches one how to transform work into play so that it becomes a vehicle of awakening, how to bring harmony into human relationships, how to diminish—even extinguish—the ego. One learns how to become one with absolute reality—first briefly and intermittently, then permanently and continuously and thus learns how to be guided in every act of life by the universal consciousness. Even the intellect may be activated so that it functions simultaneously with the intuitive and the spiritual—sometimes.

I understood for the first time that Zen teaches that suffering is caused by desire for transient things, by attachment to the impermanent, by desire for private, personal fulfillment—the individualism so proudly vaunted in our Western culture. Once perhaps this was necessary in early Western society, but now it is detrimental to the individual and destructive to society. In Zen the individual loses his individuality, his personal identity, only to gain identity with a power greater than his own small self, with the Dharma, with ultimate reality. The rain drop may merge with the sea and lose its identity, but the sea also enters into the rain drop.

With a terrific impact I finally realized that intense and prolonged practice of zazen can banish the dichotomy between the conscious mind and the unconscious, reconcile the opposites that tear man apart—reason and intuition, thought and feeling, self and others, the temporal and eternal, life and death. This final reconciliation and transcendence of opposites is the highest state of ordinary man's inner development. It is Nirvana. Certainly I had not attained all these heights fully, yet I yearned to do so before it was too late. At my age, death could be right around the corner any day.

By straining every nerve, I managed in a last burst of energy to condense, organize, clarify and unify my wealth of material. The manuscript of my chapter on Zen was completed, and met Dr. Tart's deadline. Lance worked until midnight typing the reference cards and the index. Roshi read my manuscript and made corrections of my faulty understanding of Zen, for which I was grateful. Dr. Tart read it and liked it. After several delays *Transpersonal Psychologies* was published by Harper and Row in August of 1975. It was a large handsome volume priced at $16.50. It was chosen by two psychological book clubs. Later it was issued in paperback. Several college professors read the chapter on Zen and came to workshops at the Center. One entered Zen training—at another center, alas.

I felt intensely grateful to Roshi, Tart, Buddha and Zen. Writing this chapter had been a liberal education. I might never have learned so much about Zen and the philosophical and psychological problems of life in general. It was a double education, intellectual and experiential, for my work had become my practice. It was like the practice of zazen. Writing was a purifying process, joyous and strengthening—and mysteriously clarifying.

I laughed at myself because of the mental discipline writing had imposed on me. To think, to read, to talk, even to lecture about a serious subject, is child's play compared to writing about it. Writing forces the writer to organize his knowledge, marshall his facts, clarify his ideas, be accurate and bind all the disparate parts into a cohesive and convincing whole. His love of his subject must endow dead words with living vitality. He must establish an agreeable tone heard between the lines. He is like a musician who pitches his composition in a certain key and maintains it to the end. The chief value of writing, however, is that truth slowly rises to the surface like cream to the top of milk, becoming visible for the first time after having been dissipated throughout the whole. This is a startling, unexpected, wonderful and welcome process.

The minute the manuscript had been mailed to Dr. Tart in California I succumbed from sheer exhaustion to the February flu epidemic. The doctor pronounced it the most virulent case he had ever seen and the present strain of virus the most virulent that had ever struck Snowbound. My attack was accompanied as usual by high fever and all night vomiting for several nights. At first I feared I might die. Finally I feared I might not die.

A relapse worse than the original attack left me so weak I was scarcely able to walk. As usual my Zen friends, then Helena and Edith, rushed to the rescue.

Is it something innate in my nature or my own foolish habit to overdo everything? Colds and flu were no little three-day affair with me. They invariably involved two or three weeks in bed with a high fever. I lost ten pounds in this bout.

One day the odor of the soiled fruitjuice bottles and glasses that had contained juice or milk was too much to bear. I was weak from the fever, lying in bed, and the sparse liquid diet. I rose feebly and managed to walk out into the kitchen. Yet I was utterly relaxed, not thinking, not desiring, placid and passive. Just the proper condition, I realized *after* the event, for an altered state of consciousness experience. How ironical that the ego is so strong it almost requires our physical destruction to overcome its tenacious dominance.

My life-long distaste of kitchens had never been overcome even with strenuous zazen. Today, however, as I placed the soiled dishes, bottles and glasses in the dishwasher, something unaccustomed happened. Strength entered my weakened body, it felt light, painless, my spirit soared. I danced about the kitchen slowly as if performing some delightful ballet. Ease, grace, and joy informed my every movement. It was incredible but joyous, rejuvenating. "Your work can be your practice," Roshi had said. This household chore was not work, it was pleasant play. This time it was menial, manual work that suddenly became like a deeply purifying zazen. Imagine anyone on earth enjoying dishwashing! The worse chore in any household. It was too fantastic to believe.

But what a revolutionary discovery! And of tremendous import not only for me but for people everywhere. To think that zazen or any force on earth possessed the power to transform work into play. To think that a way to change all the necessary drudgery of the world had been discovered—and proved. For here was delightful proof in my own kitchen. I recalled that St. Teresa said she "often found God among the pots and pans."

I stood there literally stunned but feeling exalted, happy, elevated to another higher plane.

Illness, fever, weakness no longer mattered. While the dishwasher swished merrily away, the truth dawned on me. I walked slowly from the kitchen into the living room. I stood before the figure of Buddha staring at it in awe. This is it! Zen Buddhism is the final solution to the problems of life which nothing else on earth seems able to solve. Not reason, not will power, not good intentions, no noble social legislation can do it. Zen is a way of life for me—forever. I've come home at long last. All doubts concerning the experiential and religious aspect have long since vanished. Now—now at long last all intellectual doubts have vanished too.

I felt a strange physical sensation that my body sitting motionless on the meditation cushion was turning about. Now I felt my body was facing Zen, the spiritual realm, and my back was turned on the world—forever. I might look and seem the same to others but to me this was a momentous turning point in my life.

Suddenly for the first time in four years a sense of total commitment filled me to the brim like a glass of champagne running over. For the first time in years of yearning, resistance, doubt, and compromise, I felt a strong urge to subordinate my life as a whole to Zen Buddhism. It was both a defeat and a victory. Defeat for my old ego, my conventional values and worldly way of life. Victory for the True-self. The battle was won. This was a crucial moment.

The same feeling invaded me as had arisen during my marriage ceremony. A moment of committing myself to a totally new and different way of life. I felt overwhelmed by the enormity of it all yet I felt secure, no longer alone in life, full of joy but afraid of the great mystery yet to unfold. Now I understood the reason Catholic nuns are called the "Bride of Christ." To commit oneself totally to a religious life, even as a lay person living in the world, was a kind of marriage. Was I a bride of the Dharma?

It was as if heretofore I had received permission from my mother to live the Zen way but had not yet received permission from my father. My mother, the feminine principle of feeling and experience; my father, the male principle of thought and reason. Heretofore only half of me had been committed to Zen. Now all of me was committed. Both reason and intuition. What a wonderful sense of completion, of closing of the circle.

Of course there were many minor matters in Zen—as in any system—and in the Center—as in any institution—that I did not accept. But now they shrank into insignificance in the realization of the dynamic, eternal, basic principle of Zen that I knew would sustain me for the remainder of my life.

I smiled as the words formed themselves in my mind: any force powerful enough to transform work into joyous play, into an art, into a vehicle for spiritual awakening is—is—There are simply no words for it.

As I sat there before the Buddha my body rocked itself back and forth in quiet joy. Now I knew that however the winds of misfortune or ill health might shake me, I would be safely cradled in the everlasting arms—safe in my place in the universe.

Now I knew beyond the shadow of a doubt I possessed a great treasure house within me on which I might draw at all times. It was my True-self, my hara, my vital center, my collective unconscious—whatever.

I knew beyond the shadow of a doubt that there existed a limitless, beginningless, endless field of energy, a source of good, inexhaustible and ever-present, with which I could become one and so banish my weakness, follies and ungoodness, and soar into a realm of joy and love, a realm at once immanent and transcendent.

I might lose sight of it at times but I knew, not only experientially but now rationally as well, that never would I be afraid again. I might grieve, be hurt, but never again would I be afraid of pain, or illness, old age, life or death. With all my being I felt grateful to the Buddha, Zen, Roshi, Tart and whatever created the human mind which is surely one of the wonders of the world.

Now both the experiential and the intellectual search for the answers to questions I had been seeking for a lifetime was ended.

I emerged from my state of absorption in my own newly evolved mind-state. I became aware of the figure of Buddha before me. I stared at the smiling imperturbable face of this great man. When I see an ideal person, I thought, a fully awakened man like the Buddha, I feel I am only half way up the mountain. I feel humble beyond words but grateful and happy beyond words—because I am on the Path.

Now, unimpeded by the fearful obstacle of my doubting rational mind, my experiential life surely will continue to grow more gloriously than ever—I hope.

My work not only had become my meditative practice, a living zazen, but it committed me intellectually to Zen Buddhism as experiential joy induced by zazen had already committed me.

Now I was totally committed to Zen—forever.

Chapter XIV
FREEDOM

There was one more commitment I had been foolish enough to make that must now be fulfilled. After that I planned to fly to Williamsburg, Virginia, home of my mother's ancestors, to recuperate. It would be the first time in years I had not escaped from the snow and spent the winter in Palm Beach, Florida.

First I must deliver my lecture on Search for Self to the American Association of University Women at their club house on East Avenue. But were they interested in inner growth or Zen? Most of the members were either business executives or retired school teachers who had already formed their opinions about everything. Or they were young married women whose main interests were their small children and their involvement in civic projects.

The *Times Union* sent a photographer and a reporter to interview me. The very pleasant reporter was an ardent Christian (I asked her). My Zen affiliation appeared to make her uncomfortable. Zen is not yet accepted everywhere. That is one reason I am writing this book—to disseminate its joy more widely.

I was so exhausted after over-working on the Tart paper I looked haggard in the photograph. After the interview appeared in the newspaper strangers commenced to call me on the phone. They were in deep distress. Is God dead? I've left the church and don't know what to believe about anything. How can I discover the Self? How can I become awakened to the good? Can you help me?

I listened. I suggested they practice meditation—that helped everyone and hurt no one. Later they might wish to investigate Zen. It was not Zen policy to urge anyone. The aspirant must be possessed by a strong desire to practice zazen. They asked if they might come to see me. I had neither the time nor the energy but how could I refuse people in such distress? One who came actually joined the Zen Center.

In the months prior to the lecture at the University Club I had been asked to talk on Zen at various Christian churches. Sometimes it was like walking into a refrigerator. To thaw out the icy atmosphere I would often begin by saying, "Didn't Jesus say, 'Unless you die and are born again, you cannot see the kingdom of heaven?' Well, zazen or meditation is simply a practical method for effecting the *death* of the ego that in turn opens the gate to the universe and brings *rebirth* of one's True-self." I attempted to demonstrate that in basic principles, all the higher religions possessed enough similarity to make intolerance illogical if nothing else. Did not every great religion strive to awaken the inherent good in man, diminish the evil, unite him with ultimate reality and integrate spiritual principles into his daily life?

The group at the University Club was a more sophisticated audience. When the evening of the lecture at the AAUW arrived, I feared I might not have the strength to stand on my feet for an hour. And I had hoped it would be one of my best talks because my lawyer and doctor and their wives had asked to come. Also Dexter and Hannah said they wished to hear it. It was the poorest performance I ever gave. Fortunately the subject of actualizing man's finest potentials is so exhilerating it sustained me.

While I struggled to overcome my disgusting fatigue, Edith came to pack for my Virginia trip. The day before I left, a startling numinous experience occurred. In the long Snowbound winters, storm and snow and ice are our daily fare. Storm clouds fill the sky at all seasons of the year. In February and March they are especially dramatic. Recently the neighbor city of Rochester had twelve feet of snow. I now feared I might not be able to reach the airport or the planes might not be able to fly.

During the four years I have lived in this apartment one of my most delightful companions has been the clouds. The sunrises are spectacular—if one rises early enough to see them. Even at sunset the clouds in the East are often tinged with pink. One of my greatest pleasures is my large spacious balcony facing East that allows a broad view of the vast panorama of sky. Six months of the year I sit out there, write there, read there with no distractions except the extraordinary cloud formations. The sky, as Emily Bronte said, is my dear companion.

This late February day I stood inside the long glass door staring at the sky drama. Everything looked different. Usually clouds seem to lie horizontal or sail across a blue sea of sky. Today there was no blue to be seen anywhere. The clouds were all perpendicular. And enormous. And thousands of them. White, grey, and menacing black. Like fabulous castles in some fairy tale, they were piled high into the sky leaning against each other as if there were not room enough for them all, even in the whole vast expanse of the heavens. Never had I beheld such a wonderous sight. The wide glass wall of the living room permitted a view of 180°, a completely unobstructed view. Never had I seen so many clouds in one sky. For miles up and down, right and left, the whole world seemed filled with gigantic storm clouds. I stared in fascination and fear. There was something uncanny about it all—a fright- ening something. Then suddenly from between a grey cloud and a black cloud I felt a current of energy fly like an invisible arrow straight through space and penetrate my chest. It inflicted not pain but joy, exciting, exalting, transforming me. I felt spiritually buoyant, happy without cause, filled with a surcharge of mysterious energy. It incited me to go out immediately and save the world, write a classic about Zen, dance across the roof tops of the world. I loved every living person, every thing—animate and inanimate. This high mindstate lasted a week or more unabated.

(Much later Roshi was to confer a Buddhist name on me—Cloudsong. It seemed peculiarly appropriate though I had never related this cloud incident to him. He was psychic anyway. I always felt he could see through me like a pane of dirty glass.)

What had those clouds done to me? Always the conceptual mind demands an explanation even of the most ecstatic experience. From the time I was ten and ran in a wild Texas Norther and merged with the wind I had been visited by what psychologists nowadays term "altered states of consciousness," moments when I lost myself, became part of a primordial power greater than I. Through the years they had been evoked by moonlight, flowers, and children, the city, writing, and dancing, sea and sand, sun and earth, dusk, and all the seven arts—music and poetry, painting and sculpture, ballet, architecture and drama.

In truth, *Awakening to the Good* is an account of these numinous incidents that culminated finally in the spontaneous awakening which lasted for twelve glorious years. At the time of their occurrence I had not understood these mysterious incidents. I called them "small ecstacies" for want of a better name. Never before, however, had I been visited by a small ecstasy occasioned by clouds. Yet many and many a time I had lain on the beach at Cape Cod in the summertime, gazing in fascination at the clouds above me, hoping they would "speak to me." They never did. Though as I lay there my body had felt deliciously ravished by the sea and sun and racing blood induced by a vigorous swim, as if a lover had been making love to me for three hours. I did not realize then that these numinous moments do not usually visit us after activity but after inactivity. I often felt guilty nowadays because I failed to keep myself continuously open to such numinous experiences, always waiting for us to open the door so that they might come flooding in. They invariably occurred when I least expected them.

Even though one experiences the beauty and mystery of reality—"immutable, irreducible, ineffable, and all-pervading," the rational mind asks, is it physically possible for anyone to be actually penetrated by cosmic energy?

Did the second law of thermodynamics apply here? It states that no living creature can exist unless energy comes to it from outside. Did this refer only to food and the physical body?

I consulted John White's *Frontiers of Consciousness*. In it Tiller says, "The basic energy is already there, it is just in an incoherent form, and our job is to make it coherent... by developing attunement with nature through our meditation, our thoughts, and our actions." He referred to "Chakra-endocrine circuits (transformers)... via which one may tap energy from the cosmos."

Of course, Zen explained it more poetically as being "in the stream," "in the cosmic How," "in harmony with Tao."

At the time there appeared no direct connection between the mind-state induced by the cloud experience and my subsequent behavior a few days later. Gradually, however, it was to become apparent that many sittings in zazen often culminate in some dramatic experience of creativity or purification, compassion or selflessness. It influences one's behavior almost imperceptibly, renders one capable of coping more wisely with the most difficult of all problems—human relationship.

It was about this time, I think, that a contretemps arose between a very close friend and I. Eleanor lived in New Haven. She had become a Buddhist but not a Zen Buddhist. I loved her deeply. We never wrote letters but frequently telephoned each other long distance and carried on endless and very expensive but very satisfying conversations.

Lately she had become painfully domineering. Every statement I made she disputed forcibly, every suggestion I offered she dismissed angrily. If I said innocently, "It looks like rain today," she retorted, "Nonsense. It won't rain." If I said, "I'm too tired to go to the Zen Center tonight," she said, "I don't believe it. You go. You need it." If I said, "Why was it so difficult for Buddha to convert his favorite, Ananda, to Buddhism?" she would say in a tone of final authority, "It was not difficult for Buddha, it was difficult for Ananda." Every word I uttered was contradicted or corrected. My forbearance was straining my affection to the breaking point.

She was not well and I should have taken that into consideration. One day, however, when I telephoned to inquire how she felt, she attacked me furiously. "Never, never ask me how I feel! That is what my mother has done every day of my life. I don't want your pity."

I was shocked and deeply hurt. "It was not pity, Eleanor. It was sympathy."

"It's pity and if that's the best you can do I don't see how we can continue to be friends." She slammed up the phone.

A few days later I called her. "I'm very upset, Eleanor."

"What's the matter?"

"Well, I have a dear friend of whom I'm very fond. She is brilliant intellectually and fundamentally a kind person. She has done me innumerable kindnesses. But recently she has allowed herself to fall into a most unfortunate habit. She contradicts or corrects every word I say. She acts as if she's Mrs. God and knows the final truth about everything. She tries by angry force and condescension to impose her ideas on me and to dominate me. I consider my ideas just as valid as hers. And even when I am concerned for her welfare she becomes angry, makes me feel I have committed a crime. I simply can't take any more so—"

"Good heavens, you mean *me*, Claire?"

"What do you think?"

"I'm sorry. I was not aware that I was acting that way."

After that matters improved.

In early March when I arrived in Virginia, the season had not yet begun. There were very few guests at the Williamsburg Inn. Most of the trees were bare. There were few flowers, though many buds. Quiet and peace were exactly what I desperately needed. I was exhausted beyond the danger point, wishing to talk with no one. I was drained to the last drop of energy and beyond.

Slowly I strolled along the footpath running parallel to the hard red brick walk, my feet grateful for the resiliance of the soft sand, welcoming the touch of the firm earth almost forgotten by my city feet.

I sank wearily to a stone bench warmed by the pale Spring sunshine, alone in the vast deserted grounds of the Inn. Grateful for the silence and healing solitude, I sat motionless, delighting in the one and only flowering magnolia tree bursting into inexplicably early white blooms. Brave little yellow crocuses boldly thrust their heads up through the green grass at my feet.

A brilliant red cardinal sat on the bare boughs of a nearby crepe myrtle, a mockingbird perched on top of the redolent boxwood hedge beside my elbow, ignoring my presence. I watched his throat pulsating with happy song, mocking every other bird with ease.

I sat there motionless, doing nothing, thinking nothing, desiring nothing—no longer pushed, pulled, coerced by people, plans, pressure, deadlines, time limits and duties. It was good to be free from work and routine. Free from doing what other people expected of me, free to do what *I* wanted to do—which was nothing, sweet restful nothing.

I reviewed my four years of discipline at the Zen Center in Snowbound. Four years of strenuous work, of submitting (of my own free will) to endless rules, of striving to meet the expectations (my teacher's and my own), obeying regulations, disciplining my rebellious body, quieting my rambunctious mind, then writing the Zen chapter under pressure of time. I was too exhausted. I longed to be free—free of everything, of everybody.

I sat there relaxing, floating idly in the stream of life. It was inexplicably sweet. Then slowly into my deadened senses, exhausted body, depleted nerves and overworked brain, something infinitely sweet commenced to flow. Like a subterranean spring, my Original-nature rose up to the surface and began to pour its life-giving waters into the dry reservoir of my being.

How long I sat there—a minute, an hour?—I shall never know. Then it happened. Suddenly my compulsive attachment to my spiritual teacher and to the Buddha fell away from my shoulders like an unneeded cloak. It was so realistic I could feel it physically. A heavy weight slipped to the ground. I felt stunned, guilty, relieved, regretful, happy. Suddenly after four years of compulsive dependence on Roshi and the Buddha - I WAS FREE!

It was unbelievable that such a sudden unexpected gift of freedom should be conferred on me. I did not rise and shout hurrah. I sat there on the bench without moving, filled with awe and gratitude and trepidation, attempting to clarify so dramatic but disturbing an event. Yet had not the Roshi stated repeatedly to all aspirants that the time should come in our progress on the spiritual path when we must dispense with a teacher and stand on our own two feet? I had never believed a word of it. I had been convinced that I should be bound to him forever. And had not even the Buddha himself warned us that until we could dispense with the Buddha we were incapable of practicing Buddhist principles properly, that we are all sufficient unto ourselves? I had never believed a word of it. I had been convinced that I should be bound to both of my teachers for the rest of my life. I had resented being dependent on any authority while at the same time, fearing to cut such ties. Like a child longing to venture forth into the world alone, yet afraid to leave home.

Freedom! I sat there savoring its sweetness. As usual Roshi was right and I was wrong. As usual Zen Buddhism was correct and I was in error—fortunately.

Gradually I emerged from this delicious mind-state sufficiently to become aware of my surroundings once again. In the distance there was a long vista of greenness as far as the eye could reach, a greensward of new green grass—young—pristine—vital. It held my gaze hypnotically. Suddenly that greenness came alive. It moved. It vibrated visibly. A sense of presence was in it, a living breathing emanation.

Silently it spoke to me, "There *is* eternal goodness at the heart of the universe. This is Mu."

I closed my eyes. Incredulity and joy surged through me. At last, had I found the solution to my koan, "What is Mu?" (Many weeks later when I reported this incident to Roshi, the glow had faded by then. He tested me and would not accept this beautiful experience as a solution to my koan. He said it was not a demonstration but a conceptual presentation. But again I consoled myself by assuming that if I had been able to see him immediately after the incident had occurred while I was still in a radiant mind-state I might have passed the test.)

For days—weeks, afterward, in fact the entire six weeks of my vacation, it was as if I were walking several feet above the earth. I felt buoyant as if approaching the primordial experience of being. Awareness of the cosmic principle permeating my body and mind and emotions was a daily delight. I felt a warm glow of harmony with nearly everyone I met: the children lonely and abandoned by their parents in the television room, the other guests, the desk clerks.

An unexpected problem arose, however. All the black waiters, doormen and bellmen, chambermaids, shuttle bus drivers, whether at the Inn or any other restaurants where I dined, were still in a state of polite but palpable hostility toward all white people. My initial reaction of affront vanished the minute I recalled their bitter struggle for equality in Virginia.

Their animosity was so strong it chilled the air surrounding them. I feared it would force me to leave Williamsburg. Other guests complained of the same thing. I felt no anger toward the blacks, only deep compassion. But they were not aware of that.

It was, however, a new and painful experience to have servants hostile to me at sight because of the color of my skin, even before I opened my mouth. I realized what blacks had been suffering from whites for centuries. I felt great warm waves of understanding and kindness. I must make them aware of that.

I smiled at every black I confronted, no matter how icy, almost to insolence, his manner. I expressed appreciation of their every good point—a pretty dress, an extra pat of butter from the waiter, helpful answers from the bus drivers to my questions concerning local matters. Gradually most of them responded warmly—too warmly on occasion. A few seemed frozen in an attitude of hostility. It would require more than smiles to thaw them out.

Every day I took the shuttle bus to the various historic buildings open to the public. I devoured with unprecedented appetite biographies of Washington, Jefferson, Thomas Paine, Governor Spotswood and Martha Washington, astounded at what I learned. My grandmother of course had told me that her ancestor, Governor William Spotswood, had built the original governor's palace. It had burned down and been restored by Rockefeller in its present form on the original foundations. It was not only that it was a little gem of Georgian architecture. It was not only that its interior was elegant and gracious. But the very presence of my ancestors could be felt especially in the garden. My feet touched the very earth that Spotswood, Jefferson and the great Washington and Martha had walked on. It was a deeply moving experience.

I took a thoughtful look at the house of Martha Dandrige Custis Washington. It is still standing in Williamsburg but not open to the public. I went to the library at William and Mary College. I read for the first time that my ancestor, Martha, had possessed 15,000 acres of land, $100,000 in gold and 300 slaves when she married George Washington.

An uncanny sensation of Washington's and Jefferson's presence pervaded my whole body when I laid my hand gently on the very billiard table at which these great men had played and talked in Raleigh's Tavern.

The original small red brick House of Burgesses still stood at the opposite end of the avenue. Here Jefferson and Thomas Paine had spoken the eloquent and noble words that saved the American Republic. All my life I, like most Americans, have taken our founding fathers for granted. Nowadays, however, the crime and corruption in the United States, the deterioration of honor and integrity among politicians, prompted me to seek out the qualities that had made those early Virginia men into great statesmen. I realized for the first time that it was the selflessness, true nobility, the vision and wisdom of men like Jefferson and Washington. They were not politicians seeking votes from the populace. They, like the Adamses of Massachusetts, made unpopular decisions if they thought them beneficial to the infant Republic. Jefferson, himself an aristocrat, insisted on establishing democracy in America.

It was appalling, almost incredible, to read of the jealousies and hate, dishonesty and intrigue among some of the early politicians, whose ego longed for fame and fortune even though it might destroy nobler men and even the young American Republic.

Ego, Ego! That seemed to be the chief source of evil in mankind just as Zen Buddhism continually warned us. Nobility—was it not one of the rarest of human characteristics? A quality that brought tears to my eyes as I stood alone in the House of Burgesses. It was a moment of truth. I felt my roots thrusting deeper into the Virginia earth. Roots that lent strength and stability to my own inner growth. Or was it because zazen had increased my awareness of the nature of reality—source of nobility and freedom?

As our plane flew above the clouds on our way back to Snowbound a sense of freedom almost lent me wings of my own. My body and nerves might still be heavy with weariness but my mind and emotions were soaring into space. I sang a little refrain under my breath, "So *this* is what four years of zazen can do!" It can bring freedom from rules and regulations, from rulers and regulators.

Chapter XV
LOVE

Lance returned to his family in Boston. He wrote a letter that pained me very much but I recognized it as a healthy sign for him. He wanted to be free of his attachment to me. It hurt but I wrote him a cheerful letter (though I did not feel cheerful) encouraging him to break his bond with me and to live a natural, normal married life. Privately I wept bitterly. I missed his tender delightful companionship. His defection was inevitable. Its inevitability did not render the loss easier to accept.

Soon he invited me to his wedding at the Zen Center and asked me to sit with his family. His mother spent the night in my apartment. I became friends with his sweet young wife. They prepared a royal dinner for me and I one for them. Then they moved back to Boston.

I felt bereft and sorry for myself yet chagrined at my weakness. The problem was, how could I live without the love of a man? Of all things in life I was most dependent on love. Now that Lance had married and left town, Haig moved forward from the background of my life, to the foreground. He began coming more often to my apartment. We cooked dinner together, laughing a great deal, and discussed Zen and the Center endlessly. He was most meticulous with all my fine crystal and Lenox china. He was by nature and habit exceedingly tidy and immaculate about his work and his person. He often took me out to vegetarian restaurants. I concealed from him my grief about Lance.

My intense relation with Dexter for two years and Lance for two years, and the pain of losing them when they married, left me cautious about becoming deeply involved with a third young man. Therefore I attempted to restrain my affection for Haig, without much success.

The explanation of these loving friendships with young men had long since eluded me. If I had been Haig's mother, grandmother and sweetheart rolled into one, he could not have been more solicitous, respectful and loving. He was practical, realistic and knowledgeable concerning many matters about which I knew nothing. He often drove me about on shopping trips and was as helpful as a considerate son. Where mechanical matters were involved I rather enjoyed being a clinging Southern vine. I simply was not interested in broken clocks and cars that refused to run.

The greatest mystery, however, was that apparently zazen awakens everyone's every faculty—including love and even the erotic. When Haig and I were alone in my apartment the atmosphere was unbelievably tense. He was 25, I think, and I was now 78, though many thought me many years younger.

Haig was extremely careful never to touch me. I think consciously the very idea would have shocked him, whatever he might have felt unconsciously. I admired the unusually broad shoulders of the former football player but had long ago ruled out taking a lover of any age. The famous sexologists, Johnson and Masters, were correct, however, when they announced that desire in a woman continues indefinitely even into her eighties.

My men friends, unaware of my advanced age, repeatedly asked, "Why don't you marry again, Claire?"

"Because my freedom is too precious. As a female I was under my father's thumb until I graduated from college at twenty. I imagined I'd be free if I left home and earned my own livelihood. Then I was under my employer's thumb—more or less. I thought I would have more freedom if I married. But that placed me under my husband's thumb. The minute he died, ironically enough, I plunged into Zen—a very confining discipline—at first. Its eventual goal, however, is complete liberation—not only from the world, people, intellect and ego, but liberation from repeated death and rebirth on earth. I am free now of father, employer, husband and religious teachers. I am free of all these men, however fond I was of them, however necessary they were to me in creating a rich full life."

My men friends would laugh but look offended and bewildered. "Oh, we aren't as bad as all that, are we?"

"My dear, I love men, I can't live without them but I am sure no man on earth can even begin to imagine how women of independent spirit feel imprisoned even by the kindest men. Nowadays I am truly like a bird out of a cage. I revel in my freedom."

"Free? What do you mean?"

"Well, it may sound simplistic or petty. But to wake in the morning and realize that I am answerable to no one but myself, that I can stay in bed without a husband complaining of having to eat breakfast alone, or a cook being offended because I do not come down to my meals when they are ready, that I do not have to rush off to a job at a certain time or incur an employer's displeasure. These are simple external manifestations of an internal freedom. The most important reaction is the inner one. I feel like a bird whose wings have been clipped all it's life or who has been in a beautiful comfortable gilded cage. Now I am free to fly—fly! To fulfill myself. To be my True-self. Oh, it's the most glorious sensation."

"But," my men friends would often protest, "a lover would not imprison you."

"Oh yes, he might. Unless he were enlightened or far advanced on the spiritual path he would be jealous and demanding. Besides, most men are very poor lovers."

"I don't believe it."

"That's because you're not a woman. Oh, they can arouse a woman easily enough but they are likely to leave her hanging on the edge of the cliff. I don't want to take that chance again. I know how beautiful and satisfying sex relations can be. And should be."

Some of the young Zen men would ask me frankly what kind of lovemaking a woman liked and I would tell them frankly. The same puritanism in which I was brought up they had thrown out the window with the greatest of ease. They refused to allow society to subject them to years of unhealthy, hypocritical guilt feelings. They were wonderfully honest and natural.

Through the Zen years I had continued to exchange dinners with Susie and Bob, Jim and Linda, and other young married couples—especially, of course, Dexter and Hannah. They now had a baby. A handsome manly little boy. Dexter asked me to be Bob's godmother and to move into the other apartment in his house.

"Why?" I asked.

"You'd be such a fine influence on little Bob as he grew up."

His trust in me was touching but for various reasons it seemed wiser not to move. I did, however, enjoy the new and moving experience of playing with the baby often. Watching the swift changes from crawling to walking, from no teeth to teeth, from babbling to words, to sentences, was enlightening. One could almost see the wheels going around in his little brain as he developed. It was the first time I had ever observed the growth of a child at close range. It was fascinating.

At the Center there was no promiscuity but many of the men and girls were living together. That was the modern form of "engagement." They did not call it an "affair" as my generation had. It was a "relationship." They did not "make love", they "had sex"—much more truthful. After a few years of experimentation they usually married. The young people still came to me for counseling about sex, neuroses and every other variety of problem.

It was not long before Haig brought Sally, his new girl friend, to dinner. She was tall, slender and pretty with long dark hair and an extremely keen mind. She had an excellent position as a computer programmer. The three of us prepared dinner together several times a week. They would usually bring a casserole. All the Zen men had learned to cook. It rather looked as if unisex was developing in the counterculture—or was it androgyny?

Working with young people was so much more delightful than working with older people. Sally would say, "Shall I wash and dry the lettuce?" "Yes, please." "All right to dry it on a dish towel?" "No, it stains it." She promptly used paper towels without a long argument. An older person might have debated every point, saying, "I never dry mine." Or "I don't think it needs it." Or "It won't stain the dish towel." Which indeed it did.

And if Haig or Dexter or any of the young men dashed out to get ice cream, they returned before I had time to twinkle an eye. Recalcitrant bottle tops in their strong young hands twisted off immediately. They were so quick, full of energy, so efficient, and understood instructions before the last word was out of my mouth. The contrast with giving instructions to various middle-aged maids in the past gave one to think. It was an absolute joy to work with the young. Preparing a meal was like a song and dance act, not like work at all.

Many a delightful hour Haig and Sally and I spent talking endlessly over a dinner table. I asked them about their childhood, their families, their jobs. They asked me about the many experiences of a long rich life. Always, of course, we discussed Zen Buddhism—an inexhaustible subject. Never had I known such harmony, such an attentive audience while I held gaily forth. Never had my ideas, my writings, my awakening, or progress in Zen Buddhism been accorded such respect.

Sometimes they listened with shining eyes. It made me feel very humble. I did not deserve such respect and appreciation but enjoyed every minute of it nonetheless. I strove more vigorously than ever to deserve the utter trust of these two highly intelligent, sensitive and affectionate young people. It was a beautiful heartwarming experience for me though I failed to see just what they derived from it.

I talked so long and so animatedly that after they left I often fell into bed with my clothes on, utterly exhausted. This was the nearest I would ever come to having a loving and lovable daughter and son. When Sally left she often hugged and kissed me saying, "You're like the mother I always wanted." Her mother had died when she was very young. I loved them both, considering them unusually fine young people with high ideals and great integrity. Our delightful dinners continued for a year. Often Haig would say at the

door, "Every time I leave this apartment I feel nearer to enlightenment."

One night Sally opened the door to carry the trash to the incinerator down the hall. "Oh, Claire, the hall is so thick with smoke I can't even see the way to the incinerator."

Haig looked out and promptly notified the fire department. "All right, Claire, stay calm. We'll get you out safely. Get your purse and keys and follow me. Sally, we must get Claire out first of all."

The entire corridor was an inpenetrable wall of grey smoke. We could see nothing. We closed our eyes and felt our way along the wall with our hands until we came to the fire stairs. Sally took one arm and Haig the other and conducted me down the steep uncarpeted steps from the third floor down to the first where there was no fire. The firemen had it out in no time. It was the blocked incinerator where some careless tenant had obstructed the chute with the wrong form of trash.

Afterward I wondered why Haig seemed so anxious to conduct me to safety. Should not his prime interest have been in Sally? But she herself seemed equally concerned with my welfare. Zen couples almost never were demonstrative toward each other. This puzzled me. I was always delighted when Haig suddenly kissed Sally's hair or paid her a compliment—and she was even more delighted. When a man loved me I wanted him to pat and pet me, kiss me, stroke my hair.

Sally seemed to vascillate between regarding me as her mother and her rival. She found an excellent position over in Massachusetts. Of course Haig accompanied her. Was it because the salary was higher? Or was her purpose to remove Haig from my presence? Did she feel he was too attached? Nothing was ever said and we all remained close friends. I missed their companionship sorely. I resolved never again to become emotionally involved with any young man. Separation was inevitable and too painful. How did real mothers endure separation from their real sons and daughters?

Somehow I felt I had failed Sally. I could not play the role of loving mother as warmly as I felt she wished. Why? Was it that it seemed natural and easy to establish a warm rapport with surrogate sons but not so easy with daughters? Never was there that irrestible magnetic attraction between the same sex as between opposite sexes. It was more than that. I felt it was my own shortcoming. I was unable to feel as excited toward daughters as toward sons. Was it because my own mother had felt that way toward me—without her own volition? But I had long since forgiven her and felt sorry that I had caused her much suffering. It was evident that she attempted to love her daughter, but then of course she had not loved her son either. It was a far sadder situation for him because our father did not approve of him either. If only parents could learn to love their children more deeply.

Sally and Haig returned to Snowbound frequently for sesshin and various ceremonies. Our reunions were always enthusiastic, Sally's eyes shining as brightly as Haig's and doubtless mine shone even more.

In the spring when I returned from Virginia they invited me to come to Massachusetts and visit them in their house for a thorough rest. Haig hitch-hiked to Snowbound in the pouring rain in order to drive me back in my car.

"Our cars are too rattletrap for an elegant lady like Claire," he said.

When we commenced our journey I announced that I would lie down on the back seat and rest while they sat in the front and drove. Haig was very solicitous. Did I want the air conditioner on? Excuse the bumps. Let him know when I grew hungry and we could stop for a meal. He leapt out to open the car door for me.

It was like being cradled in strong arms that protected me from all hurt and harm. I smiled to myself but felt I was floating in an atmosphere of love that was infinitely comforting. I strove to show my appreciation by taking them to fine restaurants. It seemed to me that others were all the time doing wonderful things for me and that I did nothing for them. I hoped I compensated somewhat by sending checks at Christmas and weddings to my young friends of both sexes. Of course also, I loved them and was concerned.

When we arrived at their house Sally asked if I wished more blankets, could she open the window for me, what groceries should she purchase for me?

"My dear Sally, don't worry about me. I want to fit right into your regular routine, not disturb it. I will eat exactly what you-all eat and like it."

There was never a moment of friction. They took their guest to gourmet restaurants, asked me to speak at their Zen group and to meet their friends. During the day my host and hostess went to their respective jobs. That left the house to me and their very affectionate cat. I relaxed, sat in the sun, read, practiced zazen in their private zendo, and played with their amusing cat. I had long ago discovered that many cats have a sly sense of humor.

There was frequent evidence that Haig and Sally were striving in a practical way to apply Zen principles in their daily lives—to each other, to all human situations, to their difficult co-workers.

One evening as we sat at the dining table after they had created an especially delicious dinner, Haig asked, "Claire, how did you obtain harmony with your co-workers in your various jobs?"

"I didn't always—especially with the women." I laughed. "I never seemed to have trouble with the men—even the ones who worked under me when I was manager of that bookshop in New York. Then after I married Thursty, our servants were my co-workers in a sense. I had Irish, Swedish, Italian, and Black. I made many awful mistakes—before my awakening in 1950. When servants failed to do a job properly I became angry and critical. That might or might not improve their work next time but it certainly caused resentment on both sides."

"But isn't anger justified?" Sally asked.

"It is really not a matter of justification. There is a different approach. As we all know, after one is enlightened one is *unable* to feel anger toward anyone. Just as Buddha said, one feels compassion. I can take no credit for it but after my awakening, the natural spontaneous thing to do was to become aware of my maids' personal identity, to feel concern for their problems, to praise them for any good work they had done and then to transform the job they had done badly into a cooperative venture, and ask for their suggestions for improvement. Then they showed a genuine interest and surprising ingenuity. I only knew how the finished product should look. They knew far more than I concerning processes. It worked like magic. It awakened their True-selves—partially. We became devoted to each other. I am sure Margaret, my cook, Katie (our chambermaid for fourteen years), and I would have laid down our lives for each other if an emergency arose."

"Oh," Sally said thoughtfully. "I am beginning to see."

"I remember," Haig said, "you once told us that the worst part of being in the hospital those four months was losing your identity. And you said Abraham Maslow's study of factory workers revealed that being treated like a mere cog in a large machine was their chief complaint. I know. With this economic depression, I took any job I could find. I'm working on an assembly line in a factory right now. I don't think I told you before, Claire."

"That all sounds very easy, Claire," Sally commented, "if one is in a state of enlightenment. But most of us are not there yet. What then? Should one *control* one's anger? I have eighteen people working for me. And there's one woman, Mary, who does excellent work but complains about something or somebody every hour of every day. She's driving me crazy."

"Well, why do you suppose Buddha formulated the Eight-fold Noble Path?"

Sally shrugged. "No one can feel compassion by will power."

"No, but if one is aware of the ideal behavior could one not act in the ideal manner by deliberate conscious planning? Isn't that the purpose of the Eight-fold Noble Path?"

The next afternoon when Haig returned from work he announced, "It works. The C.M.O. Method."

"What's the C.M.O. Method?" I asked.

He laughed. "Why, you of all people should know."

Light dawned on me. "Tell us about it."

"Well, as I've told Sally often, I work with a woman, Tina, who is very skillful but so untidy. Her work bench is a disgraceful mess. No one ever cleans their place up. So today I complimented Tina on her very great skill and speed. You won't believe it but she began to clean up the work bench voluntarily. I was so delighted I pitched in and helped her. And wonder of wonders—the whole assembly line followed suit and cleaned their places up so well you wouldn't recognize them. The foreman is always admonishing them to tidy up but they never do."

Sally made no comment at the time but a few days later she reported a similar experiment. Instead of admonishing Mary for complaining too much, Sally, her employer, praised her in the presence of others for her excellent work. "Mary has not uttered a word of complaint for the last three days."

We all laughed and hugged each other.

A look of doubt came over Haig's face. "How does the C.M.O. method accord with the Zen method which seems to me seldom pays compliments and frequently deflates the ego?"

"*They complement each other* in my opinion," I replied. "Zen represents the masculine authority principle and woman the feminine nurturing principle. Apparently we all require both. That's obvious in nature's arrangement for the father-mother upbringing of children."

"But, Claire," Sally protested, "in Roshi's book it says that in dokusan the Roshi fulfills the dual role traditionally ascribed to a father *and a mother.*"

"Have you ever talked this over with Roshi?" Haig asked.

I laughed. "No, but at the last picnic he said, 'Claire, you are always undermining my good work. You want me to always be kind and gentle with everyone. But I must be rough sometimes as a kindness.' He laughed when he said it but I think he meant it." (Later he wrote me that he was attempting to teach me by spoofing me, but I had no sense of humor.)

Haig smiled. "Roshi says—in fact, all the Zen literature says—that many people come to enlightenment because the masters, spurning honey-sweet words, open the students' minds with a verbal blow and sometimes a physical blow."

"Most women do not like to be struck," Sally murmured.

"I know," I replied. "Reluctant as I am to admit it as an advocate of gentleness, I can recall two incidents in my own life where a physical blow and a verbal blow precipitated healthy reactions. One was the time my mother slapped me and the other occured in New Haven. You may remember, my dearest friend, Clarice, struck me a terrible verbal blow. It precipitated my spiritual awakening which cured my neurosis. So I suppose as usual Zen is right and I am wrong. But not wholly wrong. I have seen kindness and appreciation work miracles—and so have you-all recently. Too much criticism and belittlement discourages some and so they give up. My point is that I believe harshness should be dealt out sparingly and not used until the person is absolutely ripe for a change. A distinction must be made between that rare moment and the long years while students are struggling on the upward path."

"But doesn't zazen itself diminish the ego?" Sally asked.

"Yes and in full enlightenment the ego is extinguished. So is it necessary to begin deflating it so early in the game? Of course, I may be entirely wrong."

Haig laughed. "Well, maybe some day soon we will all be androgynous. That may solve many of our problems."

Sally quoted Jung, "'Self-realization is a feminization process.'"

"Don't let Roshi hear you quoting Jung. He discouraged me from even reading psychologists. I can't make him realize that it would have been impossible for me to remain in Zen practice without the verification by the psychologists, philosophers and scientists of my own experiential knowledge—wonderful as it was. In my peculiar case, reading saved my Zen practice. Some people are made that way."

Sally dumped the cat from her lap and went to the kitchen to make a fresh pot of camomile tea. The cat leaped up into my lap but returned promptly to hers when she sat down again.

I shrugged. "I'm definitely second choice."

Then Sally gave a rueful little smile. "I assume you'd recommend the same method in marriage?"

"I'm afraid so," I said.

"Claire," Sally said, "tell us again how you managed to create a good marriage all those years with Thursty. You said he was a fine man but difficult."

Haig laughed. "Implying that Haig is a fine man but difficult."

"All husbands and wives are difficult," I hastened to add. "I think the crudest thing on earth that married people can do is to undermine each other's self-esteem. Yet it seems to be their favorite indoor sport."

Haig glanced knowingly at Sally. "Like Kate and Pete. He claims her constant criticism finally rendered him impotent. That's why he left her."

"What specifically did you find constructive, Claire?" Sally asked.

"Well, I made many mistakes in the early days of marriage. I grew angry and critical. That only made a bad situation worse. But I realized we were getting nowhere fast. So I learned to control my angry retorts by walking out of the room. I would think over our problem for a few days striving to see it from *his* point of view. I was appalled to see how often *I* was in the wrong. Thursty was always amenable to reasonable discussion. Later I would calmly explain my side and he'd explain his. Then we'd usually come to an amicable understanding."

"But how was it *after* your awakening?" Sally prompted.

"Ah, then everything became easy. It seemed perfectly natural to spontaneously praise his best characteristics—to him and to others in his presence. The effect was miraculous. It abolished many of his habits that had annoyed me without the necessity of ever mentioning them."

Haig laughed. "Good Lord, you mean husbands and wives *unconsciously* do things to annoy each other as a—a sort of signal about something else?"

Sally continued the idea. "But the other person doesn't know how to interpret this symbolic action?"

I smiled. "You're good psychologists. You don't need me."

"Oh yes we do," Haig reassured me. "Sally and I wouldn't have stayed together all this time if it had not been for your help."

"I doubt that."

Sally looked very thoughtful. "What you're really saying, Claire, is that the best way to create a happy marriage is to awaken one's own True-self and *that* will not only lead one to *recognition* of the other's True-self, but may even awaken it."

Haig placed his hand on Sally's. "Then we'll both have to do more zazen. But men and women are so different, they think differently, react to the same things differently. Women are so emotional, so easily hurt. I look forward to unisex."

I smiled. "Didn't Buddha say that Nirvana is the reconciliation and transcendence of opposites?"

All week long the house was permeated with affection as real as a fragrance. No friction. No conflicts. Everyone was solicitous for everyone else. When the week ended it was time to say goodbye and return to Snowbound. The three of us went out to my car with our arms around each other.

"I want you two nice people to know that this is the loveliest visit I ever made in my life. Your tender loving care cured my every ache and pain—even my insomnia. I feel simply marvelous now. You have performed a miracle."

" *We* haven't," Haig said, "*love* has. We love you and want you to come back soon."

"And I love you two dear ones and I'll be happy to come back again."

Haig put my bag in the trunk. I kissed and thanked Sally again. Her job prevented her from making this trip. Haig was driving me back to Snowbound in my car. Sally waved as we drove away. "We'll phone you often."

As we were driving along, I said, "Oh Haig, I'll never come to see you again if you hitchhike. It is simply too much of a hardship for you."

He laughed. "But, Claire, it was the only way we could get you to visit us."

I put some folded bills in his pocket. He nearly ran the car into a ditch in his haste to return them. "No, no! I won't take it!"

"Wait, Haig dear, keep it just in case it rains. Then you can take the bus. Just to please me. It took you twelve hours whereas the bus, Sally said, is about seven hours and it's six hours by private car."

Haig and I were unusually quiet. I was reviewing my visit, still amazed that love and rest were able to cure all my minor but annoying ailments.

Love, I thought, that is the magic elixir. Love pours over one like a warm balm, healing nearly every wound that life inflicts. It lends strength and confidence, purifies one's defilements, banishes ills. Love begets love. The more one is loved, the more one loves. And the more one loves, the more one is loved.

"Why," I said aloud, "is there so little love in the world? Nearly everyone I meet is hungry for love—appreciation and understanding."

"Yes," Haig said. "Surely love is the greatest benefit conferred by zazen. I think its greater than compassion or wisdom."

"A too-active ego is an obstacle to loving anyone!"

Haig laughed. "Dat ole debil—ego!"

"Honestly, when non-Buddhist people read or hear about the absolutely incredible effects of meditation or observe it, why do they not all enter meditation training the next day?"

Haig laughed.

"No, I mean it. When they learn that it can cure them of anxiety, hate and jealousy, selfishness, egotism and fear and bring joy and happiness—why do they not go to some Buddhist Center to enroll immediately—if not sooner?"

"Well, Claire, maybe you aren't considering the nature of human nature. For example, everyone in America who can read knows that smoking cigarettes may cause cancer, emphysema or heart trouble. Yet the polls report that cigarette smoking is on the increase."

"It's incomprehensible, isn't it? And television informs us every day that coffee is a drug, that butter, bacon and animal fats increase cholesterol. But at the Williamsburg Inn and the Palm Beach Hotel last winter I observed the people around me in the dining room. More than half of them smoked at breakfast, nine-tenths of them drank several cups of coffee and ordered the traditional breakfast of eggs and bacon. Don't they *care* what happens to their bodies?"

Haig's tone was playful. "I know a woman who is highly intelligent and spiritually advanced but who works too hard and writes too long. She makes her body half sick all the time from excessive fatigue." He placed his hand over mine. "Oh, that's very unkind of me."

"No, it isn't. It's kind. I need someone to reprimand me. Though honestly its a mystery. I mean, why I overtax my body constantly."

"Claire, I wish you'd take decent care of yourself. I worry about you all the time. Oh, I forgot to tell you. I think your *Awakening to the Good* should be more widely sold. I'm going to buy 100 copies from the publisher, and sell them to young people. I'll place ads in the papers the counterculture reads."

"Oh, Haig, my dear, you are *too* kind! But begin with only twenty-five. Books are not easy to sell. And in your ad you should explain briefly what the book is about. Otherwise it won't sell."

"How's this? 'The true story of a woman's spiritual awakening?'"

"Fine. My friends are really so helpful. John White is sending the hardcover *Awakening* to publishers hoping they'll issue it as a paperback—for students, he says."

"Oh, is he? Well, keep me informed. I must sell all my hardcover copies before it appears in paperback. Shall we stop for lunch pretty soon?"

While waiting for our lunch Haig handed me a paper with a quotation on it. "Sally wanted me to give this to you. Said it explains us."

"Us?"

"You and me and Sally."

I read, ". . .if a single individual devotes himself to individuation [self-realization], he frequently has a positive contagious effect on the people around him. It is as if a spark leaps from one to another. And this usually occurs when one has no intention of influencing others and often when one uses no words."

"Excellent. Who said it?" I asked.

"I'm surprised you don't recognize it. It's from *Man and His Symbols* but it's by a woman, somebody von Franz, a pupil of Jung's, I imagine."

"Colleague."

"Well, anyway, Sally wanted you to have it. Says it explains our devotion to you. You see, we can't help it."

"You know, Haig, Zen and Jung utter many of the same truths."

When we resumed our trip Haig said, "We didn't answer our own questions. The majority of people refuse to forego their sensuous but dangerous pleasures like cigarettes and coffee. So what hope is there that they'll forego their precious worldly values and habits and enter a rigorous religious discipline? Are they afraid of change? Or are nicotine and caffeine drugs that alleviate mysterious fears and conflicts whose existence they don't even admit?"

"You're right, Haig, I think. But if we Buddhists could only persuade skeptics to understand zazen. For the serious practice of meditation *increases* all sensuous pleasures ten-fold. It also gradually banishes anxieties and fears as does nothing else on earth. We know. We've been there."

"Occasionally. Briefly."

"Surely if anyone could know those basic truths *experientially*, they—he—would become a Buddhist tomorrow."

Haig laughed. "But they would have to enter training before they could experience the benefits of it. Probably that's why Roshi emphasizes the importance of the aspirants having faith."

"Doesn't Christianity also recommend faith?" I asked. "Faith, hope and charity—and the greatest of these is charity, which is actually a debased form of a Latin word for love."

"True," Haig said, "but the Buddhist aspirant must first have faith in order to practice zazen in order to awaken love."

Chapter XVI
SHARING

One balmy evening the Zen orchestra gave a concert in the garden of the Center. I dreaded going. While living in New York, I had had the opportunity of hearing "live", Toscanini, Koussevitshy, Beecham and all the other greatest conductors and orchestras of Europe and America. It was difficult to listen to amateurs. I knew Roshi, who entertained a passion for classical music, felt the same way.

Bernadine, however, was first violinist. I wanted to hear her. In stature she was small with the innocent face of a cherub but she played with the vigor and authority of a husky man.

After the concert Roshi and I agreed that it was amazingly good. "Come sit beside me and we can have a talk," he said. "You probably know that I am going to Germany and Poland next week to conduct workshops and sesshin in the affiliate groups there. Now, Claire, while I am gone, don't let anything happen to you. You are proof of the efficacy of Zen."

I was too stunned to utter a word. It was the first time in four years at the Center that my teacher had paid me a compliment. I had assumed he still considered me an ignorant schoolgirl as far as Zen was concerned. It prompted me to redouble my practice of zazen and triple my efforts to prove the efficacy of Zen in my daily life.

Later there was an even greater surprise in store for me. He asked me to come to his office. He and Dr. Prince had arranged for me to speak in Montreal at a conference of 300 scientists, all expenses paid. Dr. Raymond Prince is founder and director of the Richard Bucke Memorial Society for the Scientific Study of Religion. It was named in honor of the Canadian psychiatrist, Bucke, author of that perennial seller *Cosmic Consciousness*. This present international conference was held under the auspices of The Bucke Society in conjunction with McGill University and the Mental Hygiene Institute.

Roshi said, "I have asked Anna to deliver the talk on Zen." (She is his most advanced disciple. I am a student, not a disciple.) "Dr. Prince says he wants only one talk on Zen so you—"

"Oh, Roshi, I'd like to talk on Self-realization—Induced and Spontaneous. Of course, I'd include Zen."

My original meeting with Dr. Prince had been unusual. He, a Freudian psychiatrist then at McGill, published a paper contending that the mystical experience is a regression in service of the ego, regression to the state of infancy, and closely resembles the psychotic state. Having just enjoyed a sane joyous mystical experience I wrote a rebuttal, "The Mystical Experience—Facts and Values." It was published in *Main Currents in Modern Thought*. After Dr. Prince read it we became good friends and he had invited me to a former conference in Montreal. It was there I met the fabulous Jean Houston.

The present audience in Montreal was drawn primarily from universities in Canada and the United States. There were psychologists, Freudian psychiatrists, neurologists, anthropologists and physiologists. Who was I, I thought, to be giving a lecture to all these Ph.D.'s? They were scholars with reputations throughout the academic world. There also were Protestants, Catholic nuns and priests, Muslims, Jews and Zen Buddhists.

On the first day I listened eagerly to various erudite lectures. They were scientific analyses of the highest state of consciousness by different disciplines. These research professors presented many fascinating new facts—but offered little concerning values—nothing concerning the nature of the experience itself. It felt as if they were all skillfully prodding and dissecting an interesting but lifeless corpse. The heart was missing, the thing that lent it life, warmth, value. I felt they were missing all the concomitant joy. I could scarcely wait until my turn came.

The speakers made frequent references to Dr. Bogen's discovery of the different functions of the two hemispheres of the brain. With excitement but reluctance these scientists had accepted the observable data about the right hemisphere and its concern with intuition, imagery, and spiritual experience. This probably prepared the way for the warm reception of my unscientific presentation which it might not otherwise have received.

On the morning of the great day I nevertheless felt keen trepidation concerning the reception of my talk—not, however, about its contents—of these I was sure. It was as if the scientists had all been circumambulating around and around a priceless treasure concealed in the inner sanctum. Never once had they even attempted to enter the room where the treasure might be viewed. Why talk about it and circle about, I wondered? Why not look directly at the jewel itself—the self-realization experience?

After being introduced by a tall, handsome Catholic priest, I felt little currents of cold air flowing from certain resistant factions. I strove to warm them up immediately. In other lectures there had been a nice response when I placed the palms of my hands together in the Zen gassho gesture, bowed and smiled. I now resorted to this little ice-breaking device. An audible ripple of surprised pleasure ran over the first few rows.

I did not feel I was lecturing, teaching or preaching, or attempting to impose my ideas or Zen doctrines on others. My impulse was simply to share some beautiful and helpful concepts and experiences of self-realization with those who were receptive. Fortunately the profundity, beauty and vital urgency of my subject soon caused me to forget myself, my nervousness and self-consciousness. My ego flew out the window as it had while I was writing the Tart chapter. I felt as if I were merely a channel for the flow.

When I gazed at that great audience of faces, all turned toward me in expectation, it seemed obligatory to offer them something of vital substance. They looked vulnerable as if they had politely left their own opinions and ideas at home and were hungry for new ones.

Somehow I fell in love with that audience, the most responsive I have ever encountered. For some perverse reason I felt like a great mother feeding her hungry children. The stereotype maternal figure is usually envisioned as a short, plump woman with a large comforting bosom. I am tall and slender with small, high, unmaternal breasts. My maternal role is a paradox. I have always fondly imagined myself to be an amoureuse, a kind of minor George Sand, whose literary and erotic exploits have recently been dramatized brilliantly on television.

That day, to my relief, I felt relaxed and natural. My True-self seemed to flow forth. It felt as if I were communicating directly with their True-selves, to the best in their natures. I was speaking of a way of life that surpasses all others—the transpersonal—Buddhist or whatever. That was the message I wished to convey. I also wished to warn them of the difficulties involved. But I longed to assure my listeners that life can be harmonious and beautiful, joyous, loving and creative, that even suffering can be beneficial.

I discussed suffering—often a precipitating factor in self-realization—the stages, the psychological processes, the happy results and the beautiful life style that ensue. For examples I referred to Buddha, Roshi and the young trainees of the Sangha in Snowbound. Then I compared the induced variety with the spontaneous variety, citing Beethoven and Owens. I drew invisible graphs in the air to indicate the differences in the process of the two varieties. I listed the various stages of progress and emphasized the death of the ego as an essential to enlightenment, whether induced by external means or spontaneous.

Dr. Prince, I said, tossed out provocative remarks in order, I believed, to stimulate controversy. Before my talk he had asserted that he did not understand how any person could function without an ego. To refute him I quoted from Arthur Osborne and from my own dramatic experience of the drowning of my ego in the ocean of my collective unconscious. I described the sense of being directed by a cosmic energy after my individual consciousness identified with universal consciousness.

The audience sat motionless, gratifyingly attentive. (At the subsequent party given by Mrs. Prince, she commented, "You could literally have heard a pin drop. Mrs. Owens, you mesmerized them.")

"I was mesmerized myself. Sometimes the beauty of inner development almost makes me burst with Joy."

I became so carried away I forgot to glance at my notes on small file cards in my left hand. At one point the wonder of "seeing into one's nature" moved me so deeply I closed my eyes and stood in silence. Fortunately my old ego reminded me that this was not the time for such emotion. I shook myself and continued.

Humor—any lecture, however serious the subject, is unpalatable if humor is lacking. Alas, I was not born with the gift of wit or humor. My audiences, however, usually laughed gently during my talks, for what reason I have never been able to discover.

At the end of my talk I was in too much of a daze even to hear whether there was applause or not. The questions asked by the audience were excellent. Silently, however, I was laughing to think that these scholarly college professors were asking *me* questions; men whose knowledge so far surpassed mine. Suddenly a man rushed up to the stage and shouted that we must stop because he wanted to show his film during the lunch period.

Afterward several young men came up, grasped my hand and with tears in their eyes, murmured, "Thank you, thank you." Several professors paid very welcome compliments. Dr. Joel Elkes, director of the department of psychiatry at John Hopkins Medical School circled my wrist with his hand. "Beautiful, beautiful. Just what we need." Later he wrote me a friendly letter suggesting that we exchange reprints of our talks. I was asked to be on television and radio. All new and exciting to me. The editor of the *Journal of Altered States of Consciousness* asked me to contribute a paper to his magazine. "Why not print my talk?" I suggested.

When the issue was published I carried a copy of the journal to Roshi. He laid it on his desk. "I find it hard to read magazines, don't you?"

"I don't expect you to read the whole magazine. Just my essay."

I sent reprints to my friends in various universities and was gratified by their comments, especially those of Dr. Stanley Dean, at the University of Florida. Later to my utter amazement requests for reprints of my essay on Self-realization poured in from all directions—the Sorbonne in Paris, research institutes in Switzerland and Czechoslovakia, two universities in Canada, two in California, two in Ohio and a research institute in Maryland.

On Sunday afternoon Roshi dropped in at my apartment unexpectedly. While I gave him rose-hip tea he reminded me again that Zen did not need psychology.

To my surprise I rose up in my own defense. "Roshi, you seem to think because I wrote about the psychology of Zen for Dr. Tart's book that everything I write is psychology. So you won't read them. I write primarily about spiritual experiences—usually those induced by zazen. The psychologists in the universities seem to like my essays—not because they are psychological but because they offer the actual raw experiences."

I rushed on before my courage failed. "This printing of my talk on Self-realization—it is *not* psychology. It concerns Roshi and Buddha and the Sangha—with a little added about Beethoven and me. It explains how suffering seems to precipitate spiritual awakening—whether induced or spontaneous. You see, Roshi," I said, pouring out more tea automatically, "I came into Zen too late in life to imbibe everything in Zen, the way the young people do. Isn't it *inevitable* that I, and perhaps some other mature Americans, should integrate Western psychology and philosophy into Zen thinking and writing? We are already saturated with them. We can't just throw all our lifetime study out the window." The next time I was at the Center, Roshi said, "Claire, I've read your paper on Self-realization. I was impressed."

In an issue of the *Zen Voice* there were several papers suggesting that when Zen was presented to Americans in an American way there was little resistance, that Buddha himself stated that Buddhism must be adapted differently to different cultures and that many Eastern accretions must be eliminated for Western Zen Buddhists.

Haig and Sally drove over from Massachusetts to hear the tape recording of my speech and to hear all about my Montreal trip. I invited Dexter and Hannah to join us over ice cream and cake. When the tape ended Haig exclaimed, "Why, Claire, you didn't tell us there was such a roar of applause at the end of your lecture."

"I didn't know it. I was in too much of a daze, I reckon."

My guests discussed my lecture, pleased that I had emphasized suffering as a frequent forerunner to awakening.

"Hearing one's own voice played back on a tape recorder can be quite a shock," I protested. "My voice sounds so horribly refined and lady-like. I don't talk like that in real life."

The young people all laughed. "You sound exactly like that."

"Where does your accent come from?" Sally asked. "I detect remnants of Southern inflection and idiom."

"Sounds like New Yorkese to me," Dexter said.

"Sounds like an English accent to me," Hannah murmured.

I laughed. "Several strangers have asked me, 'When did you leave England?' 'Two hundred years ago,' I say. Last winter in Florida one of the college boys said, 'I thought you were an English baroness or something.' There happened to be an unusual number of titled people at the hotel that winter—the ones who used to go to the Riviera, I reckon."

Dexter laughed. "No English baroness would ever say, 'I reckon.'"

I smiled. "I reckon not. But when Thursty and I were in England, everyone thought we were colonials—Canadian or Australian. On the continent they thought we were English. Once in Bonn, Thursty instructed the taxi man to drive us to the American embassy. He drove us to the British embassy."

"How did your lecture to the scientists make *you* feel?" Dexter asked, who was himself a scientist.

"Fulfilled. Purified. Enriched. Like a deep zazen session."

"But physically?" Haig asked.

"Drained. So never again. I am giving up lecturing. Too exhausting physically."

"But wasn't it worth it?" Sally asked.

"Yes, once. You know lecturing is a dangerous occupation. It gives the speaker tremendous power over others. One can make people laugh or cry, believe untruths, or swallow any sort of propaganda, even if it's evil."

"Like Hitler," Hannah murmured.

"Yes. The world's prime example of the hypnotic power of the human voice over others. It can also inflate the ego of the speaker. Public applause is intoxicating. One could live on that kind of intoxication. But it is an unhealthy diet. In the case of Zen spiritual talks, however, the subject itself humbles the speaker. In fact, I did not feel I was lecturing. I felt I was simply sharing some beautiful truths with others. But never again."

"But you can continue to share Zen with others through your writing, can't you?" Sally urged.

"I hope so. It is a strange reciprocal process. The more one gives others, the more one receives. I never believed that before."

"That must explain why Roshi endures and thrives on delivering hundreds of lectures and teishos year after year," Hannah commented. "He certainly pours it out to others every day."

"Yes indeed. You-all are too young to have been forced to memorize that very sanctimonious poem in high school by Whittier or Lowell—some minor poet. 'To give is more blessed than to receive.' I always considered that merely a moralistic concept which was not true in real life. One learns—slowly."

Chapter XVII
UNITY THROUGH SELF

One day I received a reprint from the *Journal of Humanistic Psychology*. It was a list of books on the study of consciousness. It had been compiled for his students by Dr. Kenneth Ring, a professor of transpersonal psychology at a New England university.

The list not only contained the best books in the field but comments on each that were so astute, so generous, yet gently skeptical and humorous, that they revealed a very unusual mind behind them.

Any man with such a rare combination of virtues deserved widespread recognition. So I promptly wrote and told him so. Thus began a warm stimulating correspondence. I read everything he had written and he read everything I had written.

At the end of a year of this delightful correspondence he wrote, "I am coming to see you this summer. I may bring my wife or I may not. She is an ardent Jungian."

"I shall be delighted to see either or both of you," I hastened to reply. "I shall put you-all up as my guests at a nearby inn."

He came alone late on a Thursday to stay through Sunday. Dr. Ring was a man about forty, attractive and instantly friendly. I prepared dinner for him with candles and flowers and all the trimmings. We talked until midnight, primarily about ourselves, our families and our childhoods.

As he said goodnight, he laughed. "Well, if its going to be as pleasant as this, I may not even go to the Zen Workshop on Saturday."

"Oh, no, do go. I want you to meet Kolberg, and Zen should appeal to anyone interested in transpersonal experiences. That's what it's all about."

On Friday we talked all day—fifteen hours—through breakfast and lunch and dinner until I completely lost my voice, but I didn't care. I was excited and happy.

All the usual superficial barriers between strangers did not melt away, they simply were absent from the first minute. We accepted each other as human beings without reservations. It was the most "instant friendship" I'd ever known. The kind that seems possible only to those on the spiritual path. It was as if our true unadorned inner selves were meeting.

It was a delight to hear him talk. His voice was low and musical. His vocabulary prodigious, his ideas flowed as naturally and clearly as a pellucid river. He conversed as well as he wrote. I write better than I talk. I was brought up in a society that considered it so affected to use a word of more than two syllables that one was laughed at. Yet I longed to be a scholar with a rich academic vocabulary like Kenneth's.

Unlike most men Kenneth Ring listened attentively to what I, a woman, had to say. Too many men expect a woman to be merely an admiring audience. I had been that all my life and was sick of it. He accepted me—not as

a woman and consequently an inferior, but as an equal. He not only understood my every nuance, but seemed to anticipate my every feeling and
thought as if he were a mind reader. It was indeed an exciting meeting of
minds. Never had I been able to converse so effortlessly or with such intense
pleasure.

Hour after stimulating hour we talked on and on. We discussed Buddhist
principles and how Zen appeared to integrate them into daily life more than
the systems of Christ, Socrates or Jung, Tart's state-specific science, the difference between insight and concentration meditation, the probable influence
of altered states of consciousness on the highest state. We compared the principles enunciated by Stanislav Grof (who had been Ken's guest when he lectured at his university) with those of Masters and Houston, Jung and Zen
Buddhism. We questioned the various levels of the unconscious, the para-
doxical inequality of women in spiritual India, Kundalini, Jung's intellectual
colleagues in America. We compared Buddha and Socrates, Ananda and
Alcibiades, the frustration and surrender of the conscious mind in koans and
in Socratic dialectic.

We talked of Laing's psychology, electromagnetic fields, the existence or
non-existence of a soul, how energy was never lost but transformed, astral
bodies, the meaning of out-of-the body experiences, the cause and cure of
evil, reincarnation, sesshins, Kolberg, the Zen Center, Ken's new project concerning the mystical experiences of the dying, Aldous Huxley, Jean Houston,
Maslow and the validity or invalidity of his theory that basic needs must be
met before the actualization of man's noblest potential is possible.

We spoke of Sutich, Fadiman, Lilly, Tiller and John White. We speculat-
ed on Bogen's concept of the function of the right hemisphere of the brain
and the role of the corpus callosum—could knowledge not only pass from the
unconscious to the conscious mind but could knowledge pass from the conscious to the unconscious?

I asked him why it was that in Grof's psychedelic experiments where the
highest state of consciousness was induced, the subjects experienced the
trauma of *physical* birth and why this did not occur in the spontaneous variety of self-realization as witness Whitman, Millay, Beethoven and Owens?
Might Zen makyo sometimes include this painful memory? We wondered if
it was always necessary to cure the neuroses before one could penetrate the
deepest religious level. What of schizophrenics who frequently were visited
by mystical experiences yet were in a state of total disorientation?

We discussed humanistic psychology and transpersonal, whether man
was the measure of all things, why in ordinary meditation one seems to taste
some of each of the stratifications of the unconscious as if they were vertical.
Yet in deeper zazen, in sesshin, one seems to penetrate downward through
various horizontal layers in the unconscious. We found no answer.

We examined objective reality and experiential reality, scales of values,
my writings and his, *Introduction to Zen*, *Hara* and *Tao of Physics*.

It was like fishing in an unfathomable ocean teeming with riches. We
were deep-down honest with each other without fear of those value judgments that most human beings consider their god-given right, passing per-

sonal judgments on others whom they may scarcely know. No pretensions, no false modesty, no fear. There was a feeling of mutual understanding and empathy, complete acceptance of exactly what we were—no more and certainly no less. It was rare and absolutely wonderful. I felt as if all the fresh winds of the world were sweeping my dusty brain clean of debris.

I phoned Roshi and told him Dr. Ring was coming to the workshop on Saturday and would like to meet him.

"Why don't you come to the workshop too, Claire?" Roshi asked.

"Oh, thanks, I'd like to Roshi, but if I stay there all day I get too tired." I did not tell him that I still would have a dinner to cook for my guest requiring all the energy I possessed.

"Then come to lunch."

"Thank you, I shall be happy to."

On Saturday I went to the Center early and helped to carry the food outdoors. The buffet lunch was in the garden. The sun seemed to have come out especially for it after several days of rain. Martha and the kitchen staff had prepared a beautiful yellow mound of egg salad surrounded with alfalfa sprouts, homemade bread, Russian borscht soup, hot herb tea and homemade cookies made with honey, not the injurious refined white sugar.

I met Ken and we lunched together. I said to Roshi, "It's always so crowded here at the Center nowadays with all the people in the special long training program. I honestly thought you might prefer to have the older members not come too often so as to leave room for the newer people."

"But, Claire, you are our shining example."

Again I felt too stunned and happy to say a word. After so many years of struggle and discouragement it soothed my wounded feelings like a magic salve.

"And Claire, you used to come to all the Tuesday night Dharma dialogues. Now you never come."

"Oh Roshi, I should have told you. There have been so many muggings and rapes around here lately that it isn't safe for a woman to drive out alone at night. But all right. I'll come. And I *do* come every Sunday morning to listen to your teishos and always tell the Roshi when he has been in especially good form, don't I?"

He laughed, taking both my hands in his, saying nothing. It is the Zen way.

Why did Roshi like for me to appear at the Center? He often said it was good for the young people to have older people present. He never explained the reason and I didn't have sense enough to ask. One day a visiting mother of one of the young members furnished a clue. Her son reported it to me. There had been a picnic for parents. None of the older members of the Center were present—except the Roshi.

This mother had said to her son contemptuously, "Zen may be all right for the young but it's no good for mature people."

At today's workshop most of the visitors were middle-aged—a good portent. Roshi always asked me to mingle with the workshop people. When they asked me how long I'd been here and I replied, "Five years and I find Zen more wonderful every year," their eyes opened in surprise.

On Sunday night Blanch drove Kenneth and me to the airport, and we dined there. I had wanted them to meet.

As Kenneth kissed me goodbye, he said, "Zen is not for me, but I'm coming to see you again next summer, Claire."

A few weeks later he wrote that he had entered training at a Zen Center nearer his university. It was a fourteen hour drive to Snowbound or an expensive trip by air by way of New York City, entailing a change of planes.

I was absolutely exhausted after the three exciting days of Ken's visit. As I lay resting, however, I felt deeply satisfied, nourished in more ways than one. How unbelievably wonderful that men and women who are striving to realize their finest potentials can be friends without sex, without love, without romance, though pleasantly aware of each other as man and woman. This was like the beautiful friendships I had enjoyed with Northrop and Sinnott at Yale and had missed so painfully. It is the kind of deep trusting unjealous friendships that men enjoy so often with men but women with women so seldom.

As I lay resting I reviewed the various men I had known. It suddenly became evident that the men I had cared for most in my life had been aware of me as a human being as well as a woman—such as Theo, Leslie, Hans, Dexter and Lance and Haig, Northrop, Sinnott and Kolberg. And now Kenneth.

The following Sunday Kenneth returned with his daughter and they spent the day with me. He had driven her to Canada for her vacation, returning by way of Snowbound. The harmonious relationship of father and daughter was pleasant to observe.

During Kenneth's first visit his wife and I had held a long conversation on the telephone and afterward exchanged long friendly letters.

I now debated whether I should send her a quotation that might explain my warm relationship with men—including her husband—a relationship where sex, age, race, marital or social status, or ideologies no longer matter!

"It is ultimately the Self that. . . regulates one's human relationships.... Spiritually attuned... people find their way to one another.... The familiar bond of kinship or common interests are replaced by a different type of unity—a bond through the Self."

Chapter XVIII
SEVEN WONDERS OF THE INNER WORLD

It is against all the rules governing influenza to contract it so early in the Autumn season as September. But that is what I did. On the Friday preceding Labor Day I was brought to bed with an unusually virulent attack of flu. High fever, excruciating pains like clashing knives in the intestines and retching all night. Always in the middle of the night—never in the daytime.

I felt so chagrined at allowing myself to be ill that probably to punish myself, I fell and gashed my leg so deeply it was necessary to call the doctor. Usually when I was ill faithful friends came rushing to the rescue, regardless of germs. Blanch would always bring soup and flowers. Hannah would bring soup, Dexter fruit juices. He would sit beside my bed and hold my hand. Dexter and Lance and Haig through the years had made me feel so well loved that I was badly spoiled.

This time the phone never rang once. No one came, not even Marian with whom I was in constant communication. I felt weak, abandoned, unloved. I began to feel sorry for myself and ashamed that any good Buddhist should fall into such an ignominious state.

I well knew that seven of my closest friends were out of town for the Labor Day weekend. That didn't matter, I still thought they should at least phone me, though none of them even knew I was ill. I felt like an unreasonable child. I lay on my stomach to keep my spine straight and practiced zazen intermittently. It always lessened any illness and usually cheered me up tremendously. This time it did not cheer me up.

As I lay there alone, feeling forgotten, weak from fever, from vomiting, lack of sleep and food, an incredible incident occurred. It was as if a subterranean river of whose existence I was unaware suddenly rose to the surface, flowing over and around me until it all but drowned me.

The very *essence* of my beautiful experiences in Zen floated to the surface of consciousness. I sat up, took the large blue-lined notebook and pen always ready at my bedside and began to write rapidly—what do you suppose? Poetry—of all things—though I am not a poet—alas.

The first one was "Seven Wonders of the Inner World" to reassure myself that I—that all human beings—should count their blessings. It flowed smoothly—swiftly with scarcely a change necessary. Incredible as it may sound, I wrote 25 poems, enough for a small book. The poetry was poor but the content was interesting.

I wrote "The Magic of Meditation," "The Mystery of Music" (after listening to a Beethoven symphony), "The Joy of Aging" (to a woman deep in meditative practice), "Kundalini," describing the essence of my extraordinary experience with Dexter in New Haven, and a poem to Spring trees.

In our immediate neighborhood there are a score of fine houses with beautiful grounds filled with Japanese maples, magnolia, weeping elms, forsythia, lilacs, fragrant linden, maples with red or green flowerets, evergreens, honey locusts, ginkgoes and crab apples. In fact we have a dozen small, graceful, pink and white flossoming crab apple trees that surround our apartment buildings. They are as delicate as a Japanese print.

Frequently I walk about our neighborhood to note the progress of growing things. One day all barriers were lowered. I seemed to step over into the world of nature. The beauty of the trees flowed into me so intoxicatingly it was almost more than I could endure. So *now* I wrote a poem about it, "I Walk In Beauty."

The creative stream carries all before it, wrecking everything in its path—rest, sleep and meals. Like the Mississippi at the flood, it cares nothing for its victim's convenience or health. It obeys no laws but its own. It possesses the strength and ruthlessness of an elemental force of nature.

I wrote on and on for several days, unable to stop. Weakness disregarded, illness ignored. I no longer seemed to have control over my own life. Apparently zazen sets inner forces of creativity in motion and things merely happen without one's volition.

Later I gave several of these poems to Roshi. He said, "I am no judge of poetry, but I think they are beautiful. 'The Magic of Meditation' should be put on the bulletin board and I'll give it to Freddie to print in the *Zen Voice*." They never were, why I never knew.

Later at Christmas I had some of them xeroxed and sent in place of my usual letter of progress to my list of 100 out of town friends to whom I never had time to write.

Only one poem I considered good enough to submit to a magazine. That was the first one I wrote and the best. After the response to my article, "Self-realization—Induced and Spontaneous" in the *Journal of Altered States of Consciousness*, they promptly published it. The poem was:

SEVEN WONDERS OF THE INNER WORLD

i: NATURE AND THE COSMIC RHYTHM

Why should I tremble
For my future
Why should anyone doubt
The innate nature of man
When all men are endowed
With fabulous inner resources,
With the seven wonders
Of the inner world,
Proven means of actualizing
Our noblest potentials,
Inherent means of realizing the self?

How can I,
How can anyone despair—
However weary our body—
Or weighed down by the strife

And suffering of the world—
When the provocative Spring breeze on our cheek
Is a kiss of promise,
When the burst of Spring blossoms
Renews the hope we feared had died,
When the misty greenness
Of new leafing trees
So young and tender,
So pure and perfect
Awakens the beyond within,
When the unending expanse of sky
Filled with hundreds of majestic storm clouds
Built up like fabulous castles
Of white and gray and black,
Suddenly reveals in its very midst
An unknown something, a current of energy,
A presence,
And the sunrise one morning,
Flung like gold over a gray world,
Brings the eternal into the now;
How can we ever despair
So long as nature can restore us
To the rhythm of the universe?

ii: ART AND PURIFICATION

Why should I lament
My own imperfections
Or those of sentient beings in general
So long as man
Struggling in pain and poverty,
Is capable of creating music
That renews our inner harmony
With a symphony by Beethoven, for example,
Creates a Gothic cathedral
That leaves us strangely purified,
Exalts us with a glimpse of eternal beauty
In a painting by Leonardo,
Integrates our fragmented senses,
Intellect and inner self
Through the poetry of Dante?
How can we ever forget
The forgotten potentials of the race,
So long as man can create by means of art
A momentary manifestation
Of Absolute beauty
And so long as we can be purified
By man's made beauty?

iii: PASSION AND HARMONY

How can I or anyone
Be a stranger and afraid
When there can be unleashed in us a passion
So intense, so integrative,
We become one with another human being
And are made whole again—
For a moment?
How can we feel alienated
In a world we never made
When a shattering climax
Arouses emotion so elemental
It plunges us to the very roots of life,
Seeming to answer all questions,
Offer solutions to all problems,
Obliterate tensions and conflicts—
For an hour?
How can we feel out of tune
With the scheme of life
When the force of our own passion
Is so primordial
We die an ecstatic little death
And are born again radiantly in harmony
With ourselves, with others and life itself—
For a day?

iv: LOVE AND LOVE OF MANKIND

How can I weep for loneliness
When it is possible for me,
For all sentient beings,
To know love,
Even if only once—past or present?
For to receive love
Is to live in an eternal Spring
Filled with sweetness so poignant
It can scarcely be borne.
And to give love
Is to be imbued with a selflessness
That enriches us forever.
How can we ever mourn
For the transciency of love
When we remember personal love
Is but a rehearsal
For the higher love—
Of which we all—potentially—are capable
Love of mankind?

v: a) THOUGHT AND COMPASSION

How can I,
How can anyone
Fear that Western man
Is debilitated by his neuroses,
When we can explore
The dangerous country of the unconscious,
See the misleading maze of human motivation—
Our own and others'—
Flooded to the far corners
With the dazzling light
Of the Freudian science of psychology
And the Jungian psychology of religion,
When we observe and acquire
Illumined comprehension
Of the causes and solutions
Of other men's problems—
And our own,
When we discover
That the self is born with unbelievable potentials,
Is imbued with the virtues of ideal man
Striving to free itself
From neurotic entanglements,
From imprisonment by the modern ogre—
The ego,
And we are shown a way to freedom
That is known as self-realization
By an experienced guide known as Carl Jung?
How can anyone protest
That the struggle is futile
Having witnessed and participated
In the heroic adventure—
Of human thought at its boldest and bravest,
Gaining thereby understanding of human beings—
Unloved and unenlightened—
That fills us with selfless compassion?

v: b) THOUGHT AND WHOLENESS

Who can allow illness or misfortune
To depress or discourage,
When reason can be exercised
Like a fabulous horse
Bearing us on its flight with Plato
Mounting like a winged horse
Into the realm of eternal Ideas,

Until we feel accepted opinions and appearances
Fall away like unsubstantial dust,
Until—beholder and experiencer
Of eternal verities—
We return to earth eager to pursue the good,
The true and the beautiful?
Having witnessed and experienced
The majesty of reason,
The masculine principle of the universe,
Having felt it awaken and unite with intuition,
The feminine principle,
We know a wholeness never known before.
Was this the secret goal
Of the subtlest of all masters of dialectic:
That reason and intuition
Should reign together
In the good life
And the good society?
Thus we are privileged through thought—
If abstract and profound and exalted enough—
To unite our reason and intuition
In the pure ambience
Of the immortal Socrates,
And perhaps some sweet day, through dialectic,
To experience self-realization.

vi: CREATIVITY AND ENTERING THE
UNIVERSAL STREAM

How can we ever complain
That we are unfulfilled,
When evolution or heredity
Bestows on us the capacity for creativity,
When, creating,
We engage in an inner cleansing,
Discarding our most cherised errors,
Our most brilliant opinions—unsubstantiated,
Our half-truths and wishful thinking,
Because we are searching in fear and trembling
For the most dangerous and elusive treasure
This earth has to offer—
Ultimate truth?
How can we fail
To express ourselves fully
When, creating,
We construct a new world of our own making
Where there are no wasteful social obligations,
No wearying domestic chores,

No distracting personalities,
Or worldly responsibilities—
Necessary but time-consuming,
Where bodily ailments are transcended,
Ego diminished
And we seem to enter the universal stream
Enabling us to speak to—
And for—all men?
These are the privileges and powers granted
If we create something of beauty and truth
To nourish all man.

vii: MEDITATION AND SELF-REALIZATION

How can we ignore the human potential
For psychic growth
Or the natural laws
That govern spiritual development,
If ever once we have deeply meditated,
Followed the Zen path of the universal Buddha
Or the noble Tibetan, Hindu or Sufi way,
Quieted the discursive intellect,
Diminished the troublesome ego,
Released the deeper unconscious,
Awakened the True-self
And liberated the latent good,
The compassion, selflessness and wisdom
Inherent in all men?

How can we deny that meditation
May lead to full realization of the self
If ever once we have known
The actualization of the self—
That cataclysmic psychic drama
 Precipitated by death of the ego,
When everything on earth is obliterated
By a blaze of light,
When our intuitive mind
Identifies with the Universal mind
And we unite with ultimate reality
In ineffable ecstasy,
And are reborn
Purified beyond our own belief;
When we experience intuitive insights
Into the nature of things,
See that the universal scheme is good,
That man's Original-nature is good,
That man suffers because he is in conflict

With the laws of life,
In conflict with the laws of the universe,
Out of touch with his own True-self,
Out of tune with the cosmic rhythm,
When we see that all things are one
And that we love all people
Regardless of social status, sex or age
Religion or the lack of it?
After being blinded
By the beauty of cosmic consciousness—
The highest state of consciousness
Possible to man—
We find, to our surprise,
Our behavior and values transformed;
Our lives,
Heretofore dominated by ego, ego, EGO,
Now, to our astonishment,
Seem directed by universal consciousness,
And our days filled
With love and service,
Certitude and creativity,
Wisdom and joy—
Always joy.

So how can I,
How can anyone doubt
That life possesses purpose and meaning,
When every man is endowed
With the inherent capacity
To participate wholly or partially
In these seven wonders
Of the inner world:
Restoration to the rhythm of the universe
Through nature,
Purification through art,
Harmony with life through passion,
Love of mankind through personal love,
Compassion and wholeness through thought,
Entrance into the universal stream
Through creativity—
And above all—self-realization
Through meditation—
A spiritual plane
Where we can look back and see
That nature and art,
Passion and love,
Thought and creativity,
Are but means of purification,

And our responses but preparation
For the completest of all forms of purification
Self-realization or the spiritual experience,
Said to be the only psychological process
Known to man
That actualizes his finest potentials,
Sweeps away anger,
Fear and hate,
Worldly values,
Desires for transient things,
Sensory indulgence
And other defilements,
Replacing them with permanent values
Of the uncreated,
The unborn, the undiscriminated?
How can we disregard
The primary function of man:
Acceleration of the next step
In his own evolution
By means of the seventh resource
Of the inner world,
As perhaps the only way
For the race to survive
Its own destruction—
Now steadily advancing?

No longer shall I fear
For my personal destiny.
No man should fear for the eventual fate
Of the human race
When we know that self-realization
Is possible to all men,
That it can guide the changing man of today—
While he is simultaneously changing the world—
Into a better society for all men
In the New Age now dawning.

Chapter XIX
BLISS AND LIBERATION

Frequently in his talks at the Zen Center the Roshi reminded the aspirants that both physical and emotional problems are excellent incentives to the deeper practice of zazen. We seldom recognized the connection. He also emphasized the fact that the East believes body-mind is one, not two separate entities as believed in the West.

I ushered in this New Year of 1975 with a prize example of influenza which exacerbated my large collection of minor ills. In February I was off to Florida for my winter vacation. I was so weak I could walk through the airport only because I leaned heavily on the arm of my solicitous friend, Blanch. I was ten pounds underweight. During the four hour flight I practiced zazen with great fervor for fear I might not be able to walk off the plane under my own power.

After arriving in Palm Beach I was still unable to walk even two blocks. I was obliged to take the hotel limousine everywhere I felt it necessary to go. Usually medical doctors are not interested in functional ailments. Only organic diseases, for which they can prescribe quantities of medication.

Never once did any doctor investigate my mode of living to determine the possible cause and cure of my various ills. They only saw the physical, never the psychological, and treated symptoms. They never suggested anything but sleeping pills and tranquilizers which I refused to take. My body seemed to reject any form of medication as if it were an insult. Some doctors dismissed all my ailments as "just old age." I knew this was not true.

My incapacitated condition was still a mystery to me in the winter of 1975 and a painful anachronism. It was deeply mortifying for anyone on the spiritual path to allow herself to succumb to so many disabilities. It was refutation of all I believed in concerning the nature of zazen. Chagrined, I told no one the details. There was no escaping Roshi's eagle eye, however, and he offered several helpful suggestions. I was utterly disgusted with myself. I felt guilty that I had allowed such infirmities to develop.

At the hotel in Palm Beach when I practiced zazen on Mondays, everything seemed better. When I practiced it on Tuesday my back grew too tired. I practiced a mild form of yoga on Wednesday and it helped. On Thursday yoga caused my heart to pound. A walk of a block refreshed me one day and the next day was too exhausting. I would read a serious book to take my mind off myself and it was relaxing. Next night I read the same book and it caused a sick pain in the back of my head. Nothing was consistent. Nothing provided reliable guidelines. Worst of all, I had lost my appetite. Yet I was living in a hotel famous for its cuisine and its excellent chef. What irony, what wasted opportunity.

Despite all my incapacities I managed to live through the days fairly well. It was at night that my bed was transformed into a battle field. All the ailments that seemed afraid of the daylight crept out to attack at night in the dark, like vicious mice, if mice are ever vicious.

The recital of these intimate details might appear indelicate, in poor taste or inexcusable except for the major role they were to play in my inner development. Arthritic pains in my fingers, left arm and right hip stabbed me like so many knives in the night. Always the pain was far more intense at night when I was not using these joints than in the daytime when I was—ironically enough. Diverticulosis awakened me in the middle of the night, filling the transverse colon with very hard bricks. Skin eruptions here and there and everywhere were so irritating I could have screamed from sheer frustration.

And there was a generous assortment of other unmentionable aches and pains. About three o'clock every morning I awakened with a violent start, my heart pounding wildly. First I lay still, then practiced Jacobsen's progressive relaxation. The conscious mind instructs each voluntary muscle separately and progressively down the body to "let go." And it does just that—usually—but not now. So I would sit up and read for several hours every night. In former nights reading generally caused drowsiness. No more. Now nothing worked. I awakened each morning with my pajamas dripping with perspiration. It was all mortifying, painful, debilitating, stupid and I felt quite unnecessary.

I was desperate. I needed help and immediately. So I succumbed to a naturopath. His vitamins and minerals were all reputed to be natural products, not synthetic chemicals. He prescribed eight pills with each meal, enzymes made from pineapple and dessicated liver. He injected B-12 into my thigh every other day—all at a cost of hundreds of dollars. I warned him that vitamins induced erotic dreams in me. He said they activated the sex hormones but scoffed at my idea. Soon erotic dreams awakened me violently in the night. I was obliged to discontinue all vitamins.

I even endeavored to interpret my dreams, something I had never been able to do despite my admiration for Freud and Jung. Mine were always unhappy dreams. I was forever searching for something I could not find. I went on trips, became lost and no one could or would direct me. I went shopping for some mysterious something which I was forever unable to find. Often in my dreams people rebuffed me and wounded my feelings. That seemed strange, for in real life most people were extremely kind to me most of the time. If not—I said nothing. I buried my hurt. I reminded myself that Jung said dreams are designed as a compensation to maintain a balance between the conscious mind and the unconscious. I did not care for this kind of balance, thank you. I went back to my old childhood prayers to a *personal* God in which I had not believed since I was twenty-five, when the prevalence of evil in the world had argued him out of existence. Nothing did the slightest good.

There was one assignment, however, which I must honor, no matter how I felt. Jean Rindge, editor of the *Human Dimensions* quarterly, had requested that I write a paper for her describing my spontaneous spiritual and psychological awakening in New Haven. I felt extremely grateful to her so I strove to meet the deadline.

I smiled ruefully to think that she was the first editor who had ever asked for such a personal document. All the new human potential magazines contained endless and brilliant essays on self-realization from every angle—but one—the experiential. There was an unwritten law that no respectable, scholary, analytical, scientific journal would dare demean itself by publishing true personal accounts of the highest state of consciousness, about which the scientists were all writing theoretically. What irony?

I was too ill to write for more than one hour every morning. Finally it was finished. The deadline was met and the manuscript mailed off to John White, who was the guest editor for this next issue.

Later my paper illicited a comment that proved particularly restorative to me. The Yale philosopher Northrop, author of *Meeting of East and West*, wrote me, "It shows your autobiographical genius."

It didn't, of course. I was no genius in anything. I only wished I were. But it proved more rejuvenating than an injection of B-12 in my thigh. My body was a nuisance to me and I was extremely annoyed at my physical condition. I was also completely mystified. I knew Roshi repeatedly told us that body-mind were one. Yet that winter of 1975 I was a total mess—hopeless and helpless. I was not too unhappy though. How could I be, with all my beautiful spiritual experiences of the past and better ones in the future? I hoped.

The next winter of 1976 when I flew down to Florida, I reclined in my seat as we flew above the clouds—rather a sacrilegious act, I always felt. I planned a very different regimen for this vacation. I was determined to recover my health or die in the attempt. Now I knew the cause and cure.

Recently I had read books and seen documentaries on television that explained one of our most prevalent modern ills—stress. The concept of stress was entirely new to me. Stress means an overload of the nervous system with a greater load than it can adequately cope with. Stress also causes death of certain body cells about which I am still ignorant. Stress—to my utter astonishment, can be caused by a variety of things—even too much happiness (me), too great stimulation (me), overwork (me), exhaustion—mental or physical (me) and loss of sleep (me).

In some cases stress in adults may be psychological in origin, causing psychosomatic ailments. In that case it originates in infancy or childhood if one failed to give natural physical expression to the pain or hurt inflicted by others. The natural primitive reaction still alive in us all, though supressed by our civilized society, is to strike out with the hands or kick with the feet—or both. Usually a child does neither because she longs above everything to be loved. She buries the hurt or anger in her unconscious and even in adulthood it may erupt as physical ills.

Good heavens, I thought, even while playing with the lunch the pretty stewardess set before me, did I belong in this distressing category? The machinations of the unconscious I considered fascinating and helpful. Not frightening or shameful. Certainly in childhood and girlhood I had been admonished every day to "act like a little lady," not get angry, not cry, not strike back either physically or verbally.

(When my tray was removed I continued my interior dialougue.)

Or was the source of my difficulties also that I was too intense about everything, pleasure as well as pain? Roshi had said to me, "Claire, you respond to everybody and everything so intensely you drain yourself of energy. You give too much of yourself."

Or, I asked myself, have I too great a zest for life? I enjoy everything. I want to do everything, see everything, learn everything, experience everything—sorrow as well as joy.

My common sense, however, said, The trouble is, Claire, you never listen to your own common sense. You're a fool to destroy your own health for no earthly reason. Other people possess sufficient instinct of self-preservation to stop when they're exhausted. Oh, no, not you. You think there's great merit in working until you collapse on the floor. Rest and sleep you consider a waste of precious time.

But how did it all start? I wondered. What causes this driving passion? Am I like most Americans—a victim of the Protestant work ethic? All my life I have considered it a virtue to fill every sixty minutes of every hour with eighty minutes of activity. I feel guilty if I am not busy every second though I know Zen teaches us, and experience has demonstrated to me, that the greatest spiritual growth occurs when one is doing nothing, not when one is active.

I reviewed my life. An inner voice said, Well, Claire, it all began with you a long time ago. It is cumulative. Even in high school and college you exhausted your strength. Maybe you have a mesomorphic drive with a weak ectomorphic physique.

But that can't be. Didn't Dr. Sheldon somatotype my physique in his laboratory in New York as a 4-4-4 in endomorphy, mesomorphy and ectomorphy, respectively?

Well, never mind that now. When you were manager of that bookshop in New York you worked eight hours, six days a week, went out to dine or dance or see a play every night in the week and wrote like mad on your book on Sundays and holidays. And for those two weeks before Christmas every year you worked every night until midnight in the bookshop and spent all Christmas day in bed with a high psychic fever from sheer exhaustion. And incidentally, you never earned an extra penny for all that overtime.

I shrugged. I never thought of that before.

There are many things you never thought of before, young lady, and its high time you did. And when you were married to Thursty, with a nice husband and three devoted servants to help you, you still managed to work beyond the danger point. You've been an idiot and you deserve to pay for all your folly as you are jolly well doing right now. And another thing, Claire. You expended too much time and energy unnecessarily on all that research for your Zen paper for *Transpersonal Psychologies*.

Oh no, oh no. I learned so much that—

And you have too active and too gay a social life. (Some sudden turbulence caused me to open my eyes and quickly close them again, admonishing myself to "Relax, relax!") Even when you had those beautiful friendships with Dexter and Lance, they were delightful but too, too intense. (Haig and

Sally are more temperate.) You were in a state of excitement and happiness twenty-four hours a day. The nervous system cannot sustain such a continuous strain.

Roshi warned you several times that you had too active a social life but oh, no, you would not heed his words of wisdom. Even today when you go shopping with Edith to help you, do you stop and go home when you are tired? Oh no, you continue until you have purchased every item on your list. Then you drag yourself home like a sack of potatoes. Even an idiot would have more common sense.

Well, I protested in self-defense, remember I inherited a weak nervous system from my father.

And your mother was never sick a day in her life.

Well, I know you're right. So I promise when we arrive in Florida this winter I won't lift a finger, think a thought, or write a word, not even letters to my friends.

You never write letters anyway. I wonder that you have a friend left to your name.

I won't even talk but devote my days to doing sweet nothing. I will conserve every ounce of energy. Quiet, solitude, silence, no social life, and no doctors, thank you. All writing and spiritual life must await their turn. My physical health will take precedence over everything.

During all of my 79 years my will power had assumed that it knew better what was good for my body than it did. For the first time in my life I must listen to it.

This winter I had left Snowbound in mid-January and was flying directly to Miami to visit Seymour and Patty Tate for ten days. Later she would drive me from Miami Beach to Palm Beach. The Tates had invited me to be their guest at their beach club.

They installed me in an elegant suite facing the ocean. Seymour was on the board of directors and most solicitous. Was my bed too hard or too soft? It could be changed. Did I want the air conditioning on? The window open? A paper would be left at my door every morning. Did I want breakfast in bed? Or there was a kitchenette in the suite in case I cared to use it. This was the way the refrigerator worked and this was the way to turn on the stove. And here were some books he had brought me.

Previously the Tates had invited me to stay at their home in Michigan. There Patty had given me the red carpet treatment as if I were royalty. Dinner parties with all the local celebrities and constant solicitude.

I had informed them that I needed a great deal of rest and quiet this year. Every morning while they took their music lessons and practiced, I sat in their cabana. I never tired of watching the ocean and breathing the good salt air. Every afternoon while they played golf I took a long nap, practiced meditation, read and did sweet nothing.

In the evening I enjoyed dining with my host and hostess at the club. One night we had dinner in their apartment which they, with all their millions, preferred preparing themselves. It was a quiet family evening. For some reason, I forget the occasion, I said, "It is not easy being a woman alone in the world."

When we rose from the table Seymour put his arm around me, kissed my hair and murmured, "We love having you with us."

"Not half so much as I love being with you-all."

Kindness, solicitude and affection were the best medicine imaginable, added, of course, to rest and the deep relaxation of zazen. I began to feel and apparently look better. One evening when they came by my suite to take me to dinner all decked out in my only evening gown Seymour whispered in my ear, "Why, Claire, you look radiant. You must have a lover." He introduced me to his friends as "a distinguished writer with impeccable taste and very demanding standards."

What did he mean? Was I too demanding? I must watch it. Never, never did I wish to do anything to annoy Seymour. I was so deeply indebted to him for his great kindness and skilled assistance with my investments. He had lifted an intolerable burden from my shoulders. But what could one do for people who had everything—and millions besides? All I could do was give them flowers and books, appreciation, admiration and love. Does anyone ever have enough of these gifts?

At the end of my visit, Patty drove me to Palm Beach. We had a long intimate conversation. She had experienced some altered states of consciousness herself. We had a delicious lunch at the Palm Beach Hotel.

It is a quiet old-fashioned hotel built around two large patios open to the sun and sky but protected from the strong seashore winds. One could dine al fresco in the south patio. The north patio was designed for social life out of doors with sun umbrellas, tables and chairs.

During the first eleven days I continued to concentrate on rest and quiet. In the morning I sat in the patio and read the *New York Times* or fell into a pleasant reverie. It was wonderfully soothing to sit out of doors, no roofs to oppress one's head, no walls to imprison one. To be able to see the sky and clouds, to feel the warmth of the sun and the cool breeze on one's face was a delight. To hear the wind in the palm trees that sounded exactly like rain—it was all very restorative. I listened to the birds singing, the mourning doves with their provocative laments, the mockingbirds trilling away with abandon saying," "Gurdjieff! Gurdjieff!" as plain as human speech. Silently I urged them to sing, "Buddha! Buddha!" but they did not seem to hear me for some reason.

All the staff of the hotel seemed exceedingly pleasant when I spoke to them. The owner, the manager, the reservation clerk, the chef, the cashier, the telephone operator, and in the dining room or out in the patio, the maitre d'hotel, the captain, the waiters and waitresses who were usually college students. So I lived and moved and breathed in a wholly harmonious atmosphere. A situation that was essential to my well being. Friction and discord were too upsetting. Though I reminded myself continually that the Zen Buddhist goal is to become impassive and serene, transcending both joy and sorrow. Would I ever attain that high mind-state?

One day fate dropped a fly in the ointment as it invariably does sooner or later. I wonder why? To offer a challenge to greater inner growth?

One frequently overheard guests commenting to each other on what a well run hotel this was. Nevertheless, one night the only unhappy looking waiter in the dining room dumped my entire dinner on the table at once—

soup, meat and vegetables, salad and dessert, even my demitasse of decaffinated coffee. We were paying a high price to receive formal elegant service with all courses served separately.

I was horrified to find that I was angry at the waiter. Anger is impossible to a highly developed person. For twelve years after my former awakening in New Haven anger had been impossible. Two of my best friends to my astonishment had attacked me bitterly after reading *Awakening to the Good*. Something beyond my control caused me to feel spontaneous compassion for them. To my surprise I heard myself endeavoring to reestablish their self-esteem of which my book had inadvertently deprived them.

Now I did not express my displeasure at the waiter's breach of etiquette. The next time, however, he was assigned to me and I said, "Peter, you seem like a nice young fellow. Would you be terribly unhappy if you served my dinner in separate courses after this? You see, while I eat my soup, my vegetables get cold. And while I eat my meat I have to look at that dirty soup bowl and it begins to smell."

Peter never committed that sin again. But my reaction of compassion should have been automatic, not one of conscious design. I complimented him whenever possible and developed a genuine concern for his personal problems which he was only too glad to confide briefly to some interested listener.

Other guests complained of Peter's dumping their entire dinner onto the table too. I said to them, "We are strangers to this waiter. He does not hate *us*. He hates something or someone else. Aldous Huxley's wife, Laura, wrote a best-selling book called *You Are Not the Target*. This poor fellow probably had a quarrel with his girl friend or worse, with his mother or father. So he was striking out at us as substitutes."

I expected these two months to be a rest cure, nothing else. The entire day was devoted to improving the health of my body. After lunch I took a nap of two or three hours, practiced Jabobsen's progressive relaxation, sat in long deep zazen, then it was time to bathe and dress for dinner. I expected no benefits other than physical.

This new regime had been in effect for three weeks. My aches and pains were disappearing. One morning I awakened after a particularly deep sleep. I lay motionless, amazed at the little fountains of joy bubbling up in my chest for no good reason. I rose and looked out the window. There was sun after two whole days of continuous rain—unusual weather for Florida. It was surprising to find myself spontaneously raising my arms and saying aloud, "Hail to the rising sun," like some early pagan. Then I noticed all the flowers on the dresser.

"Why, it's February 11th," I said aloud. "My birthday! I'm 80 years old today and have never been happier in my life. It doesn't make sense."

Yes it does, a voice answered me silently. Nature intends for old age to be the happiest time of life because it's a beautiful spiritual preparation for a beautiful death.

I buried my nose in the bouquet of spring flowers sent me yesterday by Seymour and Patty, then the fabulous red roses sent by my faithful cook, Margaret. She sent them every year on my birthday. And the exquisite bouquet sent by Hannah and Dexter. I recalled the warm loving voices of the young men who had called me long distance last night, Dexter and Haig—not Lance this year, alas. I glanced at the pile of affectionate birthday cards and letters. From my cousins in California, Laura and Margaret, from my New York friends, Alice and Carol, from Lucy and Louise and Lois in New Haven, Peggy and Gordon in Fairfield, Doris and Eric in Weekapaug, and from Zen friends in Snowbound, Susie and Bob, Marian, Blanch and others.

How dear of all these people to remember a woman of eighty with such messages of affection. I don't understand it but I thrive on it and love them in return. It is obvious why *I* should love them but it is not obvious why *they* should love me. My body may be eighty but I feel twenty-five today.

I flung my pink pajamas on the bed and stood before the long mirror in the bathroom door scrutinizing the naked figure before it. Tall and slender, thank heavens no lumps or humps in the wrong places, though my front leaves a few things to be desired. The legs are still shapely but the arms are thin and ugly. And the face—lines—but there could be more. Hair grey—but it could be white.

I studied my face in the mirror. Today this face was suffused with a pink glow, an inner radiance from deep sleep—as it used to be after I had had a long swim in the ocean or my husband had made love to me for hours, or after prolonged zazen. I laughed to think that all four of these "exercises" produce the same external glow but very different results—deep sleep, swimming, sex and zazen.

I gazed at this face incredulously. How is it possible for any woman to look like this at eighty? It isn't possible. Has zazen discovered the fountain of youth? Wasn't it in Florida that Ponce de Leon sought for the fountain of eternal youth? He looked in the wrong place. He should have looked within himself—as we do in meditation.

After I dressed I touched the flowers and birthday cards as I left the room. The dear young Zen people, so idealistic, so inexperienced, full of energy and laughter. So loving and lovable, so solicitous of my comforts as if I were some fragile flower, so oblivious to my many faults, so appreciative of my virtues and many I do not even possess.

Feeling alive and tingling in every atom of my body I strolled through the early morning sunshine to the patio for breakfast in the open air. I no longer resented drinking herb tea instead of the over-stimulating coffee I once loved so much, spreading my toast with tasteless vegetable fat instead of butter, eating my cereal with skimmed milk instead of the rich cream I once indulged in in former years. Such trivia no longer mattered. Was my former indigestion expiation for indiscretions and ignorance concerning diet?

I sat at the table as still as a Buddha with no wasted motion—an art meditation had taught me. Sitting motionless has a sweetness about it. It allows all the richness of one's being to rise to the surface like cream. I sat in utter peace. No pressures. No coercion. No duties. Suddenly everything that had been suppressed with difficulty those last three weeks of thinkingless rest and deep meditation now leapt into renewed life. Never, I said to myself, in all my 80 years have my senses been so alive, my thinking so clear, my love of people been so—so universal, intuitive insights so quick and my body so eager and buoyant.

When I returned to my room after breakfast on that birthday morning, I was overwhelmed by an irresistible urge to write a new book. It surged through me in mighty waves. I promptly telephoned for a rental typewriter to be delivered immediately. On my 80th birthday I commenced this very book. Every morning from 9:00 to 12:00 or sometimes 1:00 (which was too long) I wrote by hand and by machine faster than human fingers are designed to move.

There were no preconceived plans, no outline. I surrendered to some power beyond my control. I just let it happen. It was as if I were merely a channel serving some force greater than I. It did all the work. Never in my long life had writing been such a joy. Never had it flowed with such ease and rapidity (far more so than when I wrote the *factual* paper for Tart's book). Now indeed "my work was my practice." It was what Roshi would call "living zazen."

But the lingering poison of Protestant Puritanism injected a feeling of guilt at such happiness. I feared some dire disaster must surely be imminent to punish me for being too happy. But Zen Buddhism teaches that nature intends for man to be happy so long as he lives in harmony with the laws of life and of the Dharma, the law of the universe. Man suffers because he has misinterpreted these laws, distorted them and deprived the human race of its natural heritage of joy.

Maintaining this euphoric state, however, was like walking a high wire. One misstep and I fell into disaster. If I talked too much, ate too much, slept too little, practiced too little meditation, or worked too long, then all my dormant ailments leapt up gleefully to attack again. Self-discipline—that is the secret of well-being, I reminded myself daily.

At noon when I forced myself to stop writing, my back ached, my fingertips tingled but I felt exhilerated, purified, filled with *joriki*—that kind of energy apparently peculiar to zazen. I was to write on this manuscript seven days a week for seven unbroken months and produce 700 pages of the first draft. I called it my seven month's baby. (I was blissfully unaware, of course, that it would require nine more months to write the second draft with Charles and Barbara to help me with the typing).

Words swept through my mind and out of my fingers like a swift, smoothly flowing river. All my other books had required four or five years to write. I did not know why I was writing this book. I was seized by a mysterious force and carried happily away. The old ego was completely inundated so long as I was writing and remained "in the cosmic order."

I wrote, I ate, I slept, I practiced zazen. I talked only to the trees and flowers. I grew happier and healthier every day. At mealtime all foods agreed with me. I discovered it was not so much *what* I ate as the state of my nerves, body and mind at that time. They must be deeply relaxed—that was the secret of good digestion. In fact, relaxation seemed to be the secret of all good things.

Every morning I awakened in amazement. Life no longer seemed such an interminable struggle. Everything came more easily now. Living had always entailed so many struggles underneath all the happiness. A struggle to keep the money one had or to make a living, a struggle to make a successful career, or a happy marriage, a struggle to keep one's friends, and an even greater one to maintain one's love, to keep one's health and looks, and the most difficult struggle of all was to abide continuously on a spiritual plane in daily living.

This winter in Florida the immediate effects of meditation or absence of it were so obvious it was frightening. It was uncanny. For zazen places in your hands a power over things, people and events that is unbelievable. I discovered that if you fail to sit for an hour before breakfast, people irritate you and you irritate people all day long. Everything goes slightly awry. The waiter is sullen because you ask for the fork he forgot; a woman bumps into you, you turn your ankle and she blames you; the melon that agreed with you yesterday gives you indigestion today; a sudden wind blows up on the way home from the hair-dresser and leaves your new coiffeur in disarray. The usual glow of life turns grey, as if the sun had disappeared behind a cloud.

If, however, morning meditation has been prolonged and profound, the waiter is all smiles, the woman assumes all the blame for your collision, the melon agrees with you like ambrosia of the gods, and no wind dares to dishevel your hair. Everything falls into its proper place. Everything behaves itself for your benefit. All life glows in the light of your own inner harmony. You feel happy, moving with the eternal flow, attuned to Tao. For minutes, hours, sometimes for consecutive days you feel in harmony with yourself, with others, with the nature of things, with the eternal Dharma.

These incidents, minor or major, advantageous or disadvantageous, appear incredible even while they are occurring. They seem so beyond the possible that you almost become superstitious, even tempted to succumb to belief in all sorts of folklore and myths. I was grateful that my experiences were grounded in Zen principles and time-tested truths, and in *personal* awareness of the primal unity of all things. Even the science of the functions of the two hemispheres of the brain did not explain such mysteries. In some of these uncanny incidents I was obliged to remind myself of Buddhist teachings—that if one is at one with reality, which is perfect, one participates in that perfection, however briefly and partially—therefore nothing can go wrong.

Living in the worldly world, no longer among religious trainees, was a severe test. To protect my fragile spiritual life and my creative work, I found myself weaving a little cocoon of privacy about myself. I attempted to reduce distractions. I shunned all social activities and superficial conversations. But fate seemed against it.

Of course, I enjoyed briefly passing the time of day with the young college students who waited on tables. At whatever table I happened to sit three or four of them came by at each meal to talk a minute or two. At home I had trained our servants never to talk in the dining room. This was different.

The first night I appeared in my passionate pink evening gown, three young men rushed up. One said, "I didn't know raspberry sherbert was on the menu tonight."

Why me? I asked myself as I ordered dinner. There are many younger, prettier women here. It doesn't make sense.

There was one special young man, James, who was to be a senior next year. He was tall, slender, and very attractive with a nice wit. We felt an instant rapport, a natural almost irresistible mutual attraction that increased steadily in warmth. He offered to xerox the reprints of my article, "Self-realization—Induced and Spontaneous." For this was the time the requests came in and I had brought only one copy to Florida. James also brought an extra serving of papaya and the largest piece of pecan pie. He asked if he might write me when he went to California at the end of the season to finish his education. Why me? It didn't make sense.

Even stranger things happened. One night at dinner a young woman sitting at the next table with another woman rose and came over to my table. We had never seen each other before in our lives. "I see you are dining alone. Why don't you eat all your meals with my sister and me as long as you're here?"

I was stunned. "Thank you. You're very kind, but that would not be possible. I'm writing a book and I'm thinking of it all the time. Even if I'm only staring out the window."

Why me? For heaven's sake. The dining room was full of women dining alone. Resort hotels are havens for lonely widows.

One sunny morning I took my manuscript and notebooks, pens and pencils, down to one of the tables in the North patio. I thought I was well barricaded against intrusions. A pretty, expensively dressed woman soon came up, introduced herself, sat down and told me that after her husband died she became manager of his factory. She manufactured pens and pencils. "I heard you were a writer so I'd like to send you some pens and pencils."

Eavesdroppers, it is said, never hear anything good about themselves. I overheard two women talking at the table behind me. "Yes, I do know who she is. Her name is Claire Myers Owens. She's a writer."

"Oh yes. I've seen her in the other patio with her books and papers. She never pays the slightest attention to anyone if she can avoid it."

"No, she's not social at all. I think its very unfriendly."

Sometimes I listened to various guests at other tables. They talked of sports, politics, and business if they were men. If they were women they talked of clothes, food, children, their ailments, the ailments of their family, friends, and friends' friends and complained of their family, friends, and servants. It filled me with terrible sadness. Here were all these wealthy women free of work, free of husbands and children, frittering their last years away on trivialities. These could be golden years of advancement on the spiritual path, enveloped in the joy it alone can bring. When would our culture bring this new way of life to them?

One morning out in the patio I was writing vigorously. An English woman walked up to me. "I hate to interrupt you but I'm told you do meditation and that's why you are so happy all the time. Will you teach me to meditate?" She had recently suffered a great sorrow and was driven to it. I did the best I could.

The only spiritual woman who spoke to me was the companion of a very rich titled woman from London. The former was an ardent Christian who had had some mystical experiences.

On another morning at breakfast a beautiful blonde young woman who looked like Zaza Gabor and had a similar Austrian accent stopped at my table. "Excuse me. I heard a typewriter going and I asked the chambermaid if someone was writing a book. She said yes, you were. What's it about?"

"Self-realization and meditation."

"Oh, I'm interested in both of those subjects. Will you have dinner with me tonight? Maybe we could dine together every night."

"Thank you. Some night soon perhaps. But frankly I am deeply engrossed in writing a book and I am also working continually on my inner development through meditation. Both require lots of solitude."

And so it went week after week. What should I do? If these women were seeking spiritual assistance I was happy to do all in my limited power. But when I discovered that the majority of them wished to discuss superficial matters, I resorted to all kinds of ruses to avoid them and felt remorseful for doing so.

But why me? There were half a dozen other women sitting alone in the patio who would probably welcome company. I had been coming to this hotel for ten years and strangers had not beseiged me before. Why now?

On sunny days that were rare even in Florida in the unprecedentedly cold winter of 1976, I would always carry my manuscript down to the North patio to work. James often passed by as he returned from some guest's room where he had taken a breakfast tray. He would stop and talk. Or if some uninvited woman was sitting with me, he would murmur as he passed by, "Bees and the honeypot."

Of all distractions from the creative or spiritual state people were the worst—nature the least. In fact nature stimulated both. It spoke directly to the unconscious. The kind of book I was writing did not seem an intellectual exercise. It all appeared to be flowing from the deep unconscious.

Now, suddenly, it seemed to be the senses that released the in-dwelling life force, the first to reveal my new relation to life. My appetite had returned. I was able to eat anything—almost. Everything—almost—agreed with me. I ate very little, for zazen decreases the rate of metabolism and one does not require much food. Yet every mouthful was an intense delight, too much so, I feared. The subtlety of papaya at the peak of perfection, the young crisp Bibb lettuce too delicate to ruin with a salad dressing, sea bass so fresh from the ocean it had no odor.

At breakfast a large, bold blackbird took a bath in the fountain, flirting the water over the amused guests nearby. At lunch a small lizard came running out of the shrubbery. He sat motionless on the flagstone to sun himself beside my chair. His eyes never once left my face, never blinked once. "Well, Mr. Lizard, you certainly have been well trained in zazen. I have never seen anyone able to sit so motionless for so long. Do lizards come to enlightenment, I wonder?"

At dinner time as I sat in the open patio, a cricket hidden in the shrubbery behind me chirped as happily as if all these noisy human beings had not intruded into her preserves. I revelled in this combination of nature and sophisticated comfort. Why not have the best of both worlds? Of course, Zen believed in simplicity—to the point of physical hardships and privation it sometimes seemed to me. My body rebelled against hardship. Even in the best of circumstances the physical struggle was difficult enough.

At night the entire dining patio was lighted up. It looked like some gay fiesta. Guests in evening clothes from outside the hotel streamed in for dinner and cocktails, always cocktails. Who needs a cocktail, I thought, when there is a source of unlimited stimulation *and* relaxation deep within oneself from which one can drink indefinitely? Is it not a sad commentary on our Western civilization that adults must resort to liquor before they can feel merry?

It may sound simplistic or simple-minded but the high point of each day was a walk before breakfast on the street beside the hotel where I knew there was always a provocative breeze from the ocean. To feel it blowing through my hair, caressing my face sensuously, filling my lungs as if with a mysterious elixir was to imagine it was conveying some subtle message from some idealistic somewhere. Was this what Plato meant by "transcendent ideas?" Was this what Buddha meant by the relative world and the absolute world? On certain days the air was so deliciously balmy it seduced one into believing that life was perfect—and with a little effort one could become perfect oneself. This is not like the provocative air of a Northern spring which promises impossible pleasures in the future. This balmy Southern air fulfills its promise—here and now—for a fleeting moment.

The town of Palm Beach met most of my peculiar needs at this time. The city officials have purposely kept it small, clean, beautiful, quiet, safe, though very expensive. A woman can walk alone on the streets unafraid even at night. One is undisturbed by traffic in daytime except in early morning and late afternoon when the workers return to their homes in West Palm Beach across Lake Worth. There are almost no stores—except on two fabulous blocks on Worth Avenue where all the luxuries of the world are on display. On South County Road, one grocery store, one drug store, banks and brokerage firms, all the rest of the town is quietly residential.

It maintains the quiet and peace of a small town with none of the disadvantages and inconveniences of provincialism. Its simplicity is combined with all the conveniences and comforts of a sophisticated city without the heavy traffic, hustle and bustle, noise and crowds. I revelled in the slow pace of my native South. It seemed the natural rhythm of life. It carried me back to childhood, when living was simple and natural, allowing leisure to enjoy the wonders of the everyday world.

When I strolled along the streets I was greeted by beauty everywhere. The clean white stucco houses in Spanish style—not always beautiful architecturally, but pleasant and romantic. Always there was a doorway or iron grill gate that delighted the eye, or steps ascending the outside of a building, luring one to who knows what. To me it was a kind of paradise. I was surrounded by beauty and peace and nature. I was free from domestic chores on which I have never wasted much affection. I was free from ordering groceries, planning menus and worst of all chores—cooking meals. All that was necessary was to stroll nonchalantly across the patio and enjoy a delicious cuisine. Thus my mind was free to let ideas for my book flow.

A car is superfluous. Everything is within walking distance—four blocks to the Four Arts Library, three to the drug store, two to the hairdresser or the fabulous dress shops on Worth Avenue where I purchased all my clothes for the entire year.

Every week as I grew stronger, another block was added to my stroll until I knew every leaf of every shrub and tree and all the attractive houses within a radius of six blocks in all directions. No one was able to tell me the names of any of the exotic plants or trees, only of the flowers—pink hibiscus, purple bougainvillea, red poinsettias and the white angels trumpet whose fragrance seemed designed for an aphrodisiac. Everywhere the green hedges were five to fifteen feet high, magnificent to behold. They separated the houses and gardens from the sidewalk and provided inpenetrable privacy for the householders. I derived peculiar pleasure from walking beside them as close as I dared. They were so lush and luxurious no one could have inserted another leaf in them. Leaves shiny, vigorous, bursting with health and succulence as if glad to be alive. Never an insect or imperfect leaf. How did they do it?

Some of the exotic tropical plants, however, were disturbing—interesting but without beauty, which I always assumed was a natural characteristic of all growing things. There were plants with green leaves spotted with white-like leprosy. There were black plants—yes, black. I thought that was against the laws of nature. There were great spears of green leaves with royal purple undersides. It did not seem quite logical. Large red-leafed shrubs with green leaves sprouting from the top as if they were not children of their own parents. Some bushes looked as if the expressionist painter Pollock had dribbled his bucket of yellow paint across them indiscriminately without pattern or purpose. There were great green leaves with broad yellow veins running vertically and horizontally. Yellow leaves with red veins. Red leaves with green veins. Nothing made any sense. These exotic plants confused me. Was nature merely experimenting, endeavoring to develop new species, or amusing itself? Or was there a diabolical spirit behind these deviations from the norm? Was there a spirit of evil emanating from them? Or was it merely nature's laughing indifference to the standards of puny man?

As the weeks passed there arose an intensity of awareness such as I had never experienced before except in too brief flashes. Everything in nature vibrated with a new beauty, colors became more vivid. Awareness of my feet as they touched the pavement, of my skin as it responded to the warm bath water flowing over it—was pleasantly surprising. Everything I did, felt, saw, tasted, heard seemed to possess a pristine purity poised on the point of revealing a great secret.

One morning my sleep had been uncommonly deep and relaxing, consequently the zazen immediately following was uncommonly deep and relaxing. Before breakfast I walked my usual one block around the hotel to breathe the new morning air. I gazed at the same trees, the same flowers I had been gazing at every morning for weeks. Today they looked different—almost too beautiful to bear. The intensity of the feeling all but made me explode with joy. A strong impulse to dance right there on the sidewalk seized me. But always, if one is no longer a child one must observe the proprieties, otherwise the world will come to an end—so *it* thinks. Why is it that if a child dances for joy it is considered charming? If an adult dances for joy she is considered balmy, if it is not at a moment decreed by convention.

In the patio I said to the captain, "You know me, Rosalie, I always like to sit at a table where I can see the palm trees blow in the wind."

She smiled as if to indulge a wayward child. I did not explain the reason to her. I did not know the reason myself. Somehow they seemed symbolic of something. I never tired of watching those long green streamers day after day floating, swaying in the breeze, first this way and that, as if the wind was a welcome playmate.

This morning a particular palm tree mesmerized me. I stared at it unable to take my eyes away. It was as if a door suddenly opened into another dimension of existence, as if a barrier had melted away, as if a veil had been lifted. I saw that palm tree in a different light, saw into the nature of the thing itself, into its true essence. It possessed a numinous quality. This was not merely a single, simple palm tree. It was a living manifestation of reality, of the ultimate mystery. Everything in me was being agitated in a sudden turmoil. Some power seemed to be regenerating the depths of my being. I sensed the primal unity of all things.

Then I heard a silent voice within my head speak these astounding words:

IT IS ENOUGH. THAT—TREE—IS—ENOUGH. I DON'T NEED ANYTHING ELSE IN THE WORLD. NOT THINGS. NOT THE WORLD. NOT PEOPLE. NOT EVEN THE LOVE OF MEN. I AM FREE!

Fear, awe, joy filled my entire body. What did it mean? Slowly, understanding came to me. It meant freedom from *compulsive* dependence on other people for their approval, admiration and affection. It meant freedom from the dependence for my happiness on the love of men—a compulsion that had imprisoned me for 80—well, at least 70 years. Until this moment I had felt all my life that I would literally die if some man was not in love with me. Yet in a way I was now free to love my friends, men and women, more than ever before, in a larger more impersonal way, love them with more understanding and compassion for their faults—with fewer demands and expectations but a deeper desire to help them, not merely receive from them.

So Buddha was right, Socrates was right, Jung was right. We become free from a narrow personal egotistic love for a few individual people and move to a universal love of all people, all things.

How long I sat there in this wonderful mind-state I do not know. Whether I went for a walk or sought the privacy of my room I do not know. I do know this state of quiet bliss was to continue unabated all day every day.

In the days that followed this extraordinary incident the glory did not fade during the performance of the necessary mundane duties, walking to my meals, paying my bills, collecting my mail, purchasing a new dress or gazing at the trees and clouds. I felt as if there were a warm light glowing within me. When I walked about the earth I felt certain I was enveloped in a great golden light that moved with me wherever I went for all to see. But I am sure it did not because no one did see. Once I lost the glow for two dismal days, why I never knew. This new state of bliss was to continue for the two months I remained in Florida.

But how very strange it all was. All I had done was to improve my health, take care of my body, let it relax so thoroughly in zazen so that it was able to heal itself as nature intends. But I never expected physical health to elevate me to a spiritual plane. Yet had not Roshi said repeatedly in his teishos that the body and mind are one and inseparable?

Ah, but Claire, a skeptical voice commented, there are hundreds of physically healthy people walking about this earth. They obviously have not been lifted to a spiritual plane. Look at the worship of the body in the international Olympic Games. I noticed nothing spiritual or loving or compassionate there—nothing but egotism and cold competition.

I recalled the time Roshi said that the practice of zazen usually gave only physical health to the Japanese samurai warriors, boxers and swordsmen because it was not done in conjunction with the religious quest. There was a vast difference.

It was surprising that my feelings were not ecstatic as they had been in my first great awakening in New Haven. Now they were quietly blissful. But had not Buddha said ecstasy is active, bliss is quiet? Nirvana is *eternal* bliss.

But how could one single, simple palm tree perform such a miracle? I recalled a statement about Zen and a tree by Huston Smith in his *Religions of Man*. I dug out a battered copy from the box of books I had had mailed to Florida. Without understanding it years ago, I had underlined it,

> "The heart of Zen training lies in introducing the
> eternal into the now, in widening the doors of per-
> ception to the point where the delight and wonder...
> [of] the satori experience... envelopes an object as
> common... as the tree in your backyard... [and] is
> seen [as] a manifestation of the infinite."

Running parallel to the quiet bliss I felt, there was an effort to analyze and understand this extraordinary liberation and the stages by which I had arrived at this wonderful culmination.

All my life I had been seeking freedom—unconsciously at first, then consciously. Did age exert an influence? I knew that Eastern religious literature, Eric Neumann and Richard Bucke, the psychologists, observed that 18—36—and 54 were especially spiritual ages.

At 20 I had announced to a weeping mother and angry father that I wished to leave home and earn my own living because I wanted to be free—to be myself—though at the time I had not the faintest idea of what "myself" was. I had first struggled for freedom from the domination of family, school, church and Southern traditions.

At 25 I had rebelled against the conventions of society, male chauvinism, puritanism about sex, and the fallacies of the Christian religion which held me in almost unbreakable bonds. For the first 25 years of my life I had believed in the Christian religion, a child believing in a father figure, a wrathful, vengeful, yet loving God who punished me when I disobeyed his laws or those of the Bible. I believed in the duality of Creator and creature. I was assured that I was innately evil because all men were responsible for the original sin, the Fall of Man and expulsion from the Garden of Eden. I never understood just what the sin was. I assumed it was sex. My religion brought me no joy and no practical method of becoming good, though I longed desperately to become good.

At 25 I underwent a traumatic experience. The prevalence of evil in the world was enough to argue the fact of an omnipotent, omniscient, benevolent being out of existence, but it didn't. The internal cleansing action of a poem did.

> "I am that which began;
> Out of me the years roll;
> Out of me god and man;
> I am equal and whole.
> Beside or above me
> Nought is there to go,
> Love or unlove me,
> Unknow me or know,
> I am that which unloves and loves, I am stricken,
> and I am the blow."

This poem, *Hertha*, shook my whole inner being. Unity of all things—for the first time in my life I faintly, briefly sensed it. For the first time I felt there might be a larger impersonal power in the universe which I scarcely dared believe. I knew no one who believed in such heresy. But I was freed of a personal god.

But there was still the Christ to deal with. Religion offered me no reason to believe he was a god. One night my little apartment in New York was filled with a great light. Standing in it there was an image of the Christ. Not until many years later did I learn that he can be a symbol of the self.

Then I had my first taste of freedom from the tyranny of society. I appeared at a formal dinner party of English artists and writers where all the women wore long gowns of cloth of gold it seemed. I was in a simple short dinner dress.

When I returned to my apartment an inner experience occurred. I beheld an image of myself climbing a great mountain. Attaining the top, I was blasted with an "excess of light" as Emerson expresses it. For a moment I felt I gazed into the glowing core of the cosmos, pierced the great enigma and saw the falseness of man-made values concerning laws, ideas, conventions, clothes, jewels, God. They all fell off me like shackles from my legs and I stood on the mountain top naked and free and unafraid. "The truth shall make you free"—but only for a golden moment. Such freedom did not last. Emerson supported yet confused me for he said, "This communication is an influx of the Divine mind into our mind." But had I not just rid myself of the concept of divinity? It was confusing.

From 25 until 54 I had no religion. The intellectuals I knew believed in Newton's mechanistic model of the universe. I could never accept that because of the "small ecstacies" or altered states of consciousness that visited me periodically when I sensed a something beyond. But I did accept the prevailing philosophy of Descartes, the separation of mind and matter—mind and body—man and nature. I equated man's identity with the rational mind rather than with the whole organism. I too believed that science and reason were able to solve all the problems of the universe which—by the time of World War II and the discovery of the atom bomb—they obviously could not. Desperately I followed one system of thought after another, dashing vainly after many misleading half-truths, never finding ultimate truth. Seeking, searching. I was always searching.

The overt behavior of man, his wars, crimes and corruption seemed to prove that mankind was inherently evil. This plunged me into despair about the state of the world. I was already in despair about a private problem that proved to be insoluble by the conscious mind when I was 54.

Age 54 was climactic. Reason, having failed me, surrendered its dominance. I saw my ego drowning in the sea of the collective unconscious. Then a cataclysmic mystical awakening was visited on me. I beheld a great golden light, merged with it, felt ineffable ecstacy and purification. I was granted intuitive insights into the nature of things, felt the oneness of all things, loved all people. I was transformed for twelve glorious years.

Then I was plunged into the Dark Night of the Soul and lost everything I had ever gained. Only Plato's *Dialogues* encouraged me to seek the next stage in inner development—the Unitive life or enlightenment. But for the next six years I lived in limbo taking care of a sick and dying husband.

At 74 I had entered Zen practice at the Snowbound Center, seeking the truth that would make me free, seeking ultimate answers to ultmate questions.

After four years of strenuous practice of daily zazen I found that my compulsive dependence on, and attachment to, my spiritual teacher and the Buddha fell off my shoulders like an unneeded cloak. It occurred without my volition while I was sitting quietly in an old deserted garden in Virginia. But I was still compulsively attached to dependence on people for their affection and the love of men. Then after six years of meditation a single, simple palm tree brought me freedom one morning in Florida when I was 80. The impact is beyond description in words.

Paradoxically enough, however, it was the experiential method that destroyed my whole Western philosophy, values, and way of life. It was not thought—not logic. Gradually though, my rambunctious rational mind accepted my inner experiences as valid—even gloried in them.

I woke up one day to find that I had *experienced* the philosophy common to all Eastern religions—Zen, Buddhism, Hinduism and Taoism. I also accepted it conceptually. For I had *felt* the basic unity of all things, the interrelatedness of all things and all people, and realized that everything is a manifestation of reality. Such simple words. But such a revolutionary experience.

As I sat at the breakfast table that unforgettable morning, that palm tree had seemed to pour the whole universe into me. I *felt* that I was the universe, though intellectually I was unable to comprehend or accept such a paradox.

I was free. No longer need I labor under the burden of an authoritative but capricious ruler who directs the world from above. I had experienced a cosmic principle that controlled me from within. Logically all things were controlled from within according to their own inherent nature.

If I ever doubted the existence of cosmic energy, I had only to recall the incident of the clouds. An invisible arrow of energy had penetrated my chest and instantly altered my life by awakening my True-nature.

So the Zen Buddhists were right—life could be one continuous song, a daily harmony with all things, all people, all work, all nature. I felt intense gratitude to my spiritual teacher, Roshi, for showing me the Way, to Buddha, for having discovered the Way and taught it to others, to my husband for having left me a comfortable income, to my financial adviser for providing me with freedom to follow the spiritual path and to my friends and lovers who gladdened my heart. I walked through my days with a singing heart, active mind, healthy body, love and spiritual fulfillment and sweet yearning.

Never in all my 80 years had I felt so happy, so healthy, so free, or so filled with quiet bliss. This was not the peak of the shining mountain but at the moment I was so grateful for my happiness that I had not the temerity to wish for any greater happiness.

But one must follow one's Karma.

Chapter XX
CONTENTEDNESS AND DEATH

One morning I had written on my book for four hours—an hour longer than I should have. Ideas were still flowing swiftly like the Mississippi at the flood. They had no intention of stopping for insignificant obstacles like rest, sleep or meals. Nevertheless I lay down for a nap, lunch forgotten. I slept three solid hours. Another of those deep dreamless sleeps that occur but rarely. One seems to sink into unfathomable depths, to go out of one's body, return to the beginningless beginning or primordial creation. When I awakened it was as if I were lying at the bottom of some deep dark ocean as if I were some primeval creature slowly arousing to life for the first time in history. My body was too heavy to move.

Gradually I struggled up into the light of consciousness. Suddenly I felt transformed, as if I was an innocent child born into the morning of the world, returning to my Original-nature. All defilements, faults and weaknesses seemed to be sloughing off. I was beginning a new life in a new world. How could the human body alone bring such a sense of utter purity? Never in my life had I felt so completely, utterly, luxuriously relaxed.

Slowly I slipped out of bed and placed the bed pillows on the floor to begin a meditation unlike any other I had known in six years. My body immediately settled itself into a comfortable and proper posture. I sat with a "sense of dignity and grandeur—like a mountain."

I sat on and on—an hour? two hours? in full lotus position—motionless. Gradually my hands melted into each other. My knees were pierced by pain. My back was aching. All this was occurring at some far distance. Trivial matters like pain did not concern me.

As time passed my body grew heavier than heavy, like some great rock embedded in the earth, like some great tree strongly rooted in the deep earth—immovable—indestructible.

I wanted never again to move my body, never again to change anything. Any state into which I might move, a state of power—wealth—fame—love—passion—could not compare with the serene state of being I was in at this moment. It was peace—deep unutterable peace.

I seemed to have arrived at the end of a long journey, the end of a rough road that had offered many inspiring views along the way. It was a beautiful plateau on which I might rest indefinitely, at which I had arrived after years of striving on the path.

I felt no desire, no ambition, no regrets. No words can describe such perfection, such completeness, fulfillment and finality.

I was intensely aware of my body yet I felt suspended bodiless in a new height. Everything within me seemed to vibrate gently in a golden light. Then everything within me was in utter stillness—like an eternal stillness. Nothing anywhere except ineffable quietness and inexpressible stillness.

I did not feel the self fuse with the absolute. I felt that the whole universe—everything that is—the uncreated—changeless, beginningless—everlasting—was in me—*was* me—for a fleeting forever.

Everything was intangible, invisible, formless and colorless—beyond the reach of the senses, above the grasp of conceptual thinking, beyond words—yet real as only reality can be. Everything was nothingness. Nothingness was everythingness.

Was it the end of everything or a new beginning for me? Was it a glimpse of the bliss of life after death? All fear of death vanished right away—forever.

All struggles were ended, all seeking forgotten, all dualities abandoned. Every hope fulfilled. Every question answered. Every problem resolved—briefly, if not for all time. I was content—utterly, sweetly—deeply content.

I could hear words speaking themselves silently inside my head—slowly—slowly,

"I—NEED—NOTHING. I—HAVE—EVERYTHING, EVERYTHING IS—IN MY MIND. EVEN UNIVERSAL MIND—IS IN MY MIND. I AM—CONTENT."

At last I knew why the Buddha said, "Everything is the Mind."

Did Buddhism claim that contentedness was a beautiful preparation for a beautiful death? If so, I welcomed both. Now I knew that "to see all things in the self... there is the great liberation."

All in one, one in All.

REFERENCES AND BIBLIOGRAPHY

Bhagavad-Gita, Trans. Prabhavananda and Isherwood, N.Y., Harper, 1951

Bible, Standard Edition, N.Y., Nelson, 1901

Blofeld, J., *Tantric Mysticism of Tibet*, N.Y., Dutton, 1970

Buddhist Bible, ed. Goddard, Boston, Beacon, 1970

Bucke, R., *Cosmic Consciousness*, N.Y., Dutton, 1948

Bogen, J., "The Other Side of the Brain, An Appositional Mind," *Bulletin of Los Angeles Neurological Societies*, 34, No. 3, 1969

Capra, F., *Tao of Physics*, Berkeley, Shambhala, 1975.

Chang, G., *Practice of Zen*, N.Y., Perennial Library, Harper, 1959

Chaun, N., in Chang, *Practice of Zen*, N.Y., Perennial Library, Harper, 1959

Cooper, J., *Taoism, the Way of the Mystic*, N.Y., Weiser, 1974

Dean, S., *Psychiatry and Mysticism*, Chicago, Nelson-Hall, 1975

Durckheim, K., *Hara*, N.Y., Weiser, 1975

Durant, W., *Story of Philosophy*, N.Y., Simon & Schuster, 1926

Elkes, N., Personal letter

Emerson, R., *Essays*, First Series, Boston, Houghton, 1903

Freud, S., in Jung, *Memories, Dreams, Reflections*, Pantheon, 1963

Goleman, D., "Buddha on Meditation and States of Consciousness," Part I., *Journal of Transpersonal Psychology*, Vol. 4, No. 1, 1972

Govinda, A., *Way of the White Clouds*, Berkeley, Shambhala, 1971.

Grof, S., "Varieties of Transpersonal Experiences, Observations from LSD Psychotherapy," *Journal of Transpersonal Psychology, 1972*, Vol. 4, No. 1.

Grof, S., "Theoretical and Empirical Basis of Transpersonal Psychology," *Journal of Transpersonal Psychology*, Vol. 5, No. 1, 1973

Hahn, T., *Zen Keys*, Intro. by Kapleau, P., Garden City, N.Y., Anchor Books. Doubleday, 1974

Hakuin, Zen Master, *Hakuin, Selected Writings*, Trans. Yampolsky, N.Y., Columbia University Press, 1971

Huxley, A., *Heaven and Hell*, N.Y., Harper, 1955

Huxley, A., *Doors of Perception*, N.Y., Harper, 1954

Huxley, A., *Perennial Philosophy*, N.Y., Harper, 1945

James, W., *Varieties of Religious Experience*, N.Y., Modern Library, Random House, 1902

Jung, C., *Psychology and Religion*, West and East, N.Y., Pantheon, 1958

Jung, C., *Collected Works*, N.Y., Pantheon, 1953-58

Jung, C., *Memories, Dreams, Reflections*, N.Y, (Pantheon), Random House, 1963

Jung, C., *Man and His Symbols*, Garden City, N.Y., Doubleday, 1964

Kapleau, P., *Three Pillars of Zen*, Boston, Beacon, 1965

Krishna, G., *Kundalini*, Boulder, Colo., Shambhala, 1975

Lao Tzu, *Tao Te Ching, Wisdom of Ancient China*, N.Y., Mentor, New Amer. Library, 1955

Maslow, A., *Toward a Psychology of Being*, Princeton, van Nostrand, 1962

Masters, and Houston, *Varieties of Psychedelic Experience*, N.Y., Delta Book, Dell, 1967

Millay, E., *Renascence*, N.Y., Harper, 1917

Morgan and King, *Introduction to Psychology*, N.Y., McGraw-Hill, 1956

Northrop, F., *Meeting of East and West*, N.Y.. Macmillan, 1946

Naranjo, C., & Ornstein, R., *On the Psychology of Meditation*, New York, Viking, 1971

Osborne, A., *Collected Works of Ramana Maharshi*, New York, Weiser, 1972

Ornstein, R., *Psychology of Consciousness*, San Francisco, W. H. Freeman, 1972

Owens, Claire, M., *Awakening to the Good*, Boston, Christopher, 1958

Owens, Claire, M., *Discovery of the Self*, Boston, Christopher, 1963

Owens, Claire M., "Mystical Experience—Facts and Values," in *Highest State of Consciousness* (ed.). White, J., Garden City, N.Y., Anchor Books, Doubleday, 1972, pp. 135-152

Owens, Claire M., "Psychology of Zen Buddhism," in *Transpersonal Psychologies* (ed.). Tart, C., New York, Harper, 1975, pp. 153-202

Owens, Claire M., "Case of Spontaneous Self-Realization," *Human Dimensions*, Summer, Vol. 4, No. 2, 1975, pp. 43-52

Owens, Claire M., "Seven Wonders of the Inner World," *Journal of Altered States of Consciousness*, Vol. 2, No. 3, 1975

Pearce, J., *Crack in the Cosmic Egg*, New York, Pocket Books, 1973

Platform Scripture, Trans. Chan, W., New York, St. Johns, 1963

Plato, *Collected Dialogues* (ed.), Hamilton, E., Cairns, H., New York (Pantheon), Random, 1961

Prabhavananda & Manchester, F., *Spiritual Heritage of India*, Garden City, N.Y., Anchor Books, Doubleday, 1964

Ring, K., "Transpersonal View of Consciousness," *Journal of Transpersonal Psychology*, Vol. 6, No. 2, 1974

Ram Dass, *Only Dance There Is*, Garden City, New York, Anchor Books, Doubleday, 1974

Saint John of the Cross, *Dark Night of the Soul*, Image Books, Doubleday, Garden City, New York (ed.). Peers, Ed., 1959

Sheldon, W., *Varieties of Temperament*, New York, Harper, 1944

Singer, June, *Androgyny*, Garden City, New York, Anchor Books, Doubleday, 1976

Sinnott, E. W., *Matter, Mind and Man*, New York, Harper, 1957

Sinnott, E. W., *Bridge of Life*, New York, Simon & Schuster, 1966

Sinnott, E. W., *Biology of the Spirit*, New York, Viking, 1955

Smith, Huston, *Religions of Man*, New York, Mentor, New American Library, 1954

Sorokin, P., *Forms and Techniques of Altruistic and Spiritual Growth*, Boston, Beacon, 1954

Suzuki, D. T., *Zen Buddhism* (ed.) Barrett, W., Garden City, New York, Anchor Books. Doubleday, 1956

Swinburne, A., "Hertha" in *Poems*, New York, Modern Library, no date

Tart, C., *Altered States of Consciousness*, Garden City, New York, Anchor Books, Doubleday, 1972

Tart, C., *Psi—Scientific Studies of the Psychic Realm*, New York, Dutton, 1977

Teilhard de Chardin, P., *Phenomenon of Man*, New York, Harper, 1959

Teresa of Avila, *Autobiography*, Garden City, New York, Image Books, Doubleday, 1960

Threefold Lotus Sutra, Trans. by Kato, Tamura & Miyasaka, New York, Weatherhill, 1975

Tiller, W., "Energy Fields and the Human Body", in *Frontiers of Consciousness* (ed.), White, John, New York, Julian, 1974

Underhill, Evelyn, *Mysticism*, London, Methuen, 1952

von Franz, M-L., "Conclusion—Science and the Unconscious," in *Man and His Symbols*, Jung, C. G., Garden City, New York, Doubleday, 1964

Walker, K., *Women Saints of East and West*, London, Ramakrishna Vedanta Centre, 1955

White, J., *What Is Meditation?* (ed.). Garden City, New York, Anchor Books, Doubleday, 1974

Whitman, W., *Leaves of Grass*, New York, Modern Library, 1921

Wilber, K., "Psychologia Perennis: The Spectrum of Consciousness," *Journal of Transpersonal Psychology*, Vol. 7, No. 2, 1975

Wolfe, T., *You Can't Go Home Again*, New York, Perennial Library, Harper, 1940

Yasutani, "Lectures I: Theory and Practice of Zazen," in *Three Pillars of Zen* (ed.), Kapleau, P., Boston, Beacon, 1967

Yogananda, P., *Autobiography of a Yogi*, Los Angeles, Self- Realization Fellowship, 1956

ALSO FROM THE BOOK TREE

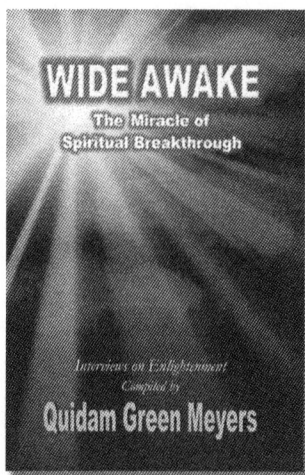

Wide Awake: The Miracle of Spiritual Breakthrough
by
Quidam Green Meyers

What is the reality of Enlightenment? How is spiritual freedom being lived in the 21st Century? In this revealing text, Quidam Green Meyers speaks to some of the West's top spiritual teachers and writers on the topic of Contemporary Awakening. Each was asked the same set of questions for the sake of comparison, yet their answers differ greatly. What is revealed is a stunning glimpse into the simple-yet-powerful life transformation that can take place when our Awakened Self is recognized and lived. Wide Awake reveals that there is no set path for Enlightenment. The men and women speaking in this book offer an impassioned plea for us to give up the search, since Truth is to be found eternally alive and present in every human Heart. Those interviewed include Matthew Fox, Alan Cohen, Rev. Michael Beckwith, Catherine Ingram, Lama Surya Das, Saniel Bonder, Isaac Shapiro, Arjuna Nick Ardagh, Satyam Nadeen, Dasarath, Neelam, Akash, Wayne Liquorman, Howard Raphael Cushner and Antonio Duncan.

BT-37X · ISBN 1-885395-37-X · trade paper · 200 pages · $18.95

CALL FOR A FREE CATALOG 1 800 700-TREE (8733)

Triumph of the Human Spirit:
The Greatest Achievements of the Human Soul and How Its Power can Change Your Life
by Paul Tice.

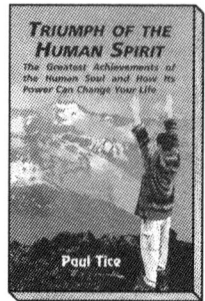

This book is about those who changed the entire course of history. They did not start with money, power, or great armies—all they had was an idea, and a passion for the truth. Gandhi, Joan of Arc, Dr. King and others died for their ideas but made the world a better place. This book outlines how an intuitive spiritual knowledge, or "gnosis," provided these people with guidance and helped to create the most incredible spiritual moments that the world has ever known. These events are all part of our spiritual evolution. We have learned from past mistakes, have become more tolerant toward others, and the people in this book have been signposts- —pointing us collectively toward something greater. This book also shows how a spiritual triumph of your own can be achieved. Various exercises will strengthen the soul and reveal its hidden power. Unlike the past, in today's Western world we are free to explore the truth without fear of being tortured or executed. As a result, the rewards are great. This is the perfect book for all those who believe in spiritual freedom and have a passion for the truth.

BT-574 · ISBN 1-885395-57-4 · 295 pages
6 x 9 · trade paper · illustrated · $19.95

Buddhist Suttas: Major Scriptural Writings from Early Buddhism
by T.W. Rhys Davids.

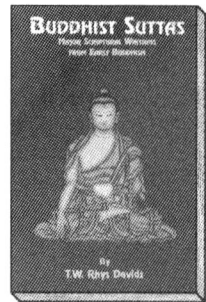

These seven scriptural writings are considered by many to be the most important of the Buddhist religion. Originally written in the Pali language, they date to the fourth and third centuries BC. This early date is what makes them so important—they form the very core of Buddhist teachings. The influence of the texts contained in this book upon the entire Buddhist world is enormous. They have been sought after and studied by monks and scholars for centuries, and there could never be a complete understanding of the true meaning of Buddhism without them. This collection of texts was not only translated by the great T.W. Rhys Davids, but edited by the renowned scholar of eastern religions, F. Max Muller, making it clearly the most reliable text of its kind in the English language.

BT-794 · ISBN 1-58509-079-4 · 376 pages
6 x 9 · trade paper · $27.95

CALL FOR A FREE CATALOG 1 800 700-TREE (8733)

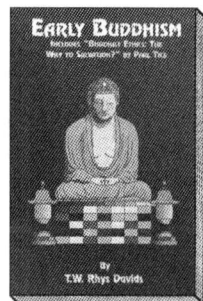

www.ingramcontent.com/pod-product-compliance
Lightning Source LLC
Chambersburg PA
CBHW022021090426
42739CB00006BA/235